One Day It Will All Make Sense: Why Your Health Matters to God

Tapiwa Chiwawa

Copyright © 2020 by Tapiwa Chiwawa
All rights reserved.
For permission requests or any other enquiries: ,
write to wtbtradio@gmail.com.
Lamp to My Feet Media
San Antonio Texas

ISBN: 9780983879145
Second edition.
United States of America.
Cover design by latoyaduncan.com

DEDICATION

To my daughter for the honor of being your father and being the motivation for me to finish this book, and my wife without whose love, prayer and belief in this project when I was at my lowest and with little faith, this would not have been possible.

CONTENTS

Chapter	Title	Page
	Acknowledgements	7
1	What is health?	9
2	Nutrition	19
3	Exercise	23
4	Rest	27
5	Water	31
6	Self Control	35
7	Air	39
8	Sunshine	43
9	Similarities: physical & spiritual health	49
10	Agape Love	59
117	It all started in Heaven	63
12	Lucifer's fall	67
13	The fall of humanity	75
14	How demons operate	83
15	The Sun of Righteousness	109
16	Bread of Life: Where are we from?	113
-	New Age Movement & Counterculture	117
-	Environmentalism	128
-	Lifestyle	141
-	Religion, spirituality & the occult	144
17	Bread of Life: Who are we – Our Origins	183
18	Bread of Life: Why are we here?	195
19	Bread of Life: Where are we going?	199

Chapter	Title	Page
-	Death as sleep?	202
-	Doctrine of Immortality of the soul	207
-	Is Hell fire eternal?	208
-	The Rapture?	216
20	Come out of her my people	231
21	Faith	235
22	Holy Spirit	241
23	Who is in control?	255
24	Rest	269
-	The Sabbath	276
-	How the Sabbath was changed	282
-	More false teachings	288
25	Fountain of Living Water	295
-	Watery grave: Baptism	302
-	Should infants be baptized?	312
26	While it is today	315

ACKNOWLEDGMENTS

First of all, praise to my Lord and Savior Jesus Christ for His Word, the inspiration to write, enabling me to even begin writing and book when I had almost given up. I am also thankful for E. G. White, Amazing Discoveries, Amazing Facts, and Constance Cumbey, whose works and courage in speaking the truth, inspired and gave me insight as I worked on the book. Unless specified, all Scripture taken from the New King James Version. Copyright © 1982 by Thomas Nelson, Inc. Used by permission. All rights reserved. Special thanks to Biblegateway.com which also made the work easier. Thanks to LaToya for the great cover and discussions which helped to refine some of the thoughts in the book. On a more personal note, I want to thank my father, for the love, wise advice, and support over the years; my mother, for your love, believing and praying even when I had doubts; my sisters for your love, support and patience with me; all my friends especially Dave, Marcia, Jim, Lily, Paida, S. Kabah, Lorato, and Sipho for your love, advice and support through the ups and downs all along the way; and finally, Abe and all the good folks at WB for your support.

1
WHAT IS HEALTH?

"This is going to be the hardest and saddest week of most Americans' lives, quite frankly. This is going to be our Pearl Harbor moment, our 9/11 moment, only it's not going to be localized. It's going to be happening all over the country" [1] said the Surgeon General Dr. Jerome Adams, as he braced the nation for a hard week of spiking COVID-19 deaths at the time.

There have been more deaths since he said this. There has also been a lot of controversy; ranging from the group which on one extreme deny its existence, or whether it is serious enough to warrant a severe response such as shutting down the world economy and mandatory face masks everywhere, to the other which believes that it is indeed a health emergency and cannot wait for a vaccine as they see it as the only way for life to return to normal. I do not know what the truth is, but I do know one thing for sure, that some people are dying from something, and underlying conditions increase the likelihood of succumbing to it. However, I want to focus on the fact that better health means one is least likely to succumb to it, and so we should strive for the best health as much as is within our control.

According to a study from Italy's National Institute of Health released on March 17, at that point, 99% of COVID-19 patients who had died in the country had at least one preexisting condition. 76.1% of patients who died from COVID-19 had hypertension, or high blood pressure, one-third had heart disease and about one-quarter had atrial fibrillation. People who previously had a stroke made up 9.6% of COVID-19 patients who died in Italy. Diabetes was the second most common condition among COVID-19 patients who died: 35.5% had the illness. 20.3% had active cancer in the past five years. The study found that 18% of people who died had chronic kidney disease. Chronic obstructive pulmonary disease — or lung diseases such as chronic emphysema and bronchitis — was present in 13.2% of the people who died. [2] Here, we have a virus that is highly likely to take the lives of those who are most vulnerable. The elderly tend to have preexisting conditions, but even in those who are considered young under 50, preexisting conditions are more likely to result in death. Even young and healthy people with no preexisting conditions are also succumbing to this virus.[3] If there has ever been anything to underline the need for good health, it is this virus. Those with good health or no preexisting conditions stand a better chance but mortality definitely increases with age and or preexisting conditions. It is showing us why it is important to have good health which is an investment in yourself if you will, if you ever encounter a disease such as this.

I believe most of us when seeing the headlines as it spread in China initially, thought it would just end up being an epidemic there and not spread to the rest of the world. It didn't occur to us that it could become a pandemic as it spreads to the rest of the world from the epicenter in Wuhan China where it allegedly started. While the 1918 Spanish flu which is estimated to have killed 50 million worldwide in a span of about 2 years, was gaining momentum, it probably did not occur to many that it would spread to wherever they were. Many suddenly were fighting for their lives, when shortly before, they were making all kinds of plans for the future and living life as usual. Besides the lives it has allegedly taken, the greater toll has been on the economy, with many businesses closed or on the brink of closing. Many are joining food bank lines for the first time in their lives as well as experiencing homelessness in unprecedented numbers as they are evicted or fail to continue paying on their homes.

We are more aware of it because we are seeing the crisis develop right before our eyes, like a plot unfolding in an apocalyptic film. I wish it was just a film but it is reality, unfortunately. There are many other things however we are not aware of that can occur suddenly in our lives. Car accidents or even plane crashes, a heart attack, diagnosis of a terminal illness like cancer, can change our lives suddenly just as the Corona virus has already changed many lives today. It is not just here in America but everywhere in the world, we are all experiencing the same challenges.

When faced with a crisis, it forces us to reevaluate and determine what is actually valuable versus what we perceive to be valuable. A crisis makes us more aware of how precious time is and how so little we have. Our perception of value can be seen in the spiritual state of the world. Before this crisis, if asked to come up with a hierarchy of valuable things, most people's lists would not include health. Homes, lands, cars, investments, tech gadgets and other possessions would all make it on there, but not health. It would be an afterthought if at all, and yet it is the most precious thing that we have and enables us to enjoy any of these other things. Everything else is dependent on it. Without it ordinary everyday activities of daily life which we normally take for granted would become difficult if not impossible in extreme cases. It is sobering when we realize that we cannot be able to work which is necessary to acquire all these other things regarded as being more valuable. A health crisis does not discriminate based on class, and even those with great wealth which can afford the very best physicians as well as the best health resources, experience terminal illness and many have passed away. So, not only can a health crisis occur suddenly without warning, it has no regard for social status.

Technology has never been more advanced and continues to improve, and yet the moral state of the world is declining at an alarming rate. In our pursuit of advancement on the technology front, the world plunges into deeper darkness, darkness due to the hopelessness and uncertainty of the future! Ever increasing lawlessness, greed and disregard for fellow man have become the way of life. The gap between the rich and the poor is increasing. There is the paradox of limited resources in the face of great waste. There is fear of a possible world war three, as there is increasing instability among the nations. Debt is piling up fast, and there is uneasiness about the economy as many dread what an economic collapse will bring.

Even nature has its own pains with mysterious die-offs of large numbers of animals reported from around the world. Hordes and hordes of fish are showing up dead on beaches or flocks of birds literally falling dead out of the sky. Drastic changes in weather patterns seem to be the norm now, with fires, droughts and flooding all over the world. Many ask why all this evil exists and if there is any explanation for all these strange happenings. Suicide is reaching unprecedented levels that we have never seen before or we thought we could ever see. Many are empty and desire for something which all the power or wealth in the world cannot satisfy, but they do not know what it is. Frustration is rampant because there is no answer for the world's problems, or so it may seem. Humanity is sicker than ever before spiritually, and desperately needs to be healed. Is there any hope of change? Is there any hope of healing for humanity?

There is hope! In understanding health in its true sense, and to act on it, we will enjoy not only good health Physically but more importantly, Spiritually. They are governed by the same principles, and so understanding one can help to understand the other. With all this in mind, I think it is well worth our time to find out what health is. Our understanding of it will be a first and crucial step in how each of us as can make the necessary changes in our lives that can enable us to have better health, not only physically but spiritually as well. What is learned can be applied anywhere and is for all humanity!

Definition of health

To understand health, we have to have an appreciation for the principles that govern it, as they are the same for spiritual well being, therefore a good foundational understanding of physical health will help us to understand spiritual health and how we can address both. The WHO's definition of health states that it is a state of complete physical, mental, and social well-being and not merely the absence of disease or infirmity.[4] In other words, Health is when we function optimally physically, socially and mentally. Therefore complete well being involves not only the absence of disease or pain, but extends to spiritual well being which has a direct bearing on mental and social health as well. Being sound spiritually means that one is sound mentally and; emotionally as a result. When the body or spirit are not sound it can result in disease or illness whether of the body and or the mind.

Physical health

When the body is functioning as it should then disease is absent and we feel good and have no signs or symptoms. Signs and symptoms serve as the body's alarm to show us that something is not right in the body. According to the Merriam-Webster dictionary, a symptom is:

a: subjective evidence of disease or physical disturbance; broadly
: something that indicates the presence of bodily disorder
2a: something that indicates the existence of something else e.g. symptoms of inner turmoil.

Since symptoms are the evidence of disorder or a problem, they alert us of a problem or disease process taking place but are not the disease. Addressing the symptom is different from addressing the root cause of the problem. To achieve and maintain health, we should be willing to get to the root cause if we truly want to eliminate the disease and therefore the symptoms as well.

Symptoms

The worldview most people espouse is that if you feel good, or there are no visible symptoms, one is healthy. This is why the general understanding of health most people have is that if you don't feel any symptoms, or if you don't show any symptoms, then you are fine. It has become the norm to address the symptoms instead of the cause. If for example a symptom is pain, then the natural thing to do is to kill the pain. If it is a rash then naturally it is to deal with the rash. We might be successful in killing the pain or removing the rash with some ointment but the root cause of the pain and rash is still there. The pain and rash are like branches and dealing with them is like trimming branches. Even if you cut down the branches, more will grow to replace them. The pain and rash return after a while or they are absent as long as they are being dealt with directly meanwhile the tree continues to grow. The tree is the disease and to deal with it is to actually uproot it. Cutting it down might work for a time but if the roots are intact, there is always the danger another stem can grow back because the tree is still alive. To address the cause by going to the root of the problem, you would have to uproot the tree so that it is truly dead and there is no chance of it growing back.

Does how we feel or look matter?

Spending on prescription medicines in the United States will increase 4-7 percent through 2021, reaching $580 billion to $610 billion, according to a report released by Quintiles IMS. [5] Staggering amounts of money are being spent on addressing symptoms such as pain and not the cause, and increasing year upon year. Feeling good and having no signs or symptoms of disease are brought about from the inside, from the optimum functioning of the body, and are long-lasting benefits.

Silent illnesses

Some illnesses advance without really showing any symptoms until it is too late in some cases. In Cardiovascular disease, the first symptom might be a fatal stroke or a heart attack. Cancer is another type of insidious illness and in many cases it progresses until it is at an advanced stage before being detected. As these silent illnesses progress, the one affected might feel like everything is alright and not see any visible symptoms of any impending health crisis. This is one of the main reasons why it is not wise to measure health by how we feel or absence of visible symptoms. Heart disease can be easier to connect to inactivity or lack of exercise and a bad diet. Cancer is more mysterious and one can still have it while living a lifestyle that would be considered healthy.

What is lifestyle?

If health is not determined by how we feel, or an absence of visible symptoms, what is it determined by? The Collins English Dictionary defines "lifestyle" as a set of attitudes, habits or possessions associated with a particular person or group. Your lifestyle can be healthy or unhealthy based on for example your food choices, activity level, sexual behavior just to name a few factors.

Physical health can be found in living a lifestyle that supports the optimum functioning of the body. The same way society is governed by laws to maintain order, health is governed by specific health laws. When civil laws are broken, disorder and chaos is the natural result and the same can be expected in the function of the body when health laws are broken. Imagine if drivers would drive at highway speeds in a 35 mph zone, or if people would just walk out of stores with items they did not pay for. These health laws are there for a reason and ignoring them endangers the function of body. Abiding by the laws of health means that one lives a lifestyle ensuring optimum or orderly function of the body which is health, while a lifestyle that does not abide by the laws of health results in disease or disorder in body function. The laws of health are the principles that contribute to not only physical, but mental and spiritual well being as well as we shall learn later.

The health Laws: necessary for healing

Before we get into what the laws of health are, we have to understand the underlying principle; that health is restored if it had been lost, or is maintained by living a lifestyle that abides by the laws of health. The process of returning to health is called healing. To heal is defined as:

1a: to make free from injury or disease: to make sound or whole.
 b: to make well again: to restore to health.
2a: to cause (an undesirable condition) to be overcome.

In the situation where health has been lost due to disease, healing would need to take place to return to health or optimum body function by addressing the cause and anything that promises healing without doing so or taking it into consideration is a vain attempt at achieving this goal.

Real healing not only addresses the cause but also has to be in harmony with the laws of health. Weight control can be a good example to illustrate this! Being overweight in most cases is encouraged by a high calorie diet which is generally nutrient deficient and catalyzed further by a sedentary lifestyle. What causes it? Lifestyle! Consuming more calories than the recommended daily intake leads to weight gain because a sedentary lifestyle does not burn them off. Even if a product is taken that supposedly burns the fat, if there is no decided change in lifestyle the weight will stay off only as long as the product is taken, if it even works. In most cases the product itself can have harmful side effects if taken especially for an extended period of time. Ceasing to take it and the weight comes right back. Whatever the latest procedure or product in the weight loss industry may be, any attempts at losing the weight without a decided change in lifestyle are in vain.

A return to health in this example would begin with a decided change in lifestyle. A change in diet to one that is more nutritious and lower in calories, and to incorporate regular physical activity to burn calories and thus prevent them from being stored as excess fat. Three laws of health are involved: self control, nutrition and exercise. The law of self-control is broken when overeating takes place versus eating enough, while the law of nutrition is broken when junk food which is bad for you is the main part of the diet instead of good nutritious food which your body needs. Finally the law of exercise when little or no exercise takes place as it is essential for maintenance of cardiovascular health, muscle tone and a host of other benefits.

Violation of these laws or principles is the cause of the problem and continued violation is a hindrance against real healing taking place, with any attempt at healing (losing weight) which ignores or involves breaking these laws but a vain attempt. In this example the person might be craving unhealthy food, overeating and sedentary because they are depressed meaning that a lack of spiritual health would be the underlying cause. Even if the three other laws are followed, the person is not completely in good health and can lapse back into emotional eating and being sedentary due to the depression. Spiritual health would still need to be addressed. This is generally the case though there are situations which can be a lot more complex than this if for example a person has hypothyroidism which then affects their metabolism. Even in these complex situations, one can still enjoy the best health possible if their lifestyle is according to the laws of health, and a complex situation should not be a reason to disregard them.

Lifestyle

Living according to the laws of health allows the body to return to order or optimum function which takes care of the symptoms because they are present only when disorderly body function or disease occurs. Address only the symptoms, and you cover them up or alleviate them only for the condition to worsen. When healing is achieved, it is important to continue abiding by the all the laws to stay in health because disregarding them can mean the return of the problem. Health is only achieved and maintained when abiding by all these laws becomes a lifestyle. Lifestyle is not a temporary 2 week diet but how you choose to eat the rest of your life. It's about the daily choices you make whether or not to exercise, what to eat and how much and so many other things that affect you physically. It is even about the choices you make in how you react to situations, or the ideas, beliefs or philosophies that you allow to shape your life as well and this is where spiritual health becomes important. For example, one can eat healthy and exercise but partake in risky sexual behavior with multiple partners. All these are examples of what contributes to lifestyle and how these lifestyle choices in turn affect our health.

The best example of lifestyle's impact on health is found in regions called Blue Zones where the highest concentration of people who live to over a hundred are found. "Blue zones" is a term first coined by Dan Buettner in the cover story of the November 2005 issue of the National Geographic, "The Secret to a long life", in which he identified 5 regions as Blue Zones: Okinawa Japan, Nicoya Costa Rica, Icaria Greece, Sardinia Italy and among the Seventh-day Adventists in Loma Linda California. He goes on to elaborate in his book The Blue Zones: Lessons for Living Longer from the People Who've Lived the Longest, that the people who live in the blue zones have the following in common:

1. Moderate, regular <u>physical activity</u>.
2. Life purpose.
3. <u>Stress reduction</u>.
4. <u>Moderate caloric intake</u>.
5. <u>Plant based diet</u> – majority of food derived from plants with legumes being a staple.
6. Engagement in family life.
7. Engagement in social life.

This gives insight into what it takes to have the best health. It is not just about eating the best diet alone. Other factors are equally as important and integral parts of health. Physical well being is just a part of a whole which is completed by spiritual well being which is influenced by social, mental and other factors. The laws of health apply not only to physical health but spiritual well being with each law like a coin with one side affecting physical health while the other spiritual health. Let us take a look at physical health and then later on we will look at the spiritual side of these same laws and how they affect spiritual health.

References

1. https://www.washingtonpost.com/politics/americans-told-to-brace-for-pearl-harbor-moment-as-trump-warns-parts-of-the-nation-to-brace-for-peak/2020/04/05/aa229d22-7774-11ea-a130-df573469f094_story.html
2. https://www.businessinsider.com/hypertension-diabetes-conditions-that-make-coronavirus-more-deadly-2020-3#chronic-liver-disease-was-the-10th-most-common-underlying-condition-among-covid-19-patients-who-died-10
3. https://www.thelancet.com/journals/lancet/article/PIIS0140-6736(20)30211-7/fulltext
4. https://www.who.int/about/who-we-are/frequently-asked-questions
5. https://www.reuters.com/article/us-usa-drugspending-quintilesims-idUSKBN1800BU

2
NUTRITION

An estimated 80,110 new cancer cases among adults 20 and older in the United States in 2015 were attributable simply to eating a poor diet, according to a study, published in the JNCI Cancer Spectrum. "This is equivalent to about 5.2% of all invasive cancer cases newly diagnosed among US adults in 2015," said Dr. Fang Fang Zhang, a nutrition and cancer epidemiologist at Tufts University in Boston, who was the lead author of the study.

The researchers evaluated seven dietary factors: a low intake of vegetables, fruits, whole grains and dairy products and a high intake of processed meats, red meats and sugary beverages, such as soda. "Low whole-grain consumption was associated with the largest cancer burden in the US, followed by low dairy intake, high processed-meat intake, low vegetable and fruit intake, high red-meat intake and high intake of sugar-sweetened beverages," Zhang said. All in all, "diet is among the few modifiable risk factors for cancer prevention," Zhang said. "These findings underscore the needs for reducing cancer burden and disparities in the US by improving the intake of key food groups and nutrients."[1]

This study is eye-opening, but it also raises a question: given these statistics, are people aware the role that diet plays in their health. For most it is intimidating, and they do not know where to start.

Diet

We have already established that lifestyle is how one chooses to do or is forced to do things due to different factors and eating is one of those things. Factors influencing diet are culture, religion, philosophy, preference, availability, and affordability. Unfortunately, it does not guarantee that all the various diets will be equally beneficial to health and some are more and others are less nutritious. Rather than go into the technical details, the best way to learn is to observe those who are reaping the benefits of eating for good health. As we learned earlier here are people who practice good nutrition among other good habits, who reside in what we learned as the Blue Zones. These are the places in the world where you find the highest concentration of people who live to over a 100 years old. The only such Blue Zone in North America is Loma Linda in Southern California which is a community with a high concentration of Seventh day Adventists. Being in America, I will focus on the Blue zone which is here. Seventh-day Adventists take the position that a plant-based diet is the original diet of man that we were designed to eat as written in scripture, "And God said, "See, I have given you every herb that yields seed which is on the face of all the earth, and every tree whose fruit yields seed; to you it shall be for food." Genesis 1:29, and for those who are non-vegetarian, they still follow the dietary law as set out in Leviticus chapter 11 which prohibits the eating of "unclean" animals such as swine and shellfish.

"Even our non-vegetarians are relatively low meat consumers," said Dr. Michael Orlich, the principal investigator of the Adventist Health Study-2, dedicated to examining the link between healthy lifestyle factors and disease in 96,000 Seventh-day Adventists in the United States and Canada.

"The average for non-vegetarians is only about two ounces of total meat a day, which is quite low," Orlich said. Low is an understatement. Based on US Department of Agriculture statistics on meat sold, Americans were expected to consume 222 pounds of red meat and poultry per person last year. In comparison, the Seventh-day Adventist meat eaters in the study consume less than 46 pounds a year.

What does that vegetarian lifestyle accomplish? A lower weight, for one. Vegans in the study had an average body mass index (BMI) of 23, well below the healthy cutoff of 25, Orlich said. Meat eaters in the study -- no matter how little they ate -- had an average BMI of 29, just shy of being considered obese. Other key factors to longevity: Only 1% of the Seventh-day Adventist community in the study smokes. Little to no alcohol is consumed. Daily exercise out in the fresh air of nature is the norm. The church advocates a life of service, so dedication to volunteering, humanitarian and mission work is typical, which contributes to a sense of community. [2] As a result of this lifestyle they live longer and are healthier well into an advanced age and are affected by the leading societal health problems at significantly lower rates for example, "The death rate from cancer for Adventist men is 60 percent lower than that of the average California male; for Adventist women, it is 75 percent lower. According to Loma Linda University, ground zero in the Adventist Health Studies, "Death from coronary heart disease among Adventist men was 66 percent [lower compared to their California peers]; for Adventist women, it was 98 percent [lower]. Stroke death rates for Adventist men were 72 percent [lower], compared to their non-Adventist counterparts. For Adventist women, death from stroke was 82 percent [lower]." [3]

Probiotics

Another aspect of nutrition which has grown in importance fairly recently is the effect of probiotics on health. There is a growing body of scientific evidence suggesting that you can treat and even prevent some illnesses with foods and supplements containing certain kinds of live bacteria. Naturally fermented food contains a lot of these beneficial microorganisms, called probiotics (from pro and biota, meaning "for life"), like yoghurt, kimchi and sauerkraut among others.

Some digestive disease specialists are recommending probiotic supplements for disorders that frustrate conventional medicine, such as irritable bowel syndrome. "Since the mid-1990s, clinical studies suggest that probiotic therapy can help treat several gastrointestinal ills, delay the development of allergies in children, and treat and prevent vaginal and urinary infections in women." [4] Research has been promising for these friendly critters. Potential benefits of probiotics have been seen in the treatment or prevention of:

- diarrhea
- irritable bowel syndrome
- ulcerative colitis
- Crohn's disease
- H. pylori (the cause of ulcers)
- vaginal infections
- urinary tract infections

- recurrence of bladder cancer
- infection of the digestive tract caused by Clostridium difficile
- pouchitis (a possible side effect of surgery that removes the colon)
- eczema in children.

References

1. Preventable Cancer Burden Associated With Poor Diet in the United States, JNCI Cancer Spectrum, Volume 3, Issue 2, June 2019, pkz034, https://doi.org/10.1093/jncics/pkz034
2. https://www.cnn.com/2019/11/25/health/longevity-blue-zone-wellness/index.html
3. https://www.theatlantic.com/health/archive/2013/02/the-lovely-hill-where-people-live-longer-and-happier/272798/
4. https://www.health.harvard.edu/vitamins-and-supplements/health-benefits-of-taking-probiotics

3
EXERCISE

In a study published in the Canadian Medical Association Journal, it was found that both men and women who reported increased levels of physical activity and fitness were found to have reductions in relative risk (by about 20%–35%) of death due to cardiovascular disease, as well as even greater reductions in the risk of death from any cause. Physically inactive middle-aged women (engaging in less than 1 hour of exercise per week) experienced a 52% increase in all-cause mortality, a doubling of cardiovascular-related mortality and a 29% increase in cancer-related mortality compared with physically active women. These relative risks are similar to those for hypertension, hypercholesterolemia and obesity, and they approach those associated with moderate cigarette smoking. Moreover, it appears that people who are fit yet have other risk factors for cardiovascular disease may be at lower risk of premature death than people who are sedentary with no risk factors for cardiovascular disease. [1]

Other than reducing risks for cardiovascular disease, exercise has a host of other benefits. Many people have the desire to exercise but do not know where to start. It is just as intimidating as how to start eating right. The good thing is that we can learn from the people who live in the Blue zones. Walking at least a mile every day, planting your own garden, cutting your own grass, riding a bike to work or school, doing plenty of work around your house, and, where reasonable, doing things yourself rather than using automatic appliances that speed things up; these are some of the everyday things they do that are activities not traditionally considered exercise but can have the same effect if done consistently and daily. These sort of activities are part of their lifestyle and they generally do not have a structured time to exercise, but it is woven into their lifestyle as activities of daily living. Keeping your body in motion is the key, and there is a term for this: "NEAT, or Non–Exercise Activity

Thermogenesis. It occurs with every activity that we perform except sleeping or performing sports- like exercises. It could be yard work, walking to work, housework, or even fidgeting."[2] The more active you are no matter how small, versus sitting all day and being sedentary, helps and adds up daily.

Benefits of exercise:

1. It Can Make You Feel Happier

Exercise has been shown to improve your mood and decrease feelings of depression, anxiety and stress. It produces changes in the parts of the brain that regulate stress and anxiety. It can also increase brain sensitivity for the hormones serotonin and norepinephrine, which relieve feelings of depression. Additionally, exercise can increase the production of endorphins, which are known to help produce positive feelings and reduce the perception of pain. Furthermore, exercise has been shown to reduce symptoms in people suffering from anxiety.

2. It Can Help With Weight Loss

Some studies have shown that inactivity is a major factor in weight gain and obesity. While dieting, a reduced calorie intake will lower your metabolic rate, which will delay weight loss. On the contrary, regular exercise has been shown to increase your metabolic rate, which will burn more calories and help you lose weight.

3. It Is Good for Your Muscles and Bones

Exercise plays a vital role in building and maintaining strong muscles and bones. As people age, they tend to lose muscle mass and function, which can lead to injuries and disabilities. Practicing regular physical activity is essential to reducing muscle loss and maintaining strength as you age. Also, exercise helps build bone density when you're younger, in addition to helping prevent osteoporosis later in life.

4. It Can Increase Your Energy Levels

Exercise can be a real energy booster for healthy people, as well as those suffering from various medical conditions. One study found that six weeks of regular exercise reduced feelings of fatigue for 36 healthy people who had reported persistent fatigue. It also helps people suffering from progressive illnesses, such as cancer, HIV/AIDS and multiple sclerosis

5. It Can Reduce Your Risk of Chronic Disease

Lack of regular physical activity is a primary cause of chronic disease. Regular exercise has been shown to improve insulin sensitivity, cardiovascular fitness and body composition, yet decrease blood pressure and blood fat levels. In contrast, a lack of regular exercise — even in the short term — can lead to significant increases in belly fat, which increases the risk of type 2 diabetes, heart disease and early death. Therefore, daily physical activity is recommended to reduce belly fat and decrease the risk of developing these diseases.

6. It Can Help Skin Health

Your skin can be affected by the amount of oxidative stress in your body. Oxidative stress occurs when the body's antioxidant defenses cannot completely repair the damage that free radicals cause to cells. This can damage their internal structures and deteriorate your skin. Even though intense and exhaustive physical activity can contribute to oxidative damage, regular moderate exercise can increase your body's production of natural antioxidants, which help protect cells. In the same way, exercise can stimulate blood flow and induce skin cell adaptations that can help delay the appearance of skin aging.

7. It Can Help Your Brain Health and Memory

Exercise can improve brain function and protect memory and thinking skills. To begin with, it increases your heart rate, which promotes the flow of blood and oxygen to your brain. It can also stimulate the production of hormones that can enhance the growth of brain cells. Moreover, the ability of exercise to prevent chronic disease can translate into benefits for your brain, since its function can be affected by these diseases. Regular physical activity is especially important in older adults since aging — combined with oxidative stress and inflammation — promotes changes in brain structure and function.

8. It Can Help With Relaxation and Sleep Quality

Regular exercise can help you relax and sleep better. In regards to sleep quality, the energy depletion that occurs during exercise stimulates recuperative processes during sleep. Moreover, the increase in body temperature that occurs during exercise is thought to improve sleep quality by helping it drop during sleep. Many studies on the effects of exercise on sleep have reached similar conclusions. One study found that 150 minutes of moderate-to-vigorous activity per week can provide up to a 65% improvement in sleep quality.

9. It Can Reduce Pain

Chronic pain can be debilitating, but exercise can actually help reduce it. In fact, for many years, the recommendation for treating chronic pain was rest and inactivity. However, recent studies show that exercise helps relieve chronic pain. A review of several studies indicates that exercise helps participants with chronic pain reduce their pain and improve their quality of life.

10. It Can Promote a Better Sex Life

This one applies to the married people. Exercise has been proven to boost sex drive. Engaging in regular exercise can strengthen the cardiovascular system, improve blood circulation, tone muscles and enhance flexibility, all of which can improve your sex life. One study found that a simple routine of a six-minute walk around the house helped 41 men reduce their erectile dysfunction symptoms by 71%. [3]

References

1. Warburton, Darren E R et al. "Health benefits of physical activity: the evidence." CMAJ : Canadian Medical Association journal = journal de l'Association medicale canadienne vol. 174,6 (2006): 801-9.
2. https://www.bluezones.com/2020/01/the-neat-way-to-exercise-for-a-longer-healthier-life/
3. https://www.healthline.com/nutrition/10-benefits-of-exercise

4
REST

A 32-year-old man was found dead in an Internet cafe in Taiwan after a marathon three-day gaming binge and it was the island's second death of an online gamer that year of 2015. [1] The cause was determined to be cardiac failure. Sadly, such occurences are becoming more common with reports of such incidences in different parts of the world due to playing for extended periods without sleep. There is widespread sleep insufficiency enough for it to be recognized as a public health concern due to its link to motor vehicle crashes, medical and other occupational errors. Unfortunately the main reason people are not getting restful sleep or enough of it is not only work anymore.

The distractions are more leisurely or social now because well into the night, people receive message notifications from social networking platforms like Twitter or facebook, or even regular text messages, and keep checking and responding to them. Given the addictive nature of social media, it is not surprising that less time is given to proper restful sleep. Getting little or no rest discourages optimum function of the body and slows down healing because important processes like tissue growth and repair take place during sleep. Sleep insufficiency is also more likely to contribute to chronic diseases such as hypertension, diabetes, depression, and obesity, as well as sleep disorders such as insomnia or obstructive sleep apnea. "An estimated 50-70 million US adults have sleep or wakefulness disorder, 37.9% reported unintentionally falling asleep during the day at least once in the preceding month 4.7% reported nodding off or falling asleep while driving at least once in the preceding month. Drowsy driving is responsible for 1,550 fatalities and 40,000 nonfatal injuries annually in the United States." [1]

What can we learn from the Blue zones about rest? In the original blue zone regions, life unfolds more slowly, more quietly, and with less urgency. People's lives aren't laced with worry, hurry, and the constant need to be elsewhere. Not coincidentally, perhaps, they live longer lives. They even find times to nap and part of the key is that they live low tech lives, as we learned above how technology has become so engaging that people are resting less. [2]

Health benefits of rest

1. Lower weight gain risk

The Nurses' Health Study is the most extensive study regarding adult sleep habits and weight, followed 68,000 middle-age American women for 16 years. The study compared women who slept seven hours a night and women who slept five hours or less. They ones who get less than five hours or less of sleep were most likely to become obese during the study. This also applies to children. The less they sleep when young increases the chances of being obese later in life.

2. Lower risk of heart disease

A 2011 European Heart Journal review of 15 medical studies involving almost 475,000 people found that short sleepers had a 48% increased risk of developing or dying from coronary heart disease (CHD) in a seven to 25-year follow-up period (depending on the study) and a 15% greater risk of developing or dying from stroke during this same time. Interestingly, long sleepers -- those who averaged nine or more hours a night -- also showed a 38% increased risk of developing or dying from CHD and a 65% increased risk of stroke. [3] In the 1980s, at the peak of the Japanese economic boom, work exhaustion and sleep deprivation were blamed for large number of deaths. Most cases of "karoshi", or "death from overwork", involved acute cardiovascular events. [4]

3. Better productivity and concentration

Research has linked getting enough sleep to better concentration, productivity, and cognition. Mounting evidence suggests that a good night's sleep seriously boosts productivity. A 2015 study in the Journal of Child Psychology and Psychiatry showed that children's sleep patterns can have a direct impact on their behavior and academic performance. [6]

4. Greater athletic performance

Getting a sufficient amount of sleep can boost a person's athletic performance. Several previous studies in team sports have demonstrated that competitive success in competition is related to increased sleep duration and quality. [8]

5. More social and emotional intelligence

Sleep has links to people's emotional and social intelligence. Someone who does not get adequate sleep is more likely to have issues with recognizing other people's emotions and expressions. sleep deprivation is associated with diminished emotional expressivity and impaired emotion recognition, and this has particular relevance for social interactions. Sleep deprivation also increases emotional reactivity. Evidence of emotional dysregulation in insomnia and poor sleep has also been reported. [9]

6. Better social life

According to a University of California Berkeley study, people who have experienced sleep loss are less eager to interact with others and on the other hand, the results also show that people who are sleep-deprived tend to come across as socially unappealing.[10]

7. Preventing depression

A study appearing in JAMA Psychiatry examined patterns of death by suicide over 10 years, concluding that lack of sleep is a contributing factor to many of these deaths. [11] In another study in the Australian and New Zealand Journal of Psychiatry it was found that people with sleep disorders such as insomnia are likely to show signs of depression. [12]

8. Lower inflammation

Too much and too little sleep appears to be associated with inflammation which can lead to many illnesses. It is being suggested that sleep disturbance or insomnia should be regarded as behavioral risk factors for inflammation, similar to the adverse effects of high fat diet or sedentary behavior. Treatments targeting sleep behavior could be a strategy for reversing the inflammation and reducing risk of inflammatory illnesses.[13]

9. Stronger immune system

Severe sleep loss jolts the immune system into action, reflecting the same type of immediate response shown during exposure to stress, a new study reports. The immune system is no exception to this relationship. Some research shows how better sleep quality can help the body fight off infection. [15]

10. Stronger bones

Getting five or fewer hours of sleep a night is associated with low bone mineral density (BMD) and higher odds of osteoporosis, according to the findings of the largest study of sleep and BMD to date among U.S. postmenopausal women. [16]

Some things a person can do to improve sleep quality are:
- Reducing stress
- Avoiding sleeping in when you have had enough sleep and try to wake up at the same time.
- Going to bed around the same time each night.
- Spending time outdoors and being more active.
- Minimizing time on social media especially at night.

References

1. https://www.sleepassociation.org/about-sleep/sleep-statistics/
2. https://www.bluezones.com/2013/09/9-blue-zones-lessons-for-slowing-down/
3. https://www.webmd.com/sleep-disorders/features/how-sleep-affects-your-heart#1
4. Nagai, Michiaki et al. "Sleep duration as a risk factor for cardiovascular disease- a review of the recent literature." Current cardiology reviews vol. 6,1 (2010): 54-61.
5. Diaz, Anjolii et al. "Children's Sleep and Academic Achievement: The Moderating Role of Effortful Control." International journal of behavioral development vol. 41,2 (2017): 275-284.
6. Watson, Andrew M. MD, MS Sleep and Athletic Performance, Current Sports Medicine Reports: 11/12 2017 - Volume 16 - Issue 6 - p 413-418 doi: 10.1249/JSR.0000000000000418
7. https://www.sciencedirect.com/science/article/pii/S1087079214001579
8. https://www.medicalnewstoday.com/articles/324678#Alienation-is-contagious
9. https://www.ncbi.nlm.nih.gov/pubmed/25133759
10. https://www.ncbi.nlm.nih.gov/pubmed/25128225
11. Michael R. Irwin, Richard Olmstead, Judith E. Carroll. Sleep Disturbance, Sleep Duration, and Inflammation: A Systematic Review and Meta-Analysis of Cohort Studies and Experimental Sleep Deprivation. Biological Psychiatry, 2016; 80 (1): 40
12. https://www.ncbi.nlm.nih.gov/books/NBK482512/
13. https://doi.org/10.1002/jbmr.3879

5
WATER

Water is life! It supports all life forms on our planet. It ranges anywhere from 55% to 75% of a human body depending on age, no wonder it is no surprise that it is vital for survival because we are primarily water. It is important not only for cellular survival but also for its cleansing properties, cleaning not only the outside but also internal organs. People who live in the blue zones tend to drink water and herbal teas like green tea in Okinawa, and in Ikaria, it is a tea made from Oregano, Rosemary and mint. The Adventists in Loma Linda tend to avoid caffeinated beverages like coffee. In all the regions, they tend to stay from beverages like sodas. [1]

Health benefits of water

1. It regulates your body temperature
Staying hydrated is crucial to maintaining your body temperature. Your body loses water through sweat during physical activity and in hot environments.
2. It protects your tissues, spinal cord, and joints
Water consumption helps lubricate and cushion your joints, spinal cord, and tissues. This will help you enjoy physical activity and lessen discomfort caused by conditions like arthritis.
3. It helps excrete waste through perspiration, urination, and defecation. Your body uses water to sweat, urinate, and have bowel movements. You also need enough water in your system to have healthy bowel movements and avoid constipation. Adequate water intake helps your kidneys work more efficiently and helps to prevent kidney stones.
4. It helps maximize physical performance
Drinking plenty of water during physical activity is essential. Athletes may perspire up to 6 to 10 percent of body weight during physical activity. You may be more susceptible to the effects of

dehydration if you're participating in endurance training or high-intensity sports such as basketball.

5. It helps create saliva

Water is a main component of saliva. Saliva also includes small amounts of electrolytes, mucus, and enzymes. It's essential for breaking down solid food and keeping your mouth healthy.

6. It helps with nutrient absorption

In addition to helping with food breakdown, water also helps dissolve vitamins, minerals, and other nutrients from your food. It then delivers these vitamin components to the rest of your body for use. Water also helps you absorb important vitamins, minerals, and nutrients from your food, which will increase your chances of staying healthy.

7. It helps you lose weight

Studies have linked body fat and weight loss with drinking water in both overweight girls and women. Drinking more water while dieting and exercising may just help you lose extra pounds.

8. It improves blood oxygen circulation

Water carries helpful nutrients and oxygen to your entire body in your blood. Reaching your daily water intake will improve your circulation and have a positive impact on your overall health.

9. It helps fight off illness

Drinking enough water can help prevent certain medical conditions which include:
- constipation
- kidney stones
- exercise-induced asthma
- urinary tract infection
- hypertension

10. It helps boost energy

One study found that drinking 500 milliliters of water boosted the metabolic rate by 30 percent in both men and women. These effects appeared to last over an hour.

11. It aids in cognitive function

Proper hydration is key to staying in tip-top cognitive shape. Research indicates that not drinking enough water can negatively impact your focus, alertness, and short-term memory.

12. It helps improve mood

Not getting enough water can also affect your mood. Dehydration may result in fatigue and confusion as well as anxiety.

13. It helps keep skin bright

Adequate water intake will help keep your skin hydrated and may promote collagen production. However, water intake alone isn't enough to reduce the effects of aging. This process is also connected to your genes and overall sun protection. [1]

How much water intake

The National Academies of Science, Engineering and Medicine recommends that men drink about 3.7 liters (about 125 ounces) a day and women drink 2.7 liters (about 91 ounces). These recommendations cover fluids from water, other beverages and food. About 20 percent of daily fluid intake usually comes from food and the rest from drinks. [2] Pale yellow urine is usually an indicator that you are well hydrated. If it is dark yellow or has a strong odor, you might be dehydrated.

These 4 factors determine your water needs:

Activity level: If you work out a lot or are moving all day long, drink more water.

Location: If you find yourself in a warmer climate, you'll probably want to increase your water intake.

Metabolism: If you consider yourself to have a faster metabolism, and your body seems to need more fuel to keep its engines revved — you may also notice that you need more water.

Size: The more you weigh, the more water your body tends to need.

But water needs fluctuate depending on:

Alcohol consumption: if you drink alcohol, drink a glass of water to rehydrate yourself and replace fluids caused by alcohol-mediated losses.

Health: Illness usually can lead to fluid loss due to vomiting or diarrhea. If you have a fever, it's a good idea to increase your daily quota of fluids by a few cups.

Physical activity: The more active you are, the more water you'll need.

Weather: You'll definitely need more water during a heatwave than a blizzard. Use your common sense.

Mild to moderate dehydration symptoms:
- Constipation.
- Dizziness.
- Dry mouth.
- Fatigue.
- Muscle cramps.

More severe dehydration constitutes a medical emergency that requires immediate attention, and can include any or all of these as well as:
- Abdominal pain.
- Confusion.
- Lethargy.[3]

References

1. https://www.nbcnews.com/better/health/blue-zones-6-secrets-borrow-people-who-live-longest-ncna921776
2. https://www.healthline.com/health/food-nutrition/why-is-water-important
3. https://www.mayoclinic.org/healthy-lifestyle/nutrition-and-healthy-eating/in-depth/water/art-20044256
4. https://health.clevelandclinic.org/how-much-water-do-you-need-daily/

6
SELF CONTROL

The abuse of tobacco, alcohol, and illicit drugs is more than $740 billion annually in costs related to crime, lost work productivity and health care in America. [1] Every day, 29 people in the United States die in motor vehicle crashes that involve an alcohol-impaired driver, which is one death every 50 minutes. The annual cost of alcohol-related crashes totals more than $44 billion. In 2016, 10,497 people died in alcohol-impaired driving crashes, accounting for 28% of all traffic-related deaths in the United States. [2]

On a different note the impact of social media usage is mind blowing, to say the least. Researchers from the University of Chicago Booth School of Business in a survey done on 250 people found that sleep and sex were the two things people most longed for during the day, but that the urges to keep on top of social networks and work were the hardest to resist. In contrast alcohol and tobacco prompted much lower levels of desire despite their reputation for being addictive.[3]

According to the North American Foundation for Gambling Addiction help, 2.6% or almost 10 million people have a gambling addiction problem. The internet has also made gambling even more accessible than ever before. 55% of it is done on laptops, 34% on PCs, and 29%/21% on mobile phones/tablets. Mobile phones are more popular with 18-44 year olds while PCs among the older population. [4]

Last but not least, Porn addiction which is now considered a public health crisis, has 42.7% of all internet users. The National Council on Sexual Addiction Compulsivity estimated that 6% to 8% of Americans are sex addicts, which is 18 million to 24 million people. More than 80% of women who have porn addiction take it offline. Women far more than men, are likely to act out their behaviors in real life, such as having multiple partners, casual sex, or affairs. [5]

Self-control is necessary to have balance and to make the best decisions for your health and your life as a whole. When we lose control to anything it becomes an addiction. By Merriam-Webster dictionary definition, an addiction is:

: a strong and harmful need to regularly have something (such as a drug) or do something (such as gamble)

The overpowering urge to engage in something even with full knowledge that it is destructive in some way and has negative consequences is the hallmark of addiction. When one lacks self-control, they are no longer in control but being controlled. It is easier to think of addiction in terms of harmful things like illicit, narcotic drugs or alcohol which have obvious harmful effects, but we can also become addicted to things that are not harmful in themselves like social media or television. They become harmful when they start taking more of your time away from important things like work or relationships. In those cases they become harmful destroying careers, relationships and even endangering health. We will look at the spiritual side of self-control later on. Addictions are good examples of lack of self-control. Here are some common examples:

- Gambling
- Alcoholism
- Recreational drugs
- Prescription drugs
- Overeating
- Sweets
- Shopping
- Sex
- Pornography
- Television
- The Internet
- Social networking
- Exercise
- Gaming

Benefits of self-control
- Good health mentally, physically, socially and spiritually
- Better use of time.

- Preserves relationships – spouse, family, friends, and work.
- Better finances

References

1. https://www.drugabuse.gov/drug-topics/trends-statistics/costs-substance-abuse
2. https://www.cdc.gov/motorvehiclesafety/impaired_driving/impaired-drv_factsheet.html
3. https://www.psychologicalscience.org/news/facebook-and-twitter-more-addictive-than-tobacco-and-alcohol.html
4. https://nafgah.org/statistics-gambling-addiction-2016/
5. https://www.addictionhope.com/sexual-addiction/

7
AIR

In a lifetime, about 250 million liters of air passes through your lungs. No wonder air quality has a major effect on health. Smoking is the one factor we can control when it comes to air pollution. The air quality in the cities where we live is largely out of our control, and unfortunately, air pollution is a great contributor to health problems. People residing in Blue zones live in small towns or lean towards a rural lifestyle, meaning less exposure compared to residents in big cities. They are also unlikely to be smokers. Unfortunately not all of us stay in the country or even in a small town, but knowing the effects of air quality on health can help to keep in mind on any of the things that are within your control which you can do to improve your situation.

Whom does air pollution affect the most?

A Children's Health Study at the University of Southern California is one of the largest studies of the long-term effects of air pollution on children and the following are some findings:

1. Higher air pollution levels increase short-term respiratory infections, which lead to more school absences.
2. Children who play several outdoor sports and live in high ozone communities are more likely to develop asthma.
3. Children living near busy roads are at increased risk for asthma.
4. Children with asthma who were exposed to high levels of air pollutants were more likely to develop bronchitis symptoms.
5. Living in communities with higher pollution levels can cause lung damage.

Other studies on women and children show that:

- Exposure can alter the size of a child's developing brain, which may ultimately increase the risk for cognitive and emotional problems later in adolescence.
- Prenatal exposure was associated with brain development effects, slower processing speed, attention-deficit and hyperactivity disorder (ADHD) symptoms, and other neurobehavioral problems in urban youth.
- In New York City, prenatal exposure to air pollution may play a role in childhood ADHD-related behavior problems.
- Prenatal exposure to particulate matter was associated with low birth weight.
- Women exposed to high levels of fine particulate matter during pregnancy, particularly in the third trimester, may have up to twice the risk of having a child with autism.
- Might increase the chance of those children having high blood pressure in early life. In California's agricultural San Joaquin Valley, women who were exposed to high levels of carbon monoxide, nitrogen oxide, or nitrogen dioxide during their first 8 weeks of pregnancy were more likely to have a baby with neural tube defects.
- In Marietta, Ohio, home to a ferromanganese refinery, manganese concentrations in blood and hair, a biomarker of air pollution exposure, were associated with lower child IQ scores.

Older adults
- In older adults, it may significantly hasten physical disabilities. The risk is more pronounced among racial minorities and lower-income people.
- Associated with accelerated memory problems and Alzheimer's-like brain declines, which was seen among women 65 years of age and older. [1]

Smoking

On average smokers die 10 years earlier than non-smokers. If smoking continues at the current rate among U.S. Youth, 5.6 million of today's Americans younger than 18 years of age are expected to die prematurely form a smoking-related illness. This represents about one in every 13 Americans aged 17 or younger who are alive today. A Smoking costs the U.S. Billions of dollars every year. Nearly $170 billion in direct medical care for adults and in excess of $156 billion in lost productivity due to premature death and exposure to secondhand smoke. Cigarette smoking is responsible for more than 480,000 deaths per year in the United States, including more than 41,000 deaths resulting from secondhand smoke exposure. This is about one in five deaths annually, or 1,300 deaths every day.[2]

Smoking can cause cancer almost anywhere in your body:
- Bladder
- Blood (acute myeloid leukemia)
- Cervix
- Colon and rectum (colorectal)
- Esophagus
- Kidney and ureter
- Larynx
- Liver
- Oropharynx (includes parts of the throat, tongue, soft palate, and the tonsils)
- Pancreas
- Stomach
- Trachea, bronchus, and lung
- Smoking also increases the risk of dying from cancer and other diseases in cancer patients and survivors. If nobody smoked, one of every three cancer deaths in the United States would not happen.

Smoking can make it harder for a woman to become pregnant. It can also affect her baby's health before and after birth. Smoking increases risks for:
- Preterm (early) delivery
- Stillbirth (death of the baby before birth)
- Low birth weight
- Sudden infant death syndrome (known as SIDS or crib death)
- Ectopic pregnancy
- Orofacial clefts in infants

- Smoking can also affect men's sperm, which can reduce fertility and also increase risks for birth defects and miscarriage.
- Smoking can affect bone health.
- Women past childbearing years who smoke have weaker bones than women who never smoked. They are also at greater risk for broken bones.
- Smoking affects the health of your teeth and gums and can cause tooth loss.
- Smoking can increase your risk for cataracts (clouding of the eye's lens that makes it hard for you to see). It can also cause age-related macular degeneration (AMD). AMD is damage to a small spot near the center of the retina, the part of the eye needed for central vision.
- Smoking is a cause of type 2 diabetes mellitus and can make it harder to control. The risk of developing diabetes is 30–40% higher for active smokers than nonsmokers.
- Smoking causes general adverse effects on the body, including inflammation and decreased immune function and is a cause of rheumatoid arthritis. [3]

References

1. https://www.niehs.nih.gov/health/topics/agents/air-pollution/index.cfm
2. https://www.cdc.gov/tobacco/data_statistics/fact_sheets/fast_facts/index.htm
3. https://www.cdc.gov/tobacco/data_statistics/fact_sheets/health_effects/effects_cig_smoking/index.htm

8
SUNSHINE

Nonsmokers who stayed out of the sun had a life expectancy similar to smokers who soaked up the most rays, according to researchers who studied nearly 30,000 Swedish women over 20 years. Compared with those with the highest sun exposure, life expectancy for those who avoided sun dropped by 0.6 to 2.1 years. Turns out avoiding the Sun is actually a risk factor for death of a similar magnitude as smoking. [1] Residents in the Blue zones tend to be people who engage in outdoor activities like gardening, yard chores like cutting grass and walking.

The sun has come under much scrutiny as the benefits of it are weighed against the dangers. Over-exposure has been linked to increased incidence in skin cancer. Though there are many health benefits to sun exposure, it is unfortunately perceived to be more harmful than it is beneficial. Many get too little exposure as a result and not only miss the benefits but also experience the negative effects of not getting enough. It seems many are more vulnerable to being sick when deficient in this vitamin.

The current Corona virus pandemic is also underlining the importance of this underappreciated vitamin, according to a University of Chicago Medicine study: "Vitamin D is important to the function of the immune system and vitamin D supplements have previously been shown to lower the risk of viral respiratory tract infections," said David Meltzer, MD, PhD, Chief of Hospital Medicine at UChicago Medicine and lead author of the study. "Our statistical analysis suggests this may be true for the COVID-19 infection."[2] Patients who had vitamin D deficiency (< 20ng/ml was used in the study) that was not treated were almost twice as likely to test positive for COVID-19 compared to patients who had sufficient levels of the vitamin.

How your body gets vitamin D

Your skin makes vitamin D3 when it's exposed to sunlight. Ultraviolet B (UVB) radiation from sunlight triggers the formation of vitamin D3 in the skin. A similar process takes place in plants and mushrooms, where UVB light leads to the formation of vitamin D2 from ergosterol, a compound found in plant oils.

Unlike dietary vitamin D, you cannot overdose on vitamin D3 produced in your skin. If your body already has enough, your skin simply produces less, but most people get very little sun. They either work indoors or live in a country that doesn't get much sunlight during the winter. If this applies to you, make sure to regularly eat plenty of food rich in vitamin D. Vitamin D3 is only found in animal-sourced foods, whereas D2 mainly comes from plant sources and fortified foods.

Dietary supplements

Vitamin D2 is cheaper to produce, which is why it is the most common form in fortified foods. Vitamin D3 is more effective at improving Vitamin D Status, however both are effectively absorbed into the bloodstream and the liver metabolizes them differently. If you are taking vitamin D supplements, consider choosing vitamin D3. There are concerns that vitamin D2 supplements might be lower quality than D3 supplements. In fact, studies suggest vitamin D2 is more sensitive to humidity and fluctuations in temperature. For this reason, vitamin D2 supplements may be more likely to degrade over time.[3]

Benefits of Vitamin D
1. Preventing stroke:
   Vitamin D may help by improving the lining of blood vessel walls to allow blood to flow freely and by reducing the harmful effects of inflammation, along with several other effects.
2. Healthier blood vessels:
   A study from Ohio University showed that vitamin D3 can repair damage to the heart and blood vessels caused by high blood pressure.

3. High blood pressure:
   Low levels of vitamin D have been linked to high blood pressure. And some research shows that taking a vitamin D pill can help to lower it, which lowers the risk of heart attacks and stroke.
4. Less susceptibility to Metabolic syndrome:
   A Brazilian study found post-menopausal women with low vitamin D levels more likely to develop metabolic syndrome. A person has metabolic syndrome when they have 3 of 5 "almost" risk factors for heart disease. For example, blood pressure is "almost high," blood sugar is "almost high," the measure of inches around the waist is "almost high," HDL cholesterol is "almost low," and/or triglycerides, another harmful blood fat, are "almost high." If you have any combination of 3 of these "almost" risk factors, it means you have metabolic syndrome and you're at a much higher risk of heart disease, stroke, and diabetes.[4]
5. Diabetes:
   Low levels of vitamin D raise the risk for pre-diabetes and type 2 diabetes, recent research shows. According to a University of California at San Diego study, lack of vitamin D in the body turned out to be a strong predictor of who would get diabetes. Those with the lowest blood levels of vitamin D were at the highest risk.
6. Bone health and muscle strength:
   Several studies link low vitamin D blood levels with an increased risk of fractures in older adults, and they suggest that vitamin D supplementation may prevent such fractures—as long as it is taken in a high enough dose. Vitamin D may also help increase muscle strength.
7. Prevent Cancer:
   Nearly 30 years ago, researchers noticed an intriguing relationship between colon cancer deaths and geographic location: People who lived at higher latitudes which get less UVB rays in the sunlight, such as in the northern U.S., had higher rates of death from colon cancer than people who lived closer to the equator. In humans, epidemiological studies show that higher serum levels of vitamin D are associated with substantially lower rates of colon, pancreatic, prostate,

and other cancers, with the evidence strongest for colorectal cancer.
8. Immune function:
Vitamin D's role in regulating the immune system has led scientists to explore a possible link to autoimmune conditions. Collectively, the current evidence suggests that low vitamin D may have a causal role in MS and if so, approximately 40% of cases may be prevented by correcting vitamin D insufficiency.
9. Prevent Flu and the Common Cold:
Vitamin D levels are lowest in the winter months and studies continue to explore the connection to colds and flu. So far it has been found that children exposed to sunlight seem to have fewer respiratory infections and adults who have low vitamin D levels are more likely to report having had a recent cough, cold, or upper respiratory tract infection.
10. Treatment and prevention of Tuberculosis:
Before the advent of antibiotics, sunlight and sun lamps were part of the standard treatment for tuberculosis (TB). Several case-control studies, when analyzed together, suggest that people diagnosed with tuberculosis have lower vitamin D levels than healthy people of similar age and other characteristics.
11. Reduced risk of premature death:
A combined analysis of multiple studies found that taking modest levels of vitamin D supplements was associated with a statistically significant reduction in mortality from any cause. [5]

Deficiency Causes

Skin type: Darker skin, for example, and sunscreen, reduce the body's ability to absorb the ultraviolet radiation B (UVB) rays from the sun. Absorbing sunlight is essential for the skin to produce vitamin D.

Sunscreen: A sunscreen with a sun protection factor (SPF) of 30 can reduce the body's ability to synthesize the vitamin by 95% or more. Covering the skin with clothing can inhibit vitamin D production also.

Geographical location: People who live in northern latitudes or areas of high pollution, work night shifts, or are home bound should aim to consume vitamin D from food sources whenever possible.

Breastfeeding: Infants who exclusively breastfeed need a vitamin D supplement, especially if they have dark skin or have minimal sun exposure. The American Academy of Pediatrics recommend that all breastfed infants receive 400 international units (IU) per day of oral vitamin D.

Symptoms of vitamin D deficiency may include:

- regular sickness or infection
- fatigue
- bone and back pain
- low mood
- impaired wound healing
- hair loss
- muscle pain

If Vitamin D deficiency continues for long periods, it may result in complications, such as:

- cardiovascular conditions
- autoimmune problems
- neurological diseases
- infections
- pregnancy complications
- certain cancers, especially breast, prostate, and colon.

How much vitamin D is ideal?

Although people can take vitamin D supplements, it is best to obtain any vitamins or minerals through natural sources wherever possible. At the least, sun exposure on bare skin for 5–10 minutes, 2–3 times per week is reasonable if you have lighter skin. This is a minimum recommendation because, the darker your skin, the more exposure you will need for longer periods. However, vitamin D breaks down quite quickly, meaning that stores can run low, especially in winter. People can measure vitamin D intake in micrograms (mcg) or international units (IU). One microgram of vitamin D is equal to 40 IU. The recommended daily intakes of vitamin D are as follows:

Infants 0–12 months: 400 IU (10 mcg).
Children 1–18 years: 600 IU (15 mcg).
Adults up to 70 years: 600 IU (15 mcg).
Adults over 70 years: 800 IU (20 mcg).
Pregnant or lactating women: 600 IU (15 mcg).

The upper limit that healthcare professionals recommend for vitamin D is 4,000 IU per day for an adult. It is best to follow your healthcare provider's dosage recommendations for your case. Since D3 is more readily assimilated into the body, if high amounts are consumed, D3 is more likely to be toxic as compared to same amount of D2. Make sure they explain what type, how much to take and for how long. Excessive consumption of vitamin D can lead to over calcification of bones and the hardening of blood vessels, kidney, lung, and heart tissues. It is usually due to consuming supplements. The most common symptoms of excessive vitamin D include headache and nausea. However, too much vitamin D can also lead to the following:

- loss of appetite
- dry mouth
- a metallic taste
- vomiting
- constipation
- diarrhea

References

1. https://pubmed.ncbi.nlm.nih.gov/26992108/
2. https://www.uchicagomedicine.org/forefront/coronavirus-disease-covid-19/vitamin-d-deficiency-may-raise-risk-of-getting-covid19
3. https://www.healthline.com/nutrition/vitamin-d2-vs-d3
4. https://www.clevelandheartlab.com/blog/new-heart-benefits-of-vitamin-d/
5. https://www.ncbi.nlm.nih.gov/pmc/articles/PMC3972416/
6. https://ods.od.nih.gov/factsheets/VitaminD-Consumer/

9
SIMILARITIES: PHYSICAL & SPIRITUAL HEALTH

Though great advancements are being made in the realm of science and technology, humanity collectively is not advancing spiritually but actually declining. The principles or laws governing physical and spiritual health are like coins with two faces, one addressing physical and the other spiritual health. This is why it helps to understand how physical health works so we can understand how spiritual health works. Just as with physical health, part of the solution is recognizing that there is a problem because we see the symptoms all around us. We also learned that every symptom has an underlying cause, and that there is a big difference between dealing with the symptoms and dealing with the cause. All these principles apply to spiritual health as well, and the laws of spiritual health help to regain spiritual health as well as to maintain it, the same way health laws help to restore and maintain health if one lives a lifestyle that abides by them. We will begin to learn what spiritual health is, which will be the first step in addressing the societal spiritual crisis.

Optimum function of the soul

If optimum function and soundness of body is health, what is it for the soul? When a soul is said to be of sound health, it functions as it should. What is optimum function for the soul?

37... 'You shall love the Lord your God with all your heart, with all your soul, and with all your mind.'

38 This is the first and great commandment.

39 And the second is like it: 'You shall love your neighbor as yourself.'

40 On these two commandments hang all the Law and the Prophets.". Matthew 22:37-40.

To love God with all our hearts, souls and minds and to love our neighbor as ourselves is optimum function of the soul. The Ten Commandments are summarized by the two commandments above with the first four about love for God and the last six, love for man (neighbor) as in Exodus 20:3-17:

The first four commandments: Love for God

3 "You shall have no other gods before Me.
4 "You shall not make for yourself a carved image—any likeness of anything that is in heaven above, or that is in the earth beneath, or that is in the water under the earth;
5 you shall not bow down to them nor [b]serve them. For I, the Lord your God, am a jealous God, visiting[c] the iniquity of the fathers upon the children to the third and fourth generations of those who hate Me,
6 but showing mercy to thousands, to those who love Me and keep My commandments.
7 "You shall not take the name of the Lord your God in vain, for the Lord will not hold him guiltless who takes His name in vain.
8 "Remember the Sabbath day, to keep it holy. 9 Six days you shall labor and do all your work, 10 but the seventh day is the Sabbath of the Lord your God. In it you shall do no work: you, nor your son, nor your daughter, nor your male servant, nor your female servant, nor your cattle, nor your stranger who is within your gates. 11 For in six days the Lord made the heavens and the earth, the sea, and all that is in them, and rested the seventh day. Therefore the Lord blessed the Sabbath day and hallowed it.

The last six commandments: Love for man by doing to them what you would have them to you:

12 "Honor your father and your mother, that your days may be long upon the land which the Lord your God is giving you.
13 "You shall not murder.
14 "You shall not commit adultery.
15 "You shall not steal.
16 "You shall not bear false witness against your neighbor.

17 "You shall not covet your neighbor's house; you shall not covet your neighbor's wife, nor his male servant, nor his female servant, nor his ox, nor his donkey, nor anything that is your neighbor's."

Love is then when the soul functions as it should. Love for God and love for man is the Law and thus optimum function for the soul and when we live according to the Ten Commandments our souls are in good health. The fulfilling of the Ten Commandments in our lives is how we love God and man, which we have been commanded to do as is written:

8 Owe no one anything except to love one another, for he who loves another has fulfilled the law.

9 For the commandments, "You shall not commit adultery," "You shall not murder," "You shall not steal," [b]"You shall not bear false witness," "You shall not covet," and if there is any other commandment, are all summed up in this saying, namely, "You shall love your neighbor as yourself."

10 Love does no harm to a neighbor; therefore love is the fulfillment of the law. Romans 13:8-10.

True love is how we relate to God and our fellow man. It begins with love for God and when we love God, then we can love our neighbor because:

"20 If someone says, "I love God," and hates his brother, he is a liar; for he who does not love his brother whom he has seen, [d]how can he love God whom he has not seen?

21 And this commandment we have from Him: that he who loves God must love his brother also." 1 John 4:20-21.

True health for the soul begins with love for God

When we love God whom we have not seen, then we can truly love our neighbour as ourselves. When we love God, and our neighbour as ourselves, we are fulfilling the Law and this is the state of health for the soul. Love is summarized in loving God first and loving our neighbor as ourselves which is His will for us. Love is the "optimum function of the soul". When we do not love God first and thus not love our neighbor as ourselves, the soul is not in a healthy state.

Disease of the soul

We learned earlier on that when the body is not functioning as it should, disease occurs. What is disease of the soul? "I said, LORD, be merciful unto me: <u>heal my soul; for I have sinned against thee</u>. Psalms 41:4 (KJV). In this verse, David is asking to be healed from his sin. Healing implies that he needs to be healed from something, or that his soul is in a diseased state. If he sinned and he needs to be healed because of his sin, then sin is a disease of the soul. If sin is a disease of the soul, then it is what is referred to in the following verse:

12 When Jesus heard that, He said to them, "Those who are well have no need of a physician, but those who are sick.

13 But go and learn what this means: 'I desire mercy and not sacrifice.' For I did not come to call the righteous, but sinners, [b]to repentance." Matthew 9:12-13. See also Isaiah 6:10 and Jeremiah 8:22.

If Jesus came to call the sinners to repentance and not the righteous, then those whose souls are in good health or are righteous do not need Him to heal them because He came to heal the sinners, those whose souls are not in good health. So this verse further illustrates how sin is the disease of the soul. What is sin? "…for by the law is the knowledge of sin." Romans 3:20. The Law in the Ten Commandments shows us how we are to relate to God and man. It shows us what is right and wrong in how we relate to God and man. When we do not relate to God or to man as we should, then it is sin.

Symptoms

We learned in the first chapter that symptoms are our friend. They alert us to health problems. You can know a disease by its symptoms, and just as a physical disease has signs and symptoms, so does this disease of the soul, sin. What are the symptoms of sin and how does it manifest?

21 For from within, out of the heart of men, proceed evil thoughts, adulteries, fornications, murders,
22 Thefts, covetousness, wickedness, deceit, lasciviousness, an evil eye, blasphemy, pride, foolishness:
23 All these evil things come from within, and defile the man. Mark 7:21-23. (KJV) Also look at Romans 1:21-32; Galatians 5:19-21 and 2 Timothy 3:1-5.

In these verses we see the symptoms or the manifestations of the disease of sin. It is clear from these verses that when we do these things we are not loving God with all our hearts, souls or minds and do not do unto others as we would like them to do unto us or love them as we love ourselves.

Diagnosis

We saw earlier in the book that symptoms are supposed to show us our true condition. They serve to warn us of any disease process taking place and are supposed to move us to seek a diagnosis to identify the cause and to know how to address it. The one who diagnoses is supposed to be qualified to do so. In the case of this sin disease, it starts in the mind and heart. Only one who can read minds and hearts is qualified to diagnose this disease. Who can read minds and hearts? God can see our hearts and can read our minds as we see in the following verses:

21 Would not God search this out? For He knows the secrets of the heart....
7 For[d] the Lord does not see as man sees; for man looks at the outward appearance, but the Lord looks at the heart."...
5 Therefore judge nothing before the time, until the Lord comes, who will both bring to light the hidden things of darkness and reveal the [b]counsels of the hearts. Then each one's praise will come from God. Psalms 44:21; 1 Samuel 16:7; 1 Corinthians 4:5.

Christ is one with His Father and so He is God in essence as is written:

1 In the beginning was the Word, and the Word was with God, and the Word was God.

2 He was in the beginning with God.

3 All things were made through Him, and without Him nothing was made that was made...

10 He was in the world, and the world was made through Him, and the world did not know Him...

14 And the Word became flesh and dwelt among us, and we beheld His glory, the glory as of the only begotten of the Father, full of grace and truth. John 1:1-3, 10 and 14. Read also Colossians 1:12-19 and 2:9.

Jesus Christ, the True Physician of our souls is the only one fit to diagnose this disease because being one with God He can also read our minds and hearts. We look on the outside and yet He "is a discerner of the thoughts and intents of the heart" through His Word and being that is the embodiment of the Word. Hebrews 4:12 (KJV). The written Word is how Christ the Physician reveals Himself to us and thus through it He diagnoses us. God the Father made Him the Judge because He can not only diagnose our sinful condition but can also Heal us because He is the Physician of our souls which is why He was sent:

38 For I have come down from heaven, not to do My own will, but the will of Him who sent Me.

39 This is the will of the Father who sent Me, that of all He has given Me I should lose nothing, but should raise it up at the last day.

40 And this is the will of Him who sent Me, that everyone who sees the Son and believes in Him may have everlasting life; and I will raise him up at the last day." John 6:38-40.

Since Jesus Christ diagnoses us and has the ability to heal from sin or give everlasting life, He is fit to judge us as well:

21 For as the Father raises the dead and gives life to them, even so the Son gives life to whom He will.

22 For the Father judges no one, but has committed all judgment to the Son,

23 that all should honor the Son just as they honor the Father. He who does not honor the Son does not honor the Father who sent Him." John 5:21-23. We learned earlier on that symptoms serve to

warn us that there is a disease process taking place and that if we ignore the disease, depending on how serious its nature, consequences can range from scars to worst case scenario, death. Sin disease on the other hand has only one outcome if we are not healed and that is death, "For the wages of sin is death"; Romans 6:23.

What makes sin such a dreadful disease is because we are all born into it. It's like a slave who is born into slavery. From the day of birth to the day of death, all that slave knows is slavery and nothing different. We are born with a sinful nature and thus are naturally prone to sin as is written: "5 Behold, I was brought forth in iniquity, and in sin my mother conceived me." Psalms 51:5. By Adam and Eve's offense of eating the forbidden fruit in the garden of Eden, sin came into the world and we see this in Genesis chapter two. "Wherefore, as by one man sin entered into the world, and death by sin; and so death passed upon all men, for that all have sinned:" Romans 5:12 (KJV). We have "all sinned and come short of the glory of God" and "the wages of sin is death." Romans 3:23 and 6:23.

We are born with a sinful nature because we inherited it from our first parents Adam and Eve. At some point between the times we were all born up until now we have all sinned at least once as well. We have not loved our neighbor as ourselves perfectly in one form or another. This illness is so serious given that we all have it. None are exempt and so all of us are in need of healing. To better illustrate how serious sin is in God's eyes, He used Leprosy as a type of sin in Leviticus chapter 13. Just as only the priest could diagnose Leprosy in those days, Christ is the only one fit to diagnose us of this Leprosy of the soul, sin. Just as one who had Leprosy was declared unclean by the priest, Christ declares us unclean or defiled because of sin as we saw in Mark 7:20-23.

To defile is to cause to be unclean. Because of sin in our hearts we become unclean in the Physician's eyes. He can see spiritual Lepers with spiritual Leprosy when He sees us. God the Father sent our Physician and Priest Jesus Christ to heal us all from this Leprosy of the soul. By the isolation of a leper out of the camp far from everyone else, He was hoping we'd understand how terrible sin is. Leprosy is a dreadful disease to behold as it eats its victim away slowly until they finally die. So does sin! Though we see its symptoms we do not see how dreadful and devastating it really is because it is a spiritual condition. If our eyes could be enabled to see spiritually, one would behold a world full of Lepers being eaten away slowly but surely by sin if they are not healed who end up dying a spiritual death. We will take a closer look later at the significance of Leprosy as a type of sin and how it applies to our healing from sin. With this sin disease there are only 2 outcomes. We choose either life or death, there is no in between:

23 For the wages of sin [is] death; but the gift of God [is] eternal life through Jesus Christ our Lord...

12 When Jesus heard that, He said to them, "Those who are well have no need of a physician, but those who are sick.

13 But go and learn what this means: 'I desire mercy and not sacrifice.' For I did not come to call the righteous, but sinners, [b]to repentance." Romans 6:23; Matthew 9:12, 13.

Jesus came to call the sinners to repentance. He came to heal the Spiritual Lepers. We are all sinners born into sin and sin is all around us. We have all sinned and fallen short of His glory. Jesus says that He came for those who are sick because the ones that are "well" or "righteous" do not need healing. If we are all sinners then His statement implies that not all will consider themselves sick or sinners. John explains that:

8 If we say that we have no sin, we deceive ourselves, and the truth is not in us.

9 If we confess our sins, He is faithful and just to forgive us our sins and to cleanse us from all unrighteousness.

10 If we say that we have not sinned, we make Him a liar, and His word is not in us.... 1 John 1:8-10.

Denying that we are sinners we make Him a liar because He is saying we are all sinners. If we accept that we are sinners and that we are sick, He will heal us. But if we choose to remain in denial and not acknowledge that we are sick we remain sick and die from sin which is unto death.

Lifestyle and sin

Earlier on we learned that the underlying cause for disease is lifestyle. Lifestyle is how we choose to live and as we learned health is determined by living a life that is in obedience to the laws of health. Disregarding them make one susceptible to disease or to have less than optimum health. Just as physical health is dependent on a life that is in obedience to the laws of health, spiritual health is just as dependent on obedience to the spiritual side of those same laws. Each of those laws is like a coin which has two faces, addressing both the physical and spiritual aspects of health. We also learned that when one is healed, for them to remain in good health they have to live a life in obedience to the laws. Even when healed, if one disregards them, disease comes back. True health exists only when they are obeyed. This applies not only to physical health but also spiritual health.

The first choice we make to be healed from our sins is to acknowledge that we are sinners and sick with spiritual Leprosy. We confess our sins and he cleanses us from our unrighteousness. We are healed and once healed, for us to stay healthy we have to obey the laws of health. So we have to choose to obey the laws of health and to live a lifestyle that helps to reduce and prevent sin from ruling our lives, just as a good lifestyle reduces the chances of illness returning and helps to prevent it. We will take a closer look at these laws of health to see how we can enjoy true health not only physically but more importantly spiritually. For us to enjoy both as much as possible is His desire for us as is written:

2 Beloved, I pray that you may prosper in all things and be in health, just as your soul prospers.
3 John 2

10
AGAPE LOVE

Physical health is measured by function and similarly spiritual health is when a soul is said to be sound and functioning as it was created to. What is ideal function for our souls? Love! To better understand what love is we have to understand how it works. Is it a warm fuzzy feeling? Is it being nice to those we like? What is it exactly? Jesus speaking about the greatest commandments said the following:

37...""You shall love the Lord your God with all your heart, with all your soul, and with all your mind.'

38 This is the first and great commandment.

39 And the second is like it: 'You shall love your neighbor as yourself.'

40 On these two commandments hang all the Law and the Prophets." Matthew 22:37-40.

The word in these verses is a type of love called Agape which according to the Thayer's Greek Lexicon means "to be full of good-will and exhibit the same". In other words it is not just the intention but also the action of good-will which accompanies it. Agape love has no conditions on who receives it or when as is written;

44 But I say to you, love your enemies, bless those who curse you, do good to those who hate you, and pray for those who spitefully use you and persecute you,

45 that you may be sons of your Father in heaven; for He makes His sun rise on the evil and on the good, and sends rain on the just and on the unjust. Matthew 5:44, 45.

God our Creator gives us an example of love by sustaining all living things, not just favoring those who are good. He is not partial in His love because He is the source of love as is written,

7 Beloved, let us love one another, for love is of God; and everyone who loves is born of God and knows God.

8 He who does not love does not know God, for God is love…

11 Beloved, if God so loved us, we also ought to love one another.

12 No one has seen God at any time. If we love one another, God abides in us, and His love has been perfected in us...

19 We love [c]Him because He first loved us.

20 If someone says, "I love God," and hates his brother, he is a liar; for he who does not love his brother whom he has seen, [d]how can he love God whom he has not seen?

21 And this commandment we have from Him: that he who loves God must love his brother also." 1 John 4:7, 8, 11, 12, 19 – 21.

To love God and our fellow human beings is Agape love. Love for God is how we can love man. Without love for God there is no agape love for man which can also be defined as "the love of God for man and the love of man for God". God is the source of love, so the power to love anyone unconditionally comes from loving Him. The love that most people exhibit are the other types of love. It might be Eros which is love "mostly of the sexual passion" and that found in marriage or between lovers.

It can be Philia which is "affectionate regard, or friendship" say in relationships between friends or siblings. It can even be storge love which is "between parents and children." All these different types of love have one thing in common: they are natural because the objects of our affection return it to us. I do not want to be misunderstood as minimizing these types of love. They are all very important and can be very deep but those loved are familiar hence why they are loved. It is more natural to love those who love us and do good to us than those who hate us and do us harm.

Agape is unnatural because it involves not only loving a God we have not seen but also our fellow human beings unconditionally, whether they are easy to love or not. The power to love strangers, or even to be kind to those who seek our hurt is a power outside of ourselves. He is our example as we see in the following passage and by His power can we also love others unconditionally:

31 And just as you want men to do to you, you also do to them likewise.

32 But if you love those who love you, what credit is that to you? For even sinners love those who love them.

33 And if you do good to those who do good to you, what credit is that to you? For even sinners do the same.

34 And if you lend to those from whom you hope to receive back, what credit is that to you? For even sinners lend to sinners to receive as much back.

35 But love your enemies, do good, and lend, [h]hoping for nothing in return; and your reward will be great, and you will be sons of the Most High. For He is kind to the unthankful and evil... Luke 6:31-35.

Why love is unnatural

It is unnatural because it goes against our default inclination towards self-preservation and self-gratification. It just seems more natural for our actions to be selfish. All these actions we see are just symptoms of the absence of Agape love. In other words, absence of Agape love results in selfishness whose fruit is sin. The following verses list different things which are all examples of selfishness or the lack of good-will and its resulting actions towards others.

1 But know this, that in the last days [a]perilous times will come:

2 For men will be lovers of themselves, lovers of money, boasters, proud, blasphemers, disobedient to parents, unthankful, unholy,

3 unloving, [b]unforgiving, slanderers, without self-control, brutal, despisers of good,

4 traitors, headstrong, haughty, lovers of pleasure rather than lovers of God,

5 having a form of godliness but denying its power. And from such people turn away!…

19 Now the works of the flesh are evident, which are: [d]adultery, [e]fornication, uncleanness, lewdness,

20 idolatry, sorcery, hatred, contentions, jealousies, outbursts of wrath, selfish ambitions, dissensions, heresies,

21 envy, [f]murders, drunkenness, revelries, and the like; of which I tell you beforehand, just as I also told you in time past, that

those who practice such things will not inherit the kingdom of God." 2 Timothy 3:1-5; Galatians 5:19-21.

These are all things that are common to humanity. "Survival of the fittest" seems more natural and fitting in this world. That is all humanity has ever known or is it? The Apostle Paul says it best:
15 For what I am doing, I do not understand. For what I will to do, that I do not practice; but what I hate, that I do...
18 For I know that in me (that is, in my flesh) nothing good dwells; for to will is present with me, but how to perform what is good I do not find.
19 For the good that I will to do, I do not do; but the evil I will not to do, that I practice.
20 Now if I do what I will not to do, it is no longer I who do it, but sin that dwells in me.". Romans 7:15, 18-20.

The right desires do not always translate into right actions. There is a great conflict taking place in our minds. Loving those who love us comes naturally, but to actively look out for the good of others even our enemies or those who hate us, unconditionally, seems other-worldly and rightly so because it is something divine, literally. It takes a power outside of us to love others just as much as we love ourselves. As natural as it might seem, it was not always so. God did not create us to be selfish beings. In fact there was no room for selfishness in all of Creation. To understand this let us take a look at how all this came to be.

11
IT ALL STARTED IN HEAVEN

In the beginning there was harmony. Everything God created was exactly as He had intended, as written, "And God saw every thing that he had made, and, behold, it was very good." Genesis 1:31. How did our world end up the way it is? Where did all these problems and disharmony come from? Is anyone responsible and if so, who? To better understand this, we have to understand what happened before humans were created.

Angels

Before we were created, there were other beings in existence as is written:
4 "Where were you when I laid the foundations of the earth? Tell Me, if you have understanding.
5 Who determined its measurements? Surely you know! Or who stretched the [b]line upon it?
6 To what were its foundations fastened? Or who laid its cornerstone,
7 When the morning stars sang together, And all the sons of God shouted for joy?" Job 38:4-7.

The morning stars or the sons of God mentioned in the verses above are the angels. They were already in existence when humans were created. God created them as well because:
16 For by Him all things were created that are in heaven and that are on earth, visible and invisible, whether thrones or dominions or [e]principalities or [f]powers. All things were created through Him and for Him.
17 And He is before all things, and in Him all things consist." Colossians 1:16, 17.

They are a great multitude:
3 [a]Is there any number to His armies?...
17 The chariots of God are twenty thousand, Even thousands of thousands; The Lord is among them as in Sinai, in the Holy Place..
11 Then I looked, and I heard the voice of many angels around the throne, the living creatures, and the elders; and the number of them was ten thousand times ten thousand, and thousands of thousands... Job 25:3; Psalms 68:17; Revelation 5:11.

Though they are many, they do not marry or reproduce as is written:
34...The sons of this age marry and are given in marriage.
35 But those who are counted worthy to attain that age, and the resurrection from the dead, neither marry nor are given in marriage;
36 ...for they are equal to the angels and are sons of God, being sons of the resurrection." Luke 20:34-36.

They are higher beings than humans:
20 Bless the Lord, you His angels, Who excel in strength, who do His word, Heeding the voice of His word. Psalms 103:20-21.

They are able to mediate God's Power over nature and events for example in the Seven Trumpets in Revelation. The blowing of a trumpet by each angel executes a specific event on the earth prophetically. (Revelation 8:7, 8, 10-12; 9:1-6 and Revelation 11:15-19) Another example of this are the 3 angels. (Revelation 14:6-11) They carry out His will such as delivering important messages from God to man, for example to Daniel in explaining his vision in Daniel 8:15-27; 9:21-23, as well as Luke 1:11-38 in delivering a message that Zacharias would have a son, John the Baptist, and to Mary to inform her that she would have a child by the Holy Spirit, Jesus Christ. They are powerful beings as seen in Luke 1:19-20 when Gabriel makes Zacharias dumb and not able to speak because of his unbelief that he would bear a son in his and his wife's old age. They are so powerful that for example when Christ resurrected from the dead
2 ...there was a great earthquake; for an angel of the Lord descended from heaven, and came and rolled back the stone [a]from the door, and sat on it.

3 His countenance was like lightning, and his clothing as white as snow.

4 And the guards shook for fear of him, and became like dead men. Matthew 28:2-4.

The stone had been sealed to make sure that none of Jesus' disciples would attempt to steal his body and also to prevent Jesus from leaving the tomb in case He did indeed resurrect, which He did. (see Matthew 27:62-66) Another instance of just how powerful they are is seen in 2 Kings 19:35 when a single angel killed a 185 000 soldiers of the Assyrian army in 1 night.

This is just a glimpse into their nature and abilities but it is humbling to learn that these beings that excel in strength are:

14...sent forth to minister for those who will inherit salvation;

11 For He shall give His angels charge over you, To keep you in all your ways;...

7 The [a]angel of the Lord encamps all around those who fear Him, And delivers them." Hebrews 1:14; Psalms 91:11; 34:7.

God has His angels watch over those who love Him and for a reason because "we do not wrestle against flesh and blood, but against principalities, against powers, against the rulers of [c]the darkness of this age, against spiritual hosts of wickedness in the heavenly places." Ephesians 6:12. The invisible foes we have were not always that way.

You may be wondering what all this has to do with all the trouble in this world. Well it has everything to do with it. Though everything was very good, trouble started brewing sometime before we were created. Though the angels worshiped and adored their Father and Creator out of love, there was one among them who became discontent.

12
LUCIFER'S FALL

12 "How you are fallen from heaven, O [d]Lucifer, son of the morning! How you are cut down to the ground, You who weakened the nations!

13 For you have said in your heart: 'I will ascend into heaven, I will exalt my throne above the stars of God; I will also sit on the mount of the congregation On the farthest sides of the north;

14 I will ascend above the heights of the clouds, I will be like the Most High...

12 Thus says the Lord God: "You were the seal of perfection, Full of wisdom and perfect in beauty.

13 You were in Eden, the garden of God;...

14 "You were the anointed cherub who covers; I established you; You were on the holy mountain of God; You walked back and forth in the midst of fiery stones.

15 You were perfect in your ways from the day you were created, Till iniquity was found in you...

17 "Your heart was [b]lifted up because of your beauty; You corrupted your wisdom for the sake of your splendor;' Isaiah 14:12-14; Ezekiel 28:12-15, 17.

Cherubim are angelic beings and a covering cherub would be one of two angels that flanked God's throne (Kings 6:23-28; 7:29; Ezekiel 1:5-28), covering it with their wings. There are other types of angels called seraphim (Isaiah 6:1-7). As a covering cherub Lucifer was directly in God's presence at His throne. To be a covering cherub was a very high position with which Lucifer was highly honored. As a created being, Lucifer coveted for the throne, glory and honor due only to his Creator. His beauty, wisdom, abilities and position got to his head and he forgot that he was still just a created being and because of this discontent, he started a rebellion in heaven. He had great influence over the other angels because of his position and managed to convince a third of them to join him in his rebellion. (Revelation 12:4) How did he achieve this? Everything had been good and harmonious till this point. All Heaven and the entire universe had known was the principle of love. Love was the source of the harmony and anything foreign to this principle of doing to others as you would want done to you would disrupt this harmony.

It is not revealed exactly how he convinced the other angels, but he had to have convinced his fellow angels to distrust God and the state of things so they could take his side and be part of what he was trying to establish. The foundation of God's government is His Law. The Law is a reflection of His character because:

8 He who does not love does not know God, for God is love…

14 For all the law is fulfilled in one word, even in this: "You shall love your neighbor as yourself."" 1 John 4:8; Galatians 5:14. All the peace and harmony had existed because of this principle or law of love.

The principle of love can be summed up in the word beneficence. According to the Merriam-Webster dictionary being beneficent is "doing or producing good; especially: performing acts of kindness and charity." Beneficence is love in action and is summarized in the following passage:

10 He sends the springs into the valleys; They flow among the hills.

11 They give drink to every beast of the field; The wild donkeys quench their thirst.

12 By them the birds of the heavens have their home; They sing among the branches.

13 He waters the hills from His upper chambers; The earth is satisfied with the fruit of Your works.

14 He causes the grass to grow for the cattle, And vegetation for the service of man, That he may bring forth food from the earth,

15 And wine that makes glad the heart of man, Oil to make his face shine, And bread which strengthens man's heart.

16 The trees of the Lord are full of sap, The cedars of Lebanon which He planted,

17 Where the birds make their nests; The stork has her home in the fir trees.

18 The high hills are for the wild goats; The cliffs are a refuge for the rock[d] badgers.

19 He appointed the moon for seasons; The sun knows its going down.

20 You make darkness, and it is night, In which all the beasts of the forest creep about.

21 The young lions roar after their prey, And seek their food from God.

22 When the sun rises, they gather together And lie down in their dens.

23 Man goes out to his work And to his labor until the evening.

24 O Lord, how manifold are Your works! In wisdom You have made them all. The earth is full of Your possessions—

25 This great and wide sea, In which are innumerable teeming things, Living things both small and great.

27 These all wait for You, That You may give them their food in due season.

28 What You give them they gather in; You open Your hand, they are filled with good.

29 You hide Your face, they are troubled; You take away their breath, they die and return to their dust.

30 You send forth Your Spirit, they are created; And You renew the face of the earth…

36 For of Him and through Him and to Him are all things, to whom be glory forever. Amen." Psalms 104:10-25, 27-30; Romans 11:36.

God is the source of all life and apart from Him there is no life. God is love! Life is bound in this principle of Love. Love is seen in beneficence, in that nothing exists for its own good but that all benefit from each other, as each benefit from God. Nature glorifies its Creator through the beauty and diversity. The galaxies, the planets, our planet, all the life on our planet all testify to how Awesome our Creator is as written:

1 The heavens declare the glory of God; And the firmament[a] shows [b]His handiwork.

2 Day unto day utters speech, And night unto night reveals knowledge.

3 There is no speech nor language Where their voice is not heard.

4 Their [c]line has gone out through all the earth, And their words to the end of the world." Psalms 19:1-4.

Even now in the fallen state where we have predators and prey, which God had not intended as death was not meant to exist, life is given to sustain another life. Nothing exists for its own glory, or for its own good. Everything glorifies God by how unique in form and function it is, which is evidence that there is a Higher Power, a Higher Intelligence behind everything as we know it, visible and invisible. Fruits are a good example of this. The more fruit is eaten, the more of its seeds are scattered encouraging more of its kind to thrive. The less it gives of itself, the less of it is eaten discouraging more of its kind to thrive, and this is a principle which can be applied to many things in life as is written:

24 There is one who scatters, yet increases more; And there is one who withholds more than is right, But it leads to poverty.

25 The generous soul will be made rich, And he who waters will also be watered himself. Proverbs 11:24, 25.

This principle in these verses can be described in another way – selflessness! The selflessness resulting from Love was the glue that held the harmony together and was the very reason it existed. God sustains everything as we know it and everything gives glory back to Him as Creator by existing to benefit the rest of creation in some way. He loves us so that we can love Him back, and love others as we want to be loved. We give as we want to receive!

The principle of Love was the foundation and standard, what had been known to be the Source of the Harmony and Peace. For the first time, a being broke this continuous flow of receiving love from God and returning it back to Him. Lucifer wanted to receive but not give. He coveted for what God had and was receiving, for himself. The throne which belonged to His Creator, he wanted for himself. The adoration and love God received from the beings He had created, Lucifer wanted for himself. He craved for the Glory and Honor that was rightfully God's as the Creator and Source of all things. For the first time ever, the principle of selfishness came into existence. Sin and all that came as a result of it: selfishness, death, sorrow, pain, disease, suffering and all the negative things we have come to associate with our lot on this planet was foreign and something new that had not been seen or experienced in the Universe. Selfishness encourages death because that is not how anything was created to be, including the angels. In the fruit example, selfishness leads to its extinction, which is death. What is the definition of selfishness?

According to the Merriam-Webster dictionary it is being: concerned excessively or exclusively with oneself: seeking or concentrating on one's own advantage, pleasure, or well-being without regard for others. Even in our everyday lives, selfishness hinders us instead of encouraging us to thrive. It can negatively affect so many areas of our lives like work and relationships. Selflessness encourages all the areas of our lives to flourish, even if returns are not seen immediately. In this sense selflessness encourages thriving and life, while selfishness encourages decline and death. Selfishness was a strange phenomenon, a new development that was foreign and unknown before this.

This new principle not only destabilized the harmony which had always existed but also meant that Love was no longer the only principle affecting how beings interacted. Life and harmony had existed because of love. Now this new principle disrupted the natural order of things introducing disharmony and chiefly death as a result of it. When Lucifer made up his mind to rebel against God, he was in essence cutting himself off from his life Source. Many ask why Lucifer felt this way, but it is a mystery. Everything had been fine, but all Lucifer had been given, the exalted position he had among the angels, the abilities, the beauty, the wisdom, perfection in every sense of the word, was not enough.

Freedom of choice

Many ask why God allowed this to even take place. God knows everything and knew what was happening in Lucifer's heart, but he allowed it to happen. Here we see the most important characteristic of love. It is freely given and freely accepted. God could have created beings that would do nothing but love, worship and praise Him without fail, but how different would they be from robots? It would not be love if His sons were designed to do all these things without a choice, but more like instinct. Love can only be love if it is freely given and freely received. Once there is no choice, it ceases to be love. God is powerful enough to make clones which would do as He pleases. Where is the love in that? God values individuality and the freedom to choose. He did not create the angels to be clones but they are individuals with names and the ability to think and choose for themselves like we do. In Luke 1:19, the angel Gabriel is mentioned by name, as an example. Even though they are so many and we don't know much about them individually other than what is revealed about Lucifer, they were created higher than mankind and therefore whatever we can do, they can as well. If we can choose, they can do the same.

Lucifer became known as Satan or the devil once his rebellion matured, and had convinced a third of the angels to join him. What does his name mean? As a word, 'Satan' is an untranslated Hebrew word which means 'adversary', while 'devil' is a translation of the Greek word 'diabolos', meaning a liar, an enemy or false accuser. He became an adversary of God and the good angels, and everything God holds dear, which as we will see later, includes humanity. He lied to the angels to convince them to turn against Him, achieving this by false accusations, becoming an enemy of God. Because of the rebellion, Satan was cast out of Heaven along with the fallen angels which believed him as we see written:

7 And war broke out in heaven: Michael and his angels fought with the dragon; and the dragon and his angels fought,

8 but they [a]did not prevail, nor was a place found for [b]them in heaven any longer.

9 So the great dragon was cast out, that serpent of old, called the Devil and Satan, who deceives the whole world; he was cast to the earth, and his angels were cast out with him....

4 His tail drew a third of the stars of heaven and threw them to the earth." Revelation 12:7-9, 4.

Many ask why God after all this, allowed Satan and his fellow rebels to live. He could have destroyed them because He created them. Their existence even now is because God allowed them to live, but why? Remember that this rebellion changed things and everything that came about because of it was new. Selfishness was a new phenomenon that the beings created by God did not understand nor had ever experienced before. Even Satan and his rebels, did not quite understand the full weight of the results of their actions, how they had changed things and would bring negativity of all forms into existence, which had been unknown before. The only way to judge fairly whether Lucifer was right after all would be for God to allow it to be seen for what it is, and to allow sin to take its course over time. Even if God explained in detail the results of this rebellion, it would be easier for the whole universe to judge according to the results, something they were still trying to understand. Lucifer and a third of the angels had committed treason. What is treason? According to the Merriam-Webster dictionary:

- the betrayal of a trust: treachery

- the offense of attempting by overt acts to overthrow the government of the state to which the offender owes allegiance or to kill or personally injure the sovereign or the sovereign's family

Even in this world we live in, death can be the sentence for those who commit it because it is a serious crime. Had they been executed immediately for their treason, the rest of the beings who remained loyal to God would still have had questions about the possibility that maybe Lucifer was right; that they never got to see him prove whether his way was right and better than God's way. In all this we see that God allowed all this to happen because though He is all powerful, He created all intelligent beings to have the freedom to choose, and to be accountable for their individual actions.

He is also fair in that He has allowed Satan's rebellion to mature, and for its results to speak for themselves as to the true nature of sin. What we are witnessing in the world today all around us are the effects of this rebellion that started long before we were created. The time will come soon when its effects will be examined to see whether in fact Satan was right in rebelling or not, and Judgment can only be passed when all the evidence has been examined so that the fate of the rebels can be decided fairly. The evidence is being collected right now, and at some point will be examined for the Judgment to be passed as we shall see later.

13
THE FALL OF HUMANITY

26 Then God said, "Let Us make man in Our image, according to Our likeness; let them have dominion over the fish of the sea, over the birds of the air, and over the cattle, over [g]all the earth and over every creeping thing that creeps on the earth."

27 So God created man in His own image; in the image of God He created him; male and female He created them…

7 And the Lord God formed man of the dust of the ground, and breathed into his nostrils the breath of life; and man became a living being...

31 And God saw every thing that he had made, and, behold, it was very good. Genesis 1:26-27; 2:7; 1:31.

As if it was not enough, when the devil was cast out of heaven, he made earth his new home and determined to disrupt the perfection and harmony down here as we learned previously. What he had failed to accomplish in Heaven, he sought to fulfill on earth his new home. He was determined to enlist humanity in this rebellion in his bid to further spread it in the Universe. We were created to be living souls, in God's image and likeness. When He created earth and everything in it including our first parents, it was perfect as intended. What went wrong? How did humanity go from perfection to where we are today? All this pain and sorrow that has become a part of daily life was not meant to be.

Life before the fall

God created humanity not only after His likeness in physical form but more importantly to reflect the image of His character and attributes. Just as everything falls under God's domain, Earth was to be man's domain because

7...You have made him [d]a little lower than the angels; You have crowned him with glory and honor,[e]And set him over the works of Your hands.

8 You have put all things in subjection under his feet."For in that He put all in subjection under him, He left nothing that is not put under him. But now we do not yet see all things put under him." Hebrews 2:7-8.

The works of God's Hands are creation, and since this planet was to be our domain, we would oversee, take care and benefit from it as it was made subject to us. Being the Creator He gave us the ability to be creative setting us apart from the rest of creation. To choose and not operate on instinct by having a conscience and freewill is another characteristic that gives mankind inherent superiority over the rest of creation here on earth.

Our first parents, Adam and Eve were created perfect, and their characters which were created to reflect that of their Creator, were not yet tainted with this new principle of selfishness.

Death after the fall

They had been created good, and everything had been perfect until the time Satan succeeded in deceiving Eve to partake of the forbidden fruit which was the first time our first parents did not heed the advice God had given them. Let us look at an account of that in the following scriptures.

15 Then the Lord God took [d]the man and put him in the garden of Eden to [e]tend and keep it.

16 And the Lord God commanded the man, saying, "Of every tree of the garden you may freely eat;

17 but of the tree of the knowledge of good and evil you shall not eat, for in the day that you eat of it you[f] shall surely die."

1 Now the serpent was more cunning than any beast of the field which the Lord God had made. And he said to the woman, "Has God indeed said, 'You shall not eat of every tree of the garden'?"

2 And the woman said to the serpent, "We may eat the fruit of the trees of the garden;

3 but of the fruit of the tree which is in the midst of the garden, God has said, 'You shall not eat it, nor shall you touch it, lest you die.'"

4 Then the serpent said to the woman, "You will not surely die.

5 For God knows that in the day you eat of it your eyes will be opened, and you will be like God, knowing good and evil."

6 So when the woman saw that the tree was good for food, that it was [a]pleasant to the eyes, and a tree desirable to make one wise, she took of its fruit and ate. She also gave to her husband with her, and he ate. Genesis 2:15-17 and 3:1-6.

We are not given an account of exactly what he told the angels to convince them to join him, but we see that if he is a good enough liar to convince them, mankind might not have fared much better in resisting his lies. He managed to plant the seed of doubt and distrust until it matured, with them unknowingly enlisting in his rebellion. He managed to convince them that God was restraining them from a higher existence than what they already had. Even though Adam and Eve had been given everything they needed, and had been content with what they had up to this point, because of the lies, they believed that maybe God was indeed restricting them from something even better. Satan implied that God was restrictive to them, and that eating the fruit would remove that restriction enabling them to the higher existence.

What makes the devil's lies so effective is that he mixes a bit of truth with lies. Obvious lies are easier to detect than when the truth is mixed in with them. Remember that God was allowing the devil to continue his existence so that sin would be seen for what it really is. Adam and Eve having freewill and the ability to choose, unfortunately made the wrong choice. The principle of Love is no different for the angels or for us. Love is love because it is freely received and freely given. Regardless of who was presenting the options to choose from, God would have wanted them to make the right choice; and though being powerful enough to make them obey Him if He wanted to, He gave them the ability to decide for themselves. Sin would result in their death, though not immediately, and the devil knew that. Life is found in God, and apart from Him there is no life. His goal was to con humanity into joining him in rebellion against God because the principle that sin separates from Him, thus separating them forever from Him as written:

2 But your iniquities have separated you from your God…

22 For as in Adam all die…

12 just as through one man sin entered the world, and death through sin, and thus death spread to all men, because all sinned…

23 for all have sinned and fall short of the glory of God…

23 For the wages of sin is death…" Isaiah 59:2; 1 Corinthians 15:22; Romans 5:12; 3:23; 6:23.

Sin separates us from God and without reconciliation to Him, death would be the result. God is the source of life and being separated from Him results in death. In John 15, we learn this principle of Christ the Vine and we being the branches. A branch does not have life in itself but has to be attached to the Vine to have life. When a branch is severed from the Vine, immediately it begins to die although it might appear to be green and alive for a little while. We are alive in God's eyes when we are connected to Him through Christ. Apart from God, we might appear to be alive as we continue to live, but in God's eyes we would be dead just as Adam and Eve who did not die immediately, but like the severed branch which appears green for a little while longer until it finally starts to show it is really dead when the leaves dry up.

The devil has mastered this throughout the ages and continues to use these same lies on us today. When they ate the fruit, that's when they realized that they were naked. It was true that their eyes were opened. All they had known was love, purity and innocence. This was a twisted truth because their eyes indeed were opened but in the sense that, they lost innocence and became fearful as they now distrusted God. They became familiar with this new principle which they had not known before, so in that sense, yes, they began to know good and evil.

8 And they heard the [c]sound of the Lord God walking in the garden in the [d]cool of the day, and Adam and his wife hid themselves from the presence of the Lord God among the trees of the garden.

9 Then the Lord God called to Adam and said to him, "Where are you?"

10 So he said, "I heard Your voice in the garden, and I was afraid because I was naked; and I hid myself."

11 And He said, "Who told you that you were naked? Have you eaten from the tree of which I commanded you that you should not eat?"

12 Then the man said, "The woman whom You gave to be with me, she gave me of the tree, and I ate."

13 And the Lord God said to the woman, "What is this you have done?" The woman said, "The serpent deceived me, and I ate."

22 Then the Lord God said, "Behold, the man has become like one of Us, to know good and evil. And now, lest he put out his hand and take also of the tree of life, and eat, and live forever"—

23 therefore the Lord God sent him out of the garden of Eden to till the ground from which he was taken.

24 So He drove out the man; and He placed cherubim at the east of the garden of Eden, and a flaming sword which turned every way, to guard the way to the tree of life." Genesis 3:8-13; 22-24.

God said that man had become like them in Heaven knowing good and evil. The universe had not been familiar with evil, until the rebellion in Heaven and as far as is revealed in Scripture, it had not spread to the rest of God's Creation as yet. Adam and Eve had been pure and had they resisted the devil's temptation, they would have continued to know only good, love, purity, harmony and peace as God had intended. By believing the lies and eating the fruit, the devil had succeeded in enlisting mankind in the rebellion. The principle of selfishness started affecting how they interacted whereas before it was only love. By eating the fruit, humanity became infected with this sin disease and immediately started showing its symptoms.

They hid from God who was looking for them, and when asked what had happened, the man blamed the woman who then blamed the serpent. Instead of taking responsibility and confessing what had happened, they both started trying to preserve themselves out of fear. The devil lied to them that they would not die, but we have learned that separation from God is death because there is no life apart from Him. They did not die right away and the devil knew that, so it was a lie mixed with the truth. God was to let sin to be seen for what it is before finally dealing with it so that the universe would know its consequences. By creating humans to have freewill, earth became a place of interest for Heaven, and it was to be seen whether they would choose God's way or not, "which things the angels desire to look." 1 Peter 1:12.

Examination of life's record

The evidence of which of the principles would be better, God's way of love or the devil's way of selfishness, would be seen in human lives, in their actions, from Adam and Eve throughout the ages to the time when Christ comes again. The results of regard for God's way and its effects would be examined, in comparison to regard for the devil's way, with the records being opened at the end as written, "And I saw the dead, small and great, stand before God; and the books were opened: and another book was opened, which is the book of life: and the dead were judged out of these things which were written in the books, according to their works." Revelation 20:12. The following is an excerpt from Stephen N. Haskell's 1914 book, The Cross and its Shadow which sheds more light on this:

"Daniel says that when the judgment was set, "the books were opened." Dan. 7:9, 10. There are several books mentioned in connection with the records of heaven. The book of remembrance records even the thoughts of the heart. Mal. 3:16. How just and merciful is our God that He takes cognizance of it when we only think upon His name! Often when pressed by temptation, our souls cry out after the living God, and a faithful record is kept of it all. Many deeds are done in darkness, hidden from even the most intimate associates; but when the books of heaven are opened, God "will bring to light the hidden things of darkness, and will make manifest the counsels of the heart." 1 Cor. 4:5. "For God shall bring every work into judgment, with every secret thing, whether it be good, or whether it be evil." Eccl. 12:14. Not only the deeds are recorded, but the motives or counsels of the heart that prompted the deed; and of the bitter tears of repentance shed in secret the Lord says, Are they not all in My book?

Our daily conversation, the words spoken without thought, we may count of little worth, but "every idle word that men shall speak, they shall give account thereof in the day of judgment: for by thy words thou shalt be justified, and by thy words thou shalt be condemned." Matt. 12:36, 37. Words are the index of the heart, "for out of the abundance of the heart the mouth speaketh." Matt. 12:34. The place of birth and the environment, everything that can in any way influence the life record, is all recorded in the books of heaven. Ps. 87:4-6.

The most wonderful book of all the heavenly records that pertain to humanity, is the book of life. This book contains the names of all who have professed the name of Christ. Phil. 4:3. To have one's name recorded in that book is the highest honor given to mortals. Luke 10:19, 20.

It is a source of great rejoicing to know that our names are written in heaven, (Luke 10:20.) but the life must be in harmony with heavenly things if our names are to remain with the righteous. The names of the wicked do not remain in the book of life; (Ex. 32:33; Rev. 13:8; 17:8.) they are written in the earth; (Jer. 17:13.) for all their hopes and affections have clung to earthly things." [1]

Many think that God should not even have allowed the fall of man but we were created free-agents with the ability to choose. Since God knows the "end from the beginning", He thankfully made the provision that there would still be a way for reconciliation to Him in case of a fall, as is written,

8 …the Lamb slain from the foundation of the world…

20 He indeed was foreordained before the foundation of the world, but was [h]manifest in these last times for you …" Revelation 13:8; 1 Peter 1:20.

What would be achieved by the fall of humanity?

No matter how powerful he is, the devil was created and there was no way he could overthrow God's government. He hates God and everything He stands for. By taking earth hostage, and by sin's devastating effects on humanity, he would grieve God in the process. Sin would be a means of torturing the hostages, humanity, so that it would pain God that humans who He had the best intentions for now had to suffer. It would be a way of grieving God since he cannot reach Him, by making those beloved of God, suffer. Satan makes false promises of true freedom in doing what you want and not caring about the consequences of our actions on ourselves or others;

and of giving true wisdom which allows humans to rise to a higher existence by their own power, but they are lies and those who subscribe to his way of doing things don't even realize that they become his slaves and unknowingly his rebel followers. The other reason is that Satan needed a place where he could fulfill the ambitions he failed to accomplish in Heaven. Earthly dominion belonged to Adam and Eve, and the only way to rightfully have it would be to cause them to disobey God. Satan knew that Adam and Eve were safe in God, and as long as they trusted Him.

Once our first parents fell, this earth became his domain and we became his subjects. In God's Kingdom the principle that governs all actions is love freely given, and freely received. The devil's kingdom down here would run on the principle of selfishness, but it would not be by choice. The devil enslaved humanity and slaves are not free. This is why every single person has sinned in some way or form throughout our lives. We are born into a sinful world, with a sinful nature inherited from our first parents. We are born into slavery as described:

5 Behold, I was brought forth in iniquity, and in sin my mother conceived me;

26...that they may come to their senses and escape the snare of the devil, having been taken captive by him to do his will;

17... Who did not open the house of his prisoners... Psalms 51:5; 2 Timothy 2:26; Isaiah 14:17.

With this sin we lost not only the dominion but also the ability to reflect God's character and started sinking lower and lower morally. "The Lord is gracious, and full of compassion; slow to anger, and of great mercy..., longsuffering, and abundant in goodness and truth..." Psalms 145:8; Exodus 34:6. These godly characteristics would have been natural for us had we not fallen. Prior to the fall we were in direct communion with God but as a result of it were banished from the garden. Toil and the pains of this life were part of the curse brought about by sin which God never intended for us or to even exist.

References

1. Stephen Haskell. The Cross and its Shadow. pp. 233-234.

14
HOW DEMONS OPERATE

The devil seeks to torment and trouble humanity as much as possible as written, "Woe to the inhabitants of the earth and the sea! For the devil has come down to you having great wrath, because he knows that he has a short time." Revelation 12:12. In the book of Job, we get some insight into the hatred and disregard the devil has towards humanity. Job during his afflictions encounters a spirit in a dream which is not identified as the devil himself but from what it says is clearly an antagonistic spirit, so it is definitely not one of God's angels:

15 Then a spirit passed before my face; The hair on my body stood up.

16 It stood still, But I could not discern its appearance. A form was before my eyes; There was silence; Then I heard a voice saying:

17 'Can a mortal be more righteous than God? Can a man be more pure than his Maker?

18 If He puts no trust in His servants, If He charges His angels with error,

19 How much more those who dwell in houses of clay, Whose foundation is in the dust, Who are crushed before a moth?

20 They are broken in pieces from morning till evening; They perish forever, with no one regarding.' Job 4:15-20.

God has a positive outlook for us as He says, "I know the thoughts that I think toward you, says the LORD, thoughts of peace and not of evil, to give you a future and a hope." Jeremiah 29:11. He looks for the positive things while the devil is seeking to undermine humanity and looking for any opportunity to bring suffering and misery because he came to "steal, and to kill, and to destroy", while Christ came that we "might have life… more abundantly." (John 10:10) One seeks to build up and make for a fuller life, the other seeks to break down and destroy. The devil is called the "accuser of brethren" (Revelation 12:10) and strives to find opportunity for us to look bad before God but thankfully, "we have an Advocate with the Father, Jesus Christ the Righteous." 1 John 2:1. A clear example of how this takes place in our own lives is seen in Job's life, in the following exchange between God and the devil where God is looking for the positive things while the devil's motive to make us look bad is revealed.

6 Now there was a day when the sons of God came to present themselves before the Lord, and [e]Satan also came among them.

7 And the Lord said to [f]Satan, "From where do you come?" So Satan answered the Lord and said, "From going to and fro on the earth, and from walking back and forth on it."

8 Then the Lord said to Satan, "Have you [g]considered My servant Job, that there is none like him on the earth, a blameless and upright man, one who fears God and [h]shuns evil?"

9 So Satan answered the Lord and said, "Does Job fear God for nothing?

10 Have You not [i]made a hedge around him, around his household, and around all that he has on every side? You have blessed the work of his hands, and his possessions have increased in the land.

11 But now, stretch out Your hand and touch all that he has, and he will surely curse[j] You to Your face!"

12 And the Lord said to Satan, "Behold, all that he has is in your [k]power; only do not lay a hand on his person." So Satan went out from the presence of the Lord. Job 1:7-12.

It is important to note that apparently the devil had already tried to reach Job in some way but could not because he realized that God protected him and his things. God to prove that Job was a good man allowed the devil access to part of Job's life but not to bring any harm to his person. God is ultimately in control and the devil has no direct access to us unless God permits it for one reason or the other. We will look at this again later on in more detail. Job's trials also show how much Satan hates God because God had made mention of how good Job was, meaning his character testified of God. The closer we get to God, the more our characters testify of Him because we reflect more of His character, the more the devil hates us. What follows reveals what the devil and demons desire to do to humanity, as Job was just an example.

Death and destruction

1. The devil moved upon the Sabeans to rob Job off his oxen and to kill his servants who were tending to them. Verse 14-15.
2. Manipulating the elements by bringing fire from the sky to burn up his sheep and servants. Verse 16.
3. Moved the Chaldeans to rob him off his camels and to kill his servants who were tending to them. Verse 17.
4. Brought about a wind, possibly a tornado to destroy one of his sons' house where all his children were gathered eating and drinking, killing all of his children at once. Verse 18-19.

Natural disasters like tornadoes happen today and they are termed, "acts of God" but in the above scriptures, we see that the devil can manipulate the weather and the environment to bring about death and destruction. In these texts we see that indeed, he came to steal, kill and to destroy. How many such atrocities happen every day, and the blame never falls where it belongs.

Today, Satan continues to take many lives through accidents and natural disasters while misrepresenting God as the one to blame for them. The devil and his demons can also move people to bring about theft, vandalism, and even death. Loss of life and property whether due to people, accidents or the weather can therefore be attributed to the devil because of his ability to manipulate people and the weather to bring about his goals of stealing, killing and destroying.

Physical and mental suffering

When God maintains that even though the devil has moved Him to allow these things to happen to Job to prove him, Satan says:

4 So Satan answered the Lord and said, "Skin for skin! Yes, all that a man has he will give for his life.

5 But stretch out Your hand now, and touch his bone and his flesh, and he will surely [b]curse You to Your face!"

6 And the Lord said to Satan, "Behold, he is in your hand, but spare his life." Job 2:4-6. (KJV)

1. Satan brought boils all over Job's body. Verses 7-10. In this instance, we see that the devil also has the ability to bring about disease and thus physical suffering upon humanity. We also see other instances in the Bible for example: a woman who was for 18 years bound by a spirit of infirmity/sickness which caused her to be bent or hunched over and could not straighten her back. Luke 13:11-13, 16.
2. A man who because of demon possession was dumb. Matthew 9:32-33.
3. A man who because of demon possession was both blind and dumb. Matthew 12:22.
4. A demon possessed man who was feared because of severe mental problems and lived among the tombs cutting himself (self-harm). Mark 5:1-20.
5. A demon possessed boy who had mental problems and would throw himself into fire. Matthew 17:14-21.
6. A demon possessed boy who would get seizures. Luke 9:37-43.

Demon possession is when a demon or evil spirit takes control of a person. As seen in the above texts it can have a physical effect like disease and inability to see or speak. It can also result in other conditions like epilepsy, losing mental control over self and constantly trying to harm themselves or even suicide attempts. Physical suffering as well as mental anguish due to trauma are among the chief ways the enemy works.

The traumas that Job went through, were a source of great mental anguish for him as seen in Job chapter 3, and even though he was able to endure, it was only because he had a spiritual anchor in his relationship with God. These traumas would be enough to cause an average person like any one of us to lose their mind. With mental problems on the rise today, it is sobering to realize that possibly a significant number of them if not all of them are attributed to demons. When the Lord rejected Saul from being King over Israel,

He allowed an evil spirit to torment Saul, as an example of demonic mental torment. (1 Samuel 16:14-23).

Drug use and mental torment

Mental illness is not normally thought to have a spiritual cause. Given the history of drug use in the occult, we can get some insight from occultists themselves, warning of some of the side effects of drug use. The following excerpt is from the Theosophical society on drug use, which gives us some insight into how drug use opens up a person to demonic opression which can then lead to mental illness.

"The experiences generated by the use of psychedelic drugs have generally been interpreted in two alternative ways—as hallucinations or as spiritual experience. For mainstream science, there is only one objective world—the one perceived by our senses. By this view, the psychedelic experience can be nothing but a hallucination produced by altering the chemical environment of the neurons.

The Theosophical view disagrees with this conclusion, stating that the cosmos has a nonphysical side that is as real and objective as the material one. Thus many of the experiences undergone under the influence of drugs can be the result of opening the doors of perception to some aspect of reality that is usually beyond the reach of the physical senses...[Drugs] bring again into the physical consciousness indiscriminate impressions from the astral world...Between the physical and the astral bodies there is a layer of etheric matter, which, while allowing the vitality (prana) and the spiritual influences to come down into the body, keeps the forces and entities of the astral plane outside the field of waking consciousness. This, as Leadbeater explains, is an important protection for those who are not ready to deal with this challenging world: "But for this merciful provision the ordinary man, who knows nothing about all these things and is entirely unprepared to meet them, could at any moment be brought by any astral entity under the influence of forces to cope with which would be entirely beyond his strength. He would be liable to constant obsession by any being on the astral plane who desired to seize upon his vehicles [of consciousness]. (Leadbeater, Chakras, 77) This "etheric web" may be harmed in several ways.

One kind of damage is produced by the excessive use of alcohol and tobacco and the consumption of drugs, and it is due to the chemical nature of these substances.

These substances may produce two different effects according to an individual's constitution. They may burn away the web, leaving "the door open to all sorts of irregular forces and evil influences," or they may produce "a kind of ossification of the web, so that instead of having too much coming through from one plane to the other, we have very little of any kind coming through" (Leadbeater, Chakras, 77–78)...When illicit drugs are ingested there is a tendency to break down this shield enabling negative influences from the astral world to enter the aura, especially through the chakras which are the psychic sense organs. These problems can range from hallucinations and delusions to a full scale obsession by a human or sub-human entity. If the process of abuse has occurred to an advanced degree—no amount of repair that I am able to do will help."[1]

What is described here is that substance abuse opens a portal as it where through which entities which we can conclude to be demons, can torment the person, besides the direct damage the substance does to the brain. They might be what is referred to as the astral entities in this excerpt. It is probably this demonic oppression which then leads to mental illness.There is a correlation between substance abuse and mental disorders according to the National Institute on Drug Abuse:

"Data show high rates of comorbid substance use disorders and anxiety disorders—which include generalized anxiety disorder, panic disorder, and post-traumatic stress disorder. Substance use disorders also co-occur at high prevalence with mental disorders, such as depression and bipolar disorder, attention-deficit hyperactivity disorder (ADHD), psychotic illness, borderline personality disorder, and antisocial personality disorder. Patients with schizophrenia have higher rates of alcohol, tobacco, and drug use disorders than the general population... Serious mental illness among people ages 18 and older is defined at the federal level as having, at any time during the past year, a diagnosable mental, behavior, or emotional disorder that causes serious functional impairment that substantially interferes with or limits one or more major life activities. Serious mental illnesses include major depression, schizophrenia, and bipolar disorder, and other mental disorders that cause serious impairment.

Around 1 in 4 individuals with SMI also have an SUD (Substance Use Disorder)."[2]

According to the CDC, 47,173 Americans died by suicide in 2017.[3] Could it be that the mental torment driving people to despair to the point of committing suicide is due to demonic oppression? Even celebrities are committing suicide which is baffling because they appear to have it all, but even with all the riches and influence that this life can offer, many find no peace: "for what profit is it to a man if he gains the whole world, and loses his own soul? Or what will a man give in exchange for his soul?" Matthew 16:26. Having everything the world has to offer doesn't guarantee peace if to obtain it means no relationship with God because Christ being the Prince of Peace is the source of real Peace as written, "Peace I leave with you, My peace I give to you; not as the world gives do I give to you." John 14:27. Real and lasting peace which is not dependent on circumstance can be found no where else but in the Prince of Peace Himself!

Self Harm

In Mark 5:1-20, we learn about the demoniac who lived among the tombs who was fierce and would cut himself, which is a form of self harm. According to the Psychology Today website, "self-harm, or self-mutilation, is the act of deliberately inflicting pain and damage to your own body and can include cutting, burning, scratching, and other forms of injury. The other forms of self-harm include consuming toxic amounts of alcohol or drugs, or participating in unsafe sex with multiple partners. While self injury can look like attempted suicide, and some who self-harm go on to actually attempt suicide, many people who intentionally hurt themselves are simply taking extreme measures to distract themselves from their problems and release themselves from unbearable mental anguish."

In addition to the immediate effects of trauma on its victims as well as those in the victim's life, its effects are also amplified when experienced as a child, having far reaching effects much later in life. Your risk for mental and physical health problems from a past

trauma goes up if you've had three or more negative experiences, called adverse childhood experiences (ACEs) which include:
- physical abuse
- sexual abuse
- emotional abuse
- physical neglect
- emotional neglect
- witnessing domestic violence
- substance misuse within the household
- mental illness within the household
- parental separation or divorce
- incarceration of a household member.

Mildly stressful events that don't necessarily meet the psychological definition of trauma can still cause problems and can include a sudden death in the family, a stressful divorce, or caring for someone with a chronic or debilitating illness. These events can still lead to a mental health disorder, such as anxiety or depression. Early childhood trauma increases the risk for almost everything, from adult depression to PTSD and most psychiatric disorders, as well as a host of medical problems, including cardiovascular problems such as heart attack and stroke, cancer, and obesity.

These effects likely reflect two factors:

Behavioral changes resulting from trauma – self harm manifests as a coping mechanism such as behaviors for example drinking, smoking, drug use, or even overeating for comfort. These habits, in turn, lead to health problems.

Physical effects related to trauma – a history of trauma may lead to stronger surges of adrenaline and experiencing them more often than someone who has not had the same history. This causes wear and tear on the body — just as it would in a car where the engine was constantly revving and racing. Stress responses have also been demonstrated in people who have experienced discrimination throughout their lives.[5]

Effects of trauma on health

This has never been more apparent than now in the Corona virus crisis which has impacted communities where people's traumatic experiences or higher likelihood of experiencing trauma increases the negative health outcomes, in addition to the disadvantages economically and in terms of health care. This we see in this excerpt from a recent McKinsey and Company study:

"Black Americans are almost twice as likely to live in the counties at highest risk of health and economic disruption, if or when the pandemic hits those counties. To assess disruption, five indicators were evaluated: underlying health conditions, poverty rate, number of hospital beds, percentage of people in severe housing conditions, and population density...39 percent of all jobs held by black Americans—compared with 34 percent held by white Americans—are now threatened by reductions in hours or pay, temporary furloughs, or permanent layoffs, totaling 7 million jobs. In addition, they are likely to experience more severe complications from the infection; black Americans are on average about 30 percent likelier to have health conditions that exacerbate the effects of COVID-19. Unfortunately, black Americans are over represented in nine of the ten lowest-paid, high-contact essential services, which elevates their risk of contracting the virus. Thirty-three percent of nursing assistants, 39 percent of orderlies, and 39 percent of psychiatric aides, 4 are black."[4] It is not just African Americans but even Native Americans and Hispanic Americans have also been affected in a somewhat similar way.

Chronic stress increases inflammation in the body, which leads to a broad range of illness, including cardiovascular disease and autoimmune diseases. Early trauma disrupts the inflammatory system which can lead to long-term aberrations in this system and chronic health problems triggered by constant inflammation.[5]

Generational trauma and sin

So far we have seen how the enemy can work through physical and mental suffering. The effects of the traumas as well as the efforts to cope with them can lead to forms of self-harm like Alcoholism or drug addiction. You see families in which there seem to be patterns of behavior or tendencies towards certain weaknesses or problems, say, a great grandfather might have been an alcoholic, as well as grandfather, father and now the child in this generation. It can be anything ranging from teenage pregnancy, drug use, adultery, being perpetrators or victims of domestic violence, to mental health issues and suicidal tendencies. Observing families including your own, you can see things that follow familial lines. They are just varying in how they visibly affect life in a negative way.

Sin as a type of spiritual trauma

Trauma in its nature is usually involuntary as a result of circumstances beyond control like the sort of events that occurred in Job's life. It can be at the hands of life events like accidents or natural disasters but is usually at the hands of people, whether familiar or strangers. But trauma is involuntary and those who experience it have no control. As we have seen in Job's situation he experienced examples of each of these, and so the devil can work effectively through all kinds of trauma as we have learned how it affects their mental and emotional health and therefore how they relate to other people as well as to God.

Sin is also a type of trauma in its own way because as we learned earlier in the book, it was not meant to exist and came into existence because of the devil. Violation of the code of conduct with mankind and with God as found in the Ten Commandments is spiritual trauma. It is a violation of God's law governing how to relate to Him and our neighbor. An extension of how we relate to Him is in how we treat our bodies or what we do with them because:

19...your body is the temple of the Holy Spirit who is in you, whom you have from God, and you are not your own?

20 For you were bought at a price; therefore glorify God in your body [g]and in your spirit, which are God's;...

16 Do you not know that you are the temple of God and that the Spirit of God dwells in you?

17 If anyone [b]defiles the temple of God, God will destroy him. For the temple of God is holy, which temple you are. 1 Corinthians 6:19-20; 3:16-17.

For the sake of explaining, I shall call trauma as we know it "Involuntary trauma" and call sin "voluntary trauma". What we do with our bodies or to our bodies, if we do not treat them as temples for the dwelling of God's Spirit is sin and that can be traumatic in the sense that an experience or event is taking place which is not intended and can have life altering consequences negatively in terms of how we relate to God and possibly others as well. If it happens to affect others negatively it will affect our relationship with God by default because:

20 If someone says, "I love God," and hates his brother, he is a liar; for he who does not love his brother whom he has seen, [d]how can he love God whom he has not seen?

21 And this commandment we have from Him: that he who loves God must love his brother also. 1 John 4:20-21.

It is a voluntary trauma because the person would have made the choice to participate and it wouldn't have been imposed on them by force or circumstance against their will. For example, a person who does not have family history or tendency towards drug use and no prior exposure to them, who is presented with drugs and uses them becoming an addict is traumatized spiritually and changed by the drug use and not the same after this. The tendency towards drug use starts with this individual and passed on to that person's future generations. It is spiritual trauma in itself except the person voluntarily put themselves in that situation, a violation in being a new thing which comes into a person's life changing the person's life while negatively affecting their relationships with God and their neighbor or those around them.

Voluntary trauma can be other things like fornication which might seem innocent but are a violation of the body as a temple, though not necessarily affecting others, would affect how that person relates to God who would not want the body violated in such a way. In "involuntary" trauma, an equivalent to fornication would be rape because the person is violated against their will and of course the violence associated with it. Another example of the body as a temple being violated would be indulgence in Alcohol or drugs which whether done to cope with the pain of an involuntary trauma or as done voluntarily for recreation, the user can become dependent nonetheless. In both cases the temple is violated thus affecting relationship with God though not necessarily affecting anyone else negatively around them, and dependence becomes the common factor but the causes are completely different. For a person with no prior individual or family history of drug or Alcohol dependency, the habit starts with them and can be perpetuated for generations to come. It is in this way that trauma involuntary or not can be relived by future descendants. This is summed up in the following scripture:

18 The Lord is longsuffering and abundant in mercy, forgiving iniquity and transgression; but He by no means clears the guilty, visiting the iniquity of the fathers on the children to the third and fourth generation. Numbers 14:18.

This scripture is describing how sin's effects can be felt exponentially to the third and fourth generation. The effects of involuntary trauma which works in the same way can also become a curse to future generations by no fault of theirs. Both groups are in bondage and need to be set free and as we shall see later, Christ can set them free because, "even the captives of the mighty shall be taken away, and the prey of the terrible be delivered; For I will contend with him who contends with you, And I will save your children." Isaiah 49:25. Understanding how this happens can shed some light on how trauma or sin can affect multiple generations of people who did not experience it first hand.

Reliving trauma as the victim or the aggressor

The following excerpt shows how those traumatized can continue to relive the trauma, although it tends to be different in how this takes place in men and women. Reliving the trauma is another weapon of the enemy to continue torturing the victims. The following excerpt outlines how this happens.

"Revictimization is a consistent finding...Victims of rape are more likely to be raped and women who were physically or sexually abused as children are more likely to be abused as adults. Victims of child sexual abuse are at high risk of becoming prostitutes. Russell, , in a very careful study of the effects of incest on the life of women, found that few women made a conscious connection between their childhood victimization and their drug abuse, prostitution, and suicide attempts. Whereas 38 per cent of a random sample of women reported incidents of rape or attempted rape after age 14, 68 per cent of those with a childhood history of incest did. Twice as many women with a history of physical violence in their marriages (27 per cent), and more than twice as many (53 per cent) reported unwanted sexual advances by an unrelated authority figure such as a teacher, clergyman, or therapist.

Victims of father-daughter incest were four times more likely than non-incest victims to be asked to pose for pornography...There are significant sex differences in the way trauma victims incorporate the abuse experience. Studies by Carmen et al. and others indicate that abused men and boys tend to identify with the aggressor and later victimize others whereas abused women are prone to become attached to abusive men who allow themselves and their offspring to be victimized further...Some traumatized people remain preoccupied with the trauma at the expense of other life experiences and continue to re-create it in some form for themselves or for others. War veterans may enlist as mercenaries, victims of incest may become prostitutes, and victims of childhood physical abuse seemingly provoke subsequent abuse in foster families or become self-mutilators. Still others identify with the aggressor and do to others what was done to them."[6]

As seen above, not only is trauma relived in the person of the one who experienced it, it is passed on and inherited in the future generations. It is studied in a branch of Genetics called Epigenetics which is the study of heritable phenotype or gene expression changes that do not involve alterations in the DNA sequence. It is not easy to study the biological basis for those effects in humans and so the mechanism is explained in the following study on mice.

How trauma is transferred to future generations

"Ressler and his colleague Brian Dias opted to study epigenetic inheritance in laboratory mice trained to fear the smell of acetophenone, a chemical the scent of which has been compared to those of cherries and almonds. He and Dias wafted the scent around a small chamber, while giving small electric shocks to male mice.

The animals eventually learned to associate the scent with pain, shuddering in the presence of acetophenone even without a shock.

This reaction was passed on to their pups,...despite never having encountered acetophenone in their lives, the offspring exhibited increased sensitivity when introduced to its smell, shuddering more markedly in its presence compared with the descendants of mice that had been conditioned to be startled by a different smell or that had gone through no such conditioning. A third generation of mice — the 'grandchildren' — also inherited this reaction, as did mice conceived through in vitro fertilization with sperm from males sensitized to acetophenone. Similar experiments showed that the response can also be transmitted down from the mother. These responses were paired with changes to the brain structures that process odors. The mice sensitized to acetophenone, as well as their descendants, had more neurons that produce a receptor protein known to detect the odor compared with control mice and their progeny. Structures that receive signals from the acetophenone-detecting neurons and send smell signals to other parts of the brain (such as those involved in processing fear) were also bigger.

The researchers propose that DNA methylation — a reversible chemical modification to DNA that typically blocks transcription of a gene without altering its sequence — explains the inherited effect. In the fearful mice, the acetophenone-sensing gene of sperm cells had fewer methylation marks, which could have led to greater expression of the odorant-receptor gene during development. But how the association of smell with pain influences sperm remains a mystery."[7]

A way to illustrate how this happens is to think of the changes that occur as switches over specific parts of the DNA code. The environment or experiences of the mice, in this case, zapping them after they smell acetone, turns on a switch for fear of the acetone, and the DNA itself is unchanged but the specific gene expression of fear as a response to the acetone smell is passed on to offspring as switches in the ON position. The switches remain in the ON position with subsequent generations. That's why the acetone smell triggers in them fear although they never experienced zapping like the first generation.

Environmental factors

Since the devil knows that the effects of sin which starts with one person can affect future generations because they will have a tendency towards that weakness, he reinforces effort in the areas that he already knows are weakest. If he already knows that a person has a weakness in the area of Alcohol, he will make sure that the person has easy access to it and many others to drink with, or to influence him to drink. He will not waste time presenting other things which he knows are not that person's weak areas, but emphasizes effort in the area for efficiency, although as people we can have multiple areas of weakness. If the weakness is rage leading to violence, then he ensures that the person has no shortage of situations which can enrage. Whatever weakness we have, he exploits it as much as possible so that the bondage deepens.

Regional operation of demons

Unlike God who is the only one that is Omniscient and Omnipresent (Psalms 147:5; Jeremiah 23:23-24.), the devil does not know everything and cannot be everywhere at the same time, so to ensure that this work of bringing sin and trauma upon many is done, he has the demons help him by delegating authority to them. "Principalities...powers, ...rulers of the darkness of this world, ... spiritual wickedness in high places." Means that there is organizational structure to how the devil and demons operate. Ephesians 6:12.

According to the Strong's concordance, principalities means chief (in various applications of order, time, place, rank.) meaning they have a ranking system, of some sort. In Vine's expository dictionary, it is used to denote the extremities or "corners", implying the corners or extremities of something, possibly a domain. Powers according to the Strong's concordance is derived from the Greek word Exousia meaning the "freedom of action, right to act." Rulers or Pantokrator "almighty" denotes a ruler of the world. According to the Vine's expository dictionary states, they are "spirit powers who under the permissive will of god, and in consequence of human sin, exercise Satanic and therefore antagonistic authority over the world."

The devil is called the "prince of this world" (John 12:31) and according to the Strong's concordance, he is a prince as in a first (in rank or power): chief (ruler), magistrate, prince, ruler. From all this we gather that he is the prince or chief among the demons, and that they have a domain which is this earth. They have to some extent the freedom and right to act (Matthew 4:8-9) but thankfully, because he is a prince means that there is a King, One higher than Him who has Absolute Power and that is God!

For them to know our weaknesses so well might mean that they have to be able to observe us long enough. If that is the case, the power structure is possibly broken down into regional domains as well because in Mark 5:10 when Christ is casting demons out of the fierce man who lived among tombs, they beg Him "not send them away out of the country." Staying in the same area would mean working with people they are already familiar with and have been focusing on them. Generational tendencies would also be easier to continue their propagation because when children are young, they are in the care of parents who can have the right conditions around them to continue their tendencies. The devil knows full well the effects of early child development can have on the rest of life because it is written to "train up a child in the way he should go, [a]And when he is old he will not depart from it." Proverbs 22:6.

The same must also be true that if they are taught the wrong way or have the best conditions around them to encourage a life of sin, ensuring a foundation is laid for them to continue and deepen bondage in adulthood. The young are enslaved while they are still part of the family nucleus, concentrating all the work in one place. When they move later in life, the foundation is already laid to deepen their bondage, as well as to transmit these tendencies to their own children and hence the cycle continues while the devil's grip gets tighter with each generation.

Undoing trauma

Fortunately, just as there can be tendencies towards negative things or curses, there can also be tendencies towards and familial patterns in good things or blessings. The devil knows and understands this very well because when God pronounced blessings or curses, they would be inherited to the third and fourth generations. (2 Kings 10:30; 2 Kings 15:12; Numbers 14:18.) Blessings and tendencies towards blessings can also be passed on to future generations. Just as it is easy to go into bondage for generations, the devil also knows that God is more than powerful to set one person free which frees future generations which would otherwise end up in bondage. He knows that all it takes is for one person to come into bondage, and he could successfully have the generations to follow, down to the fourth. This means that the effect of sin exponentially affects so many people, not only the original perpetrators of the sin or the original victims of the trauma but also subsequent generations down to the fourth generation. If the individuals in subsequent generations are unsuccessful in breaking the cycle of sin or of the trauma effects, then it continues down to their respective fourth generation. Unless there is intervention, so many people would be in bondage to the devil "that opened not the house of his prisoners." Isaiah 14:17. Literally only Divine intervention, the working of God's power on our behalf, can set us free from this cycle of sin and trauma:

7 To open blind eyes, To bring out prisoners from the prison, Those who sit in darkness from the prison house;…

26 that they may come to their senses and escape the snare of the devil, having been taken captive by him to do his will;…

7 keeping mercy for thousands, forgiving iniquity and transgression and sin, by no means clearing the guilty, visiting the iniquity of the fathers upon the children and the children's children to the third and the fourth generation." Isaiah 42:7; 2 Timothy 2:26 and Exodus 34:7.

Trauma and sin violates us in a spiritual way because it affects our understanding of who we are in God's eyes, therefore how we relate to Him as well as to our neighbor. Trauma distorts our identity as God's children that He loves and desired to to the extent of His Only Son Jesus dying for us to reconcile us back to Him. This is why many loathe themselves and feel unworthy of other people's love, let alone God's. The verse above in 2 Timothy talks about us coming to our senses. Our understanding of the fact that God loves us so much is especially distorted by trauma as well as sin. In both cases people participate whether willingly or out of necessity in self harm because the sin and or trauma causes them to feel unworthy of living. Remember that bondage of any kind to the devil is spiritual, and so it takes Spiritual Power to deliver from such. Only by His Mercy and the working of His Divine Power through being born again can those in bondage be delivered and also break the transmission of these tendencies to future generations for:

20 I have been crucified with Christ; it is no longer I who live, but Christ lives in me; and the *life* which I now live in the flesh I live by faith in the Son of God, who loved me and gave Himself for me;

17 Therefore, if anyone is in Christ, he is a new creation; old things have passed away; behold, all things have become new." Galatians 2:20 and 2 Corinthians 5:17.

Freedom only comes with being born again because "I say to you, unless one is born [a]again, he cannot see the kingdom of God." John 3:3.

Just as sin's consequences can be experienced by future generations, the benefits of righteousness can also be experienced by future generations, although they still have to decide to have Christ in their lives individually as recipients of His mercy which He is extending to all mankind.

How trauma is reversed

We have learned so far that trauma can be transmitted to future generations epigeneticially. The enemy exploits this, as well as ensuring that the environment nurtures the negative effects of and responses to the trauma, thus deepening the bondage to the enemy. The good news is that by the same mechanisms, trauma can also be undone, and the effects can also be reversed as the following excerpt from a study by Isabelle Mansuy, Professor of Neuroepigenetics at the University of Zurich and ETH Zurich, during investigations carried out in mice on the subject outlines:

"If male mice exposed to trauma in early postnatal life live in pleasant conditions as an adult, their behavior and the behavior of their offspring returns to normal. "Long after the traumatic experiences themselves, living in enriched conditions reverses the behavioral symptoms in adult animals and also prevents the transmission of these symptoms to the progeny," summarizes Isabelle Mansuy the new findings.

Lead author Katharina Gapp and her colleagues exposed newborn male mice to traumatic stress by separating them from their mothers at irregular intervals and stressing their mother unpredictably during separation. Subsequently, the male mice and their male offspring behaved significantly differently from the control mice when exposed to challenging situations. Examples related to their natural avoidance of bright light or their behavior when confronted with complex and constantly changing tasks, for example to obtain a water ration when thirsty.

At the molecular level, these behavioral alterations are associated with an increased level of the glucocorticoid receptor in the hippocampus – a brain area essential for cognitive processes and that contributes to stress responses. This altered expression results from an epigenetic dysregulation of the gene for the receptor that binds stress hormones like cortisone. The activity of this gene is normally reduced by DNA methylation, an epigenetic mark that silences genes. Traumatic experiences lead to the removal of some of these DNA methylation marks which results in an increase in gene activity and an increased production of the glucocorticoid receptor.

The epigenetic alterations are not only found in the hippocampus of the offspring of traumatized mice, but also in the germ cells of their fathers. The scientists thus assume that alterations in DNA methylation are transmitted to the progeny through the sperm. Isabelle Mansuy and her team have now shown that the impact of childhood trauma can be corrected by a low-stress and enriched environment in adult life. At the same time, the correction of the DNA methylation pattern prevents the symptoms from being inherited by the offspring."[8]

It is encouraging to know that trauma does not have to determine the course and outcome of a victim's life as well as those to come after, but that it can be undone. Trauma can be the beginning but does not have to be the end. The environment as a tool of the devil can enhance the effects of trauma deepening bondage to him, while the environment in the hands of God can be used to nurture the new man, strengthening spiritually while weakening the enemy's grip upon that soul. As an example, a drug addict having friends or acquaintances with the same problem and ready access to the substances of indulgence would be an environment which serves the devil's purpose of deepening bondage and destroying that person's life.

The born again drug addict is free but to continue to be free, "let him deny himself, and take up his cross [a]daily, and follow Me..." meaning also being in an environment without access to the substance of indulgence, the people to participate with or encourage participation in the destructive habit. Luke 9:23. The person's effort is in staying dead to the old nature by being born again daily, allowing "God who works in you both to will and to do for *His* good pleasure..." Philippians 2:13 which is to love Him first and to love your neighbor as yourself. (read 1 Corinthians 3:16; 6:19-20; and Matthew 22:37-40).

This can be applied to anything. Being in a good environment can help to an extent without being born again but lasts only as long as one is in the environment. To truly be set free, one has to be born again so that the tendency for that person as well as future generations toward the destructive habit is destroyed, whether they are in a good environment or not because God can work regardless, "Therefore, if anyone is in Christ, he is a new creation; old things have passed away; behold, all things have become new." 2 Corinthians 5:17. It does help to have an environment which nurtures one to grow closer to God and minimizes the presence or access to temptations but by itself is temporary without being made new in Christ. True and lasting freedom can only be found in Christ.

God restoring Job

Some might question why God would allow a man who was so good to even go through such tragic experiences. I do not claim to understand or know why but in my opinion, he went through everything he went through because God knew the kind of man he was and that he loved Him regardless of circumstance. God knew that he would not fail because

13 God is faithful, who will not allow you to be tempted beyond what you are able, but with the temptation will also make the way of escape, that you may be able to [a]bear it;..

6 In this you greatly rejoice, though now for a little while, if need be, you have been [c]grieved by various trials,

7 that the genuineness of your faith, being much more precious than gold that perishes, though it is tested by fire, may be found to praise, honor, and glory at the revelation of Jesus Christ,

8 whom having not [d]seen you love. Though now you do not see Him, yet believing, you rejoice with joy inexpressible and full of glory,

9 receiving the end of your faith—the salvation of your souls.." 2 Corinthians 10:13 and 1 Peter 1:6-9.

If He allows to go through something, it is because He knows you can handle it. He knows us better than we know ourselves. No trial is comfortable but if you are going through something, take comfort in the above scripture that the Lord will not allow you to be tested beyond your capacity. The fact that you are going through it means you can bare it and more importantly, the trial of your faith like the purification of gold by heat is essential for it to grow and to be more genuine. Gold is purer the more heat is applied during the purification process, and likewise, faith is stronger and more grounded through its purification during trials.

God allowed these things to happen to Job to prove that humans can have such an intimate relationship with Him that no circumstance would be able to sever. He was to be an example for us considering how severe his trials were, yet he held on to his integrity without renouncing his relationship with God. Job was such a blessed man who lacked for nothing and had been abundantly blessed in all areas of his life. What greater vindication of God's character than a man who has it all, loses it all, and still worships and loves God through it all! The expected or more natural response would be for him to curse God or renounce his relationship with Him, which is what the devil hoped for.

God in trying to prove that there are people who love Him unconditionally, allowed these things to happen and in the process His character was vindicated while also exposing the devil's agenda and how he works against humanity. Job was showing how a human being can regardless of circumstance, willingly and unconditionally love his Creator. It was God's way of also pulling the veil and showing us the same struggles each and every one of us face though in varying degrees, the great conflict taking place which we cannot see with our eyes, "for we wrestle not against flesh and blood, but against principalities, against powers, against the rulers of the darkness of this world, against spiritual wickedness in high places." Ephesians 6:12 (KJV).

Without God's help, an average person can most likely commit suicide or resort to forms of self-harm like Alcohol or drugs to self-medicate and divert the mind from such severe trials. This is what is happening to most of the people in the world today as they go through different trials. Every person will face a trial at some point in their lives but to cope and endure, it takes a strength beyond themselves and that strength and peace in a storm can only be found in God. There is a great conflict taking place in each and every one of our lives. We just cannot see it with our eyes but we see the effects of it in the circumstances we face throughout our lives.

Because of these forces working against us, God's Angels fight on our behalf against the wiles of the devil and his demons. When we have near death experiences, survive what seems like certain death, whether calamities or disease, if God still has a purpose for our existence or still giving us more time so hopefully we can accept His Salvation, it is because God's Angels are fighting on our behalf. It is not by chance! Whether believer or not, we are still alive because just as in Job's case, God sets the limit on what the devil can do. If Satan could get his way, he would kill at the first opportunity because:

44 He was a murderer from the beginning;...

12 For the devil has come down to you, having great wrath, because he knows that he has a short time." John 8:44; Revelation 12:12.

The devil knows he has a short time and he is working hard to take as many as he can with him. He wants as many as possible to die in their sins without being saved because he wants us to share in the fate God intended only for him and the fallen angels (Matthew 25:41.) God desires to save if possible, every single person including those who appear in our eyes to be the most sinful, if they take advantage of the opportunity be saved. God would have been preserving their life for them to be saved, regardless of their past. This is Good News for all of us because no matter what we might have done in the past, how we might have been, God's ultimate goal is to save as many as will accept His Salvation, as Jesus said,

38 For I have come down from heaven, not to do My own will, but the will of Him who sent Me.

39 This is the will of the Father who sent Me, that of all He has given Me I should lose nothing, but should raise it up at the last day.

40 And this is the will of Him who sent Me, that everyone who sees the Son and believes in Him may have everlasting life; and I will raise him up at the last day." John 6:38-40.

Another day we are alive is an opportunity to take advantage of Salvation; "while it is said: "Today, if you will hear His voice, Do not harden your hearts as in the rebellion."..." Hebrews 3:15. In the end because Job held on to his integrity "the LORD blessed the latter end of Job more than his beginning" blessing him with more than he had before which he lost, as well as 7 sons and 3 daughters. (Job 42: 12-17.) Each and every one of us will face trials in our lives because we have an enemy who is fighting against us we cannot see. Job had a happy ending but we are not promised that we will have happy endings like his.

We can take comfort however in the promise that if we are going through something, it is because He knows we will be able to endure it (1 Corinthians 10:13) and that "...all things work together for good to those who love God, to those who are the called according to His purpose." Romans 8:28. Our faith is the most precious thing in God's eyes because:

8 by grace you have been saved through faith, and that not of yourselves; it is the gift of God;..." for "1 faith is the [a]substance of things hoped for, the [b]evidence of things not seen;…

6 without faith it is impossible to please Him, for he who comes to God must believe that He is, and that He is a rewarder of those who diligently seek Him. Ephesians 2:8; Hebrews 11:1, 6.

Without faith we cannot be saved, so faith is the most valuable thing to have. The trials themselves can serve a higher purpose and be for our blessing but:

12 do not think it strange concerning the fiery trial which is to try you, as though some strange thing happened to you;

13 but rejoice to the extent that you partake of Christ's sufferings, that when His glory is revealed, you may also be glad with exceeding joy;…

3 Blessed be the God and Father of our Lord Jesus Christ, who according to His abundant mercy has begotten us again to a living hope through the resurrection of Jesus Christ from the dead,

4 to an inheritance [b]incorruptible and undefiled and that does not fade away, reserved in heaven for you,

5 who are kept by the power of God through faith for salvation ready to be revealed in the last time.

6 In this you greatly rejoice, though now for a little while, if need be, you have been [c]grieved by various trials,

7 that the genuineness of your faith, being much more precious than gold that perishes, though it is tested by fire, may be found to praise, honor, and glory at the revelation of Jesus Christ,

8 whom having not [d]seen you love. Though now you do not see Him, yet believing, you rejoice with joy inexpressible and full of glory,

9 receiving the end of your faith—the salvation of your souls. 1 Peter 4:12-13; 1:3-9.

The ultimate goal is salvation of our souls and everything that comes with it namely Eternal life. Trials are not comfortable but each one is an opportunity to exercise faith and deepen our trust in God. Smooth sailing through life does nothing for our faith just as much as no heat does nothing to purify gold. Faith is necessary to believe and trust in God we have not seen, and a deeper belief and trust in Him can only come through trials.

References

1. .https://www.theosophical.org/publications/quest-magazine/3521-drugs-and-spirituality-an-occult-perspective
2. .https://www.drugabuse.gov/publications/research-reports/common-comorbidities-substance-use-disorders/part-1-connection-between-substance-use-disorders-mental-illness
3. https://www.nimh.nih.gov/health/statistics/suicide.shtml
4. https://www.mckinsey.com/industries/public-and-social-sector/our-insights/covid-19-investing-in-black-lives-and-livelihoods#

5. https://www.health.harvard.edu/diseases-and-conditions/past-trauma-may-haunt-your-future-health
6. Psychiatric Clinics of North America, Volume 12, Number 2, Pages 389-411, June 1989. The Compulsion to Repeat the Trauma Re-enactment, Revictimization, and Masochism Bessel A. van der Kolk, MD
7. https://www.scientificamerican.com/article/fearful-memories-passed-down/
8. https://ethz.ch/en/news-and-events/eth-news/news/2016/06/traumata-rueckgaengig-gemacht.html

15
THE SUN OF RIGHTEOUSNESS

The Sun is essential for life on this planet and also promotes good health as we have already learned. Other than these benefits, the Sun serves primarily as a light separating night from daytime. Imagine if there was no Sun, it would be perpetual darkness with never-ending night time. One of Christ's names is Sun of Righteousness:

2 For behold, the darkness shall cover the earth, And deep darkness the people; But the Lord will arise over you, And His glory will be seen upon you.

3 The Gentiles shall come to your light,…

2 But to you who fear My name The Sun of Righteousness shall arise With healing in His wings; Isaiah 60:2-3. Malachi 4:2.

Christ heals us dispelling the darkness of sin "…who called you out of darkness into His marvelous light…" 1 Peter 2:9. The Sun not only heals but also sheds light so that we can see. When Christ shines upon us He reveals the areas in our lives that need to conform to His will. If our desire is to truly continue to grow in our relationship with Him, we have to be willing to allow Him to reveal these weak areas to us. When He reveals something, are we willing to accept His correction or do we think that He is wrong and we cling to our will? Do we put our will over His?

Do we choose our way over His which is the truth? If we are to truly enjoy good spiritual health, we have to allow the Sun of Righteousness to shine on our lives and to heal us. If we reject His correction, then we choose to remain in darkness refusing the healing the Sun brings as is written:

19 And this is the condemnation, that the light has come into the world, and men loved darkness rather than light, because their deeds were evil.

20 For everyone practicing evil hates the light and does not come to the light, lest his deeds should be exposed. John 3:19-20.

How do we get revelations about areas that need change? God reveals His will to us through His Word. When we read the Word, it can shed light on an area which needs to be addressed as is written:

12 For the word of God is living and powerful, and sharper than any two-edged sword, piercing even to the division of soul and spirit, and of joints and marrow, and is a discerner of the thoughts and intents of the heart.

13 And there is no creature hidden from His sight, but all things are naked and open to the eyes of Him to whom we must give account.

16 All Scripture is given by inspiration of God, and is profitable for doctrine, for reproof, for correction, for [c]instruction in righteousness,

17 that the man of God may be complete, thoroughly equipped for every good work. Hebrews 4:12-13; 2 Timothy 3:16-17.

The purpose of these revelations is for us to take heed and make the necessary changes. They are supposed to help us to improve our relationships with Him and those around us. If God sheds light on something that needs to be addressed and we reject to change it, we are like the person described by James in the following verses:

22 But be doers of the word, and not hearers only, deceiving yourselves.

23 For if anyone is a hearer of the word and not a doer, he is like a man observing his natural face in a mirror;

24 for he observes himself, goes away, and immediately forgets what kind of man he was.

25 But he who looks into the perfect law of liberty and continues in it, and is not a forgetful hearer but a doer of the work, this one will be blessed in what he does. James 1:22-25.

Imagine looking at a mirror in a bathroom after lunch before going back to work and realizing that you have a thick piece of mucus dangling out of one of your nostrils. You might have attended an important employee meeting and so many other things not realizing you had this nasty thing hanging on your nose the whole time. The average person would be so embarrassed and would quickly remove it. You would think about what kind of image it might have portrayed walking around all day with a big nasty booger hanging on your nose. For those looking at you, they might think that you are unhygienic, do not pay attention to your appearance or care.

They can come to all kinds of conclusions which might not necessarily reflect who you are. It would be tragic to see it yet ignoring it as if you did not see it. Imagine those who see you enter the bathroom having seen you earlier in the day. They would be shocked to see you exit the same way you entered and whatever they thought of you would be cemented in their minds. This is what we do when God reveals a defect in our character through His Word. If we read and yet refuse to make a change choosing to hold on to whatever it is, our beholders come to their own conclusions about us and even about the God we claim to love.

There are many things that God can reveal to us. It can be a problem with lust, pride, selfishness; anything that is contrary to God's principle of loving Him first and others as we love ourselves. It might be something that does not necessarily harm those around us but it can be contrary to His will as revealed in the Word. These "boogers" in our lives misrepresent God and can cause those around us to come to the wrong conclusion about Him because of the image we portray as is written:

20 Therefore by their fruits you will know them;…

35 By this all will know that you are My disciples, if you have love for one another." Matthew 7:20; John 13:35.

The things revealed might be difficult to give up but our job is not to try to overcome anything on our own. He shines on us that same Sun of Righteousness which heals us as well. It heals by shining on us. If we hide from the sun because we do not want to change or think we cannot change, then no change takes place. Healing and spiritual health only happens when we are willing for God to reveal and address these boogers. We just have to stay in the light and allow Him to take care of these defects and to continue to grow in our relationship with Him.

All we do is surrender our will and He does the rest. Spiritual health will only thrive by not being afraid of the Sun and allowing it to shine and heal us bringing us ever close to portraying the image of God as is written:

18 But we all, with unveiled face, beholding as in a mirror the glory of the Lord, are being transformed into the same image from glory to glory, just as by the Spirit of the Lord." 2 Corinthians 3:18.

15
BREAD OF LIFE: WHERE ARE WE FROM?

Just as we have to eat nutritious food to enjoy good health, good spiritual nutrition is critical to return to and maintain good spiritual health. Just as it is needed to start the journey of reconciliation with God, it is also crucial in maintaining a relationship so the soul grows healthier and stronger in this state of being born-again. Good nutrition for the soul which is the only soul food God intended for us, is the Word of God which encourages us to choose Eternal life in Him, and to be healed from our sins, for "Man shall not live by bread alone, but by every word that proceeds from the mouth of God." Matthew 4:4.

By reading the scripture we understand who God is and how much He loves us. The more we learn of Him and understand Him, the more likely we are to love Him. The Word serves to draw us closer to Him. The same way it is absolutely essential to eat to stay alive, living and thriving in this relationship is absolutely dependent on feeding on His Word daily.

17 So then faith comes by hearing, and hearing by the word of God;...

6 But without faith it is impossible to please Him, for he who comes to God must believe that He is, and that He is a rewarder of those who diligently seek Him. Romans 10:17; Hebrews 11:6.

We hear His Word when we read it because that is how He talks to us. What pleases God is for us to love Him and to love our neighbor. To be able to do this we learn more about Him in His Word and as the relationship gets deeper and we learn to trust Him even though we have not seen Him.

Bad nutrition for the soul

If the Word is good food for the soul because it draws us closer to God by helping us understand and trust Him, anything that can cause distrust of His Word, of Him and serves to drive us away and separate us from Him is not healthy for the soul. There are a lot of philosophies and beliefs that sound good and taste good to the mind but will only serve to destroy spiritual health by encouraging disbelief and distrust of God.

The same way what is called junk food tastes good but is bad for health, any idea, philosophy or theory which sounds appealing to the mind but is ultimately destructive to the soul because it denies God or distances the soul away from Him. They attack or question God's very nature, His attributes as well as the work of His hands or completely go against His recommendations for us. This is what the Word warns against:

8 Beware lest anyone [e]cheat you through philosophy and empty deceit, according to the tradition of men, according to the basic principles of the world, and not according to Christ. Colossians 2:8.

Pew Research Center telephone surveys conducted in 2018 and 2019 show that 4% of American adults say they are atheists when asked about their religious identity, up from 2% in 2009. An additional 5% of Americans call themselves agnostics, up from 3% a decade ago.[1]

Since the turn of the century, the percentage of U.S. adults with no religious affiliation has more than doubled, from 8% to 19%...U.S. church membership was 70% or higher from 1937 through 1976, falling modestly to an average of 68% in the 1970s through the 1990s. The past 20 years have seen an acceleration in the drop-off, with a 20-percentage-point decline since 1999 and more than half of that change occurring since the start of the current decade.[2]

It is categorized upon the main points of attack namely:

1. Where are we from?
2. Who are we?
3. Why are we here?
4. Where are we going?

Where are we from?

Where are we from? This is a fundamental question whose answer can help us to understand about ourselves as humanity because of where we came. This is why this is a primary point of attack by the devil. He knows that if he can distort our understanding of where we are from, it distorts our understanding of all other areas of fundamental importance like why we are here and where we are going.

How does he achieve this? Our origins are in God, so by distorting who God is, he then distorts our understanding of ourselves as we came from Him. Once our understanding of God is distorted, we become disoriented and lose sight of why we are here and what God's ultimate goal for us which is to be reconciled back to Him.

Earlier on we learned that God allowed sin to come into existence, for the devil's way to be seen for what it is because it was something foreign which had never existed before. Had God dealt with the devil and destroyed him right then, there would have been remaining doubts among the Angels that remained loyal to Him, because they would not have had a chance to see if indeed the devil was right about his way. The only way was to let God's way of Love be seen by its fruit, and for the devil's way of sin be seen by its fruit because He:

5 will bring to light the hidden things of darkness, and will make manifest the counsels of the hearts: and then shall every man have praise of God...

10 That at the name of Jesus every knee should bow, of things in heaven, and things in earth, and things under the earth;

11 And that every tongue should confess that Jesus Christ is Lord, to the glory of God the Father. 1 Corinthians 4:5; Philippians 2:10-11.

Sin brought woe and death into existence, two undesirable things which humanity has come to associate with life. The fact that God allowed sin to not only exist but seemingly to thrive, is a reason why many in trying to grapple with this, subscribe to different ideas or philosophies.

People subscribe to all kinds of philosophies, which gives them some perspective to who or what God is to them. They sound appealing, but it does not mean that they are truth and more importantly, the disorientation as a result of these philosophies robs them of the opportunity to partake in reconciliation to Him. To partake in God's invitation to come back to a relationship with Him, and Eternal life, one has to understand who God is, what He desires for us, and what He is doing on His part to ensure our reconciliation to Him. The devil's mission is to ensure that many misunderstand who God is and what He desires for them, so that they miss out on this opportunity. Shortly we will look at how the devil achieves this, but first let look at how "spiritual" people are in America.

According to Pew Research, "most American adults self-identify as Christians, but many Christians also hold what are sometimes characterized as "New Age" beliefs – including belief in reincarnation, astrology, psychics and the presence of spiritual energy in physical objects like mountains or trees. Many Americans who are religiously unaffiliated also have these beliefs.

"Roughly six-in-ten American adults accept at least one of these New Age beliefs. Specifically, four-in-ten believe in psychics and that spiritual energy can be found in physical objects, while somewhat smaller shares express belief in reincarnation (33%) and astrology (29%)...But New Age beliefs are not necessarily replacing belief in traditional forms of religious beliefs or practices. While eight-in-ten Christians say they believe in God as described in the Bible, six-in-ten believe in one or more of the four New Age beliefs analyzed here, ranging from 47% of evangelical Protestants to roughly seven-in-ten Catholics and Protestants in the historically black tradition.

"Moreover, religiously unaffiliated Americans (those who say their religion is atheist, agnostic or "nothing in particular") are about as likely as Christians to hold New Age beliefs. However, atheists are much less likely to believe in any of the four New Age beliefs than agnostics and those who say their religion is "nothing in particular." Just 22% of atheists believe in at least one of four New Age beliefs, compared with 56% of agnostics and eight-in-ten among those whose religion is "nothing in particular."

"Americans who consider themselves to be spiritual but not religious also tend to accept at least one New Age belief. Roughly three-quarters of U.S. adults in this category hold one or more New Age beliefs, including six-in-ten who believe spiritual energy can be located in physical things and 54% who believe in psychics. And among those who say they are religious and spiritual, 65% espouse at least one New Age belief." [3]

New Age movement and the Counterculture

From these statistics, we are seeing that many people are spiritual though not necessarily religious or would not want to be classified as religious. Being spiritual today means one partakes in some of the New Age beliefs and practices. A person can be a believer in any one of the World's major religions like Christianity or Islam, and still buy into New Age practices. It has become pervasive now, but it was not always the case. Until the 60s with the counterculture movement, western society had been predominantly based on Judeo-Christian values.

With the counterculture movement came an increasing interest in Eastern philosophy and mysticism. Though that period is marked by landmark social and political changes, it had New Age spirituality as its heart and soul and can be considered a spiritual movement more than anything. The counterculture was about countering and overturning what had been to bring about new values and perspective for society at large. It not only succeeded in achieving this but continues to thrive today because of its appeal.

What makes it so appealing is because it is a "spiritual supermarket where religious consumers pick and choose the spiritual commodities they fancy and use them to create their own spiritual syntheses, fine-tuned to their strictly personal needs' [4] As one of its hallmarks, it is fashionable to be spiritual but not religious. It has the advantage over more organized forms of religion like Christianity or Hinduism in that "New Age spirituality is strictly focused on the individual and his or her personal development.

In fact, this functions as an in-built defense mechanism against social organization and institutionalization: as soon as any group of people involved with New Age ideas begins to take up "cultic" characteristics, this very fact already distances them from basic individualism of New Age spirituality" [4] Organization or structure is associated with what New Agers consider "old-fashioned patterns of dogmatism, intolerance, and exclusivism)" making them less acceptable to the cultic milieu of New Age spirituality. In New Age spirituality, is "strict emphasis on the self and on individual experience as the only reliable source of spiritual truth, the authority which can never be overruled by any religious dogma or consideration of solidarity with communal values...' [4]

For something so pervasive in society today, closer examination reveals however, that the essence of the movement is in opposition to God and what He stands for. Before we look at each of the core ideas promoted by the New Age movement, looking at the things that came about as a result of the 1960s counterculture will help us to gain a perspective on its true nature and the spirit behind it. In each point, I will also highlight how these changes have matured today.

Counterculture

Television
Though television had been around for some time, its power to reach many had yet to be seen until the counterculture movement of the 1960s. It played a pivotal role in youthful disillusionment and the formulation of new social trends and behaviors.[5] The power and reach of television has been multiplied many times over today, and it remains among the top ways of promoting New Age spirituality, as well as setting trends for lifestyle, fashion and social norms. 'Modern family' and 'I am Cait' come to mind as prominent examples of how powerful television can be in setting and normalizing new societal trends. Even children programs have become pervasive with occult themes.

New cinema
The breakdown of the Motion Picture Production code or Hays code enabled modern production values and new-found artistic freedom. It made realistic depictions of previously prohibited subject matter. Major changes included art-house, pornographic, and mainstream film production, distribution, and exhibition.

Exploitation films about the hippie counterculture depicted stereotypical situations associated with the movement such as marijuana and LSD use, sex and wild psychedelic parties. Filmmakers like Kenneth Anger were among the first to promote gay culture through cinema with the 1947 homoerotic experimental film Fireworks. His later works like Lucifer Rising promoted the New Age of Aquarius, which we'll learn to be all tied to the New Age movement or New Age spirituality.

All these changes which were big at the time have become the standard today and a normal part of our lives. Occult themes have become so common to not raise eyebrows anymore, sexual immorality the staple, and violence not as shocking as we have become desensitized to all these things. Children have also become the focus of occult themed fantasy films like the Harry Potter series, the Lord of the Rings series and Labyrinth just to name a few. The films are becoming darker and some, blatantly satanic.

New radio

In the 1960s with the increasing popularity of FM over AM, there was an explosion of rock and roll music, as well as youth-oriented news and advertising for the counterculture generation. The Beatles went on to become the face of the "psychedelic revolution" while bands and other musicians, such as the Jefferson Airplane, Grateful Dead, Quicksilver Messenger Service, Janis Joplin and the Blues Project were considered key to the counterculture movement. Radio today continues to be a powerful way for musicians to influence multitudes of impressionable youth who have no idea what their favorite musicians' beliefs are or the source of their inspiration. Music is very powerful in influencing youth in terms of drug use, sexual behavior and violence. [6]

Civil Rights

The US Civil Rights Movement, a key element of the larger counterculture movement, involved the use of applied nonviolence to assure that equal rights guaranteed under the US Constitution would apply to all citizens, especially African-Americans who had been illegally denied many rights in many states up to that point. Fast forward to the present and African-Americans continue to protest for the right to live in face of police brutality, through the Black Lives

Matter Movement. The popularity of Black Lives Matter has rapidly shifted over time. Whereas public opinion on Black Lives Matter was net negative in 2018, it grew increasingly popular through 2019 and 2020. A June 2020 Pew Research Center poll found that the majority of Americans, across all racial and ethnic groups, have expressed support for the Black Lives Matter movement.[7]

They are pushing a just cause, however, closer examination of their beliefs reveals that it is actually a spiritual movement, with supporters participating in spiritualism unawares as shown in this Tristate Voices article:

"the co-founders are all radical feminists, with two of the three identifying as queer. (Please note that I use the initials BLM to distinguish this Marxist-based movement from the important affirmation that black lives do matter. We can now trace this demonic influence one step further, with the open, unapologetic statements of two key BLM leaders. I'm speaking about BLM co-founder Patrisse Cullors and Prof. Melina Abdullah, chair of the department of Pan-African Studies at California State University, Los Angeles, and a co-founder of the Los Angeles chapter of Black Lives Matter.

Their relevant video discussion on Facebook was posted on June 13. But even before that, on June 9, Heba Farrag posted an article on the Berkeley Center website titled, "The Fight for Black Lives is a Spiritual Movement." Farrag explained how Prof. Abdullah met with a BLM group in front of the house of Los Angeles mayor Eric Garcetti: "She led the group in a ritual: the reciting of names of those taken by state violence before their time—ancestors now being called back to animate their own justice:

"'George Floyd. Asé. Philando Castille. Asé. Andrew Joseph. Asé. Michael Brown. Asé. Erika Garner. Asé. Harriet Tubman. Asé. Malcom X. Asé. Martin Luther King. Asé.'

"As each name is recited, Dr. Abdullah poured libations on the ground as the group of over 100 chanted 'Asé,' a Yoruba term often used by practitioners of Ifa, a faith and divination system that originated in West Africa, in return. This ritual, Dr. Abdullah explained, is a form of worship."

Yes, this helps fuel the fires of the BLM movement: worship of the dead; calling on the dead; asking the spirits of the dead to empower the living today.

Abdullah and Cullors discussed this openly on their Facebook video, which Abraham Hamilton, III, brought to national attention on his daily radio show on August 13, playing relevant clips, in context.

In the video, Prof. Abdullah stated that "we become very intimate with the spirits that we call on regularly. Right, like, each of them seems to have a different presence and personality. You know, I laugh a lot with Wakisha, you know, and I didn't meet her in her body. Right, I met her through this work."

Yes, the spirits of the dead even have names, like Wakisha, with whom Abdullah exchanges some laughs. Cullors, in response, explained how she has been empowered by these spirits and how the mantra to "say his (or, her) name" was more than a slogan. It was an appeal to the spirits of the deceased to rise up and work through her and others." [8]

I talk about this movement because unlike the other organizations which might be white supremacist, it is actually advocating for what any decent person can see as a good cause. It is a cause which is drawing a lot of support worldwide, but the fact that spiritualism is involved makes it dangerous. This is an unfortunate way that people who are genuinely rallying around a good cause, unwittingly participate in worship involving practices God has forbidden like divination and more specifically, necromancy. I had to go into the roots of this movement because there are many good people, some even Christian, who are participating in these practices blindly thinking they are supporting a just cause.

In its landmark 1973 case, Roe v. Wade where a woman challenged the Texas laws criminalizing abortion, the U.S. Supreme Court reached two important conclusions:

> That state abortion laws are subject to the due process clause of the Fourteenth Amendment to the United States Constitution; and

> That the procurement of an abortion was a constitutional right during the first and second trimesters of a pregnancy based on the constitutional right to privacy, but that the state's interest in protecting "potential life" prevailed in the third trimester unless the woman's health was at risk. In subsequent rulings, the Court rejected the trimester framework altogether in favor of a cutoff at the point of fetal viability (cf. Planned Parenthood v. Casey). [9]

Even though Roe v. Wade was a victory for them, pro-abortion supporters are not satisfied and desire for women to have absolute ability to have abortions at any stage of fetal development without state oversight or interference. The LGBT community continues to gain equal rights which culminated in the Supreme Court ruling in favor of same-sex marriage in 2015. Homosexuality prior to 1973 was considered a mental disorder until its removal from the DSM in 1987, and WHO removed it from its ICD-10 classification in 1992. [10]

More changes are happening with the latest being the Bostock vs Clayton County Supreme court ruling which was a landmark United States Supreme Court civil rights case in which the Court held that Title VII of the Civil Rights Act of 1964 protects employees against discrimination because of their sexual orientation or gender identity. We will no doubt continue to see changes and currently we see Transgender people vying for more rights and recognition. There are concerns that these rulings in favor of the LGBT community have opened a Pandora's box which will see groups fighting for their rights to practice anything ranging from Polygamy to Pedophilia. Only time will tell if these are legitimate concerns, but judging by the trend, I would not be surprised.

Free Speech and the New Left

The 1964 Free Speech Movement at the University of California, Berkeley, students insisted that the university administration lift the ban of on-campus political activities, acknowledge the students' right to free speech and academic freedom, and the right to support off-campus issues. Given that the Free Speech movement was started by students, it is ironic that today, students are in growing opposition to it. High-profile speakers have been disinvited from or otherwise pushed out of commencement addresses, because of students who did not want to hear what they had to say. Even comedians are not keen on performing at colleges because they say students cannot take a joke. Campuses have become "safe spaces" for all sorts of marginalized groups leading to the death of free speech. [11]

In a prank to illustrate these sentiments, filmmaker and satirist Ami Horowitz made a video on the Yale campus, asking students to sign a petition for the repeal of the first amendment. 50 Students not only signed the petition within the first hour, but repeatedly thanked the presenter for helping to prevent them from hearing words that they did not want to hear. [12]

Free Speech is still protected by the first amendment though likely not for long, but even then, it does not seem to be a guarantee for all people because Christianity has become the special target of censorship. Back in September 2011, Colby May, director of the office of governmental affairs at the American Center for Law and Justice, teamed up with other groups to examine censorship by the social media platforms, and had this to say. "There is a kind of viewpoint censorship that's going on…Right now, it's on the issue of the gay rights agenda…And when you get the explanation, it's 'Well, some people were ruffled. They felt they were offended by it… We've crossed over into this netherworld where offense is now the justification upon which the rights we have as Americans to fully engage in the culture and to debate all issues is going to be decided?'" [13]

This was back in 2011. Fast forward to 2020 and even beloved liberal celebrities like Harry Potter author J. K. Rowling cannot escape the P.C. police on social media. The following is an excerpt on the matter from a Glamour article.

"On June 6, Rowling retweeted an op-ed piece that discussed "people who menstruate," apparently taking issue with the fact that the story did not use the word women. "'People who menstruate.' I'm sure there used to be a word for those people. Someone help me out. Wumben? Wimpund? Woomud?," she wrote. That initial tweet garnered a lot of backlash, but Rowling did not relent and wrote about her views in more detail. "If sex isn't real, there's no same-sex attraction. If sex isn't real, the lived reality of women globally is erased. I know and love trans people, but erasing the concept of sex removes the ability of many to meaningfully discuss their lives. It isn't hate to speak the truth," she tweeted. "The idea that women like me, who've been empathetic to trans people for decades, feeling kinship because they're vulnerable in the same way as women—i.e., to male violence—'hate' trans people because they think sex is real and has lived consequences—is a nonsense."

She continued, "I respect every trans person's right to live any way that feels authentic and comfortable to them. I'd march with you if you were discriminated against on the basis of being trans. At the same time, my life has been shaped by being female. I do not believe it's hateful to say so."

"This isn't an easy piece to write, for reasons that will shortly become clear, but I know it's time to explain myself on an issue surrounded by toxicity. I write this without any desire to add to that toxicity," she wrote "For people who don't know: last December I tweeted my support for Maya Forstater, a tax specialist who'd lost her job for what were deemed 'transphobic' tweets. She took her case to an employment tribunal, asking the judge to rule on whether a philosophical belief that sex is determined by biology is protected in law. Judge Tayler ruled that it wasn't."

Rowling explains that she became interested in trans issues while researching a character she's writing. Rowling also outlined "five reasons for being worried about the new trans activism." ...Rowling's initial tweets and her subsequent doubling down have drawn a lot of ire from trans activists and fans of Harry Potter, many of whom found comfort in the story of an outsider finding a place where he belonged."

She received backlash not only from fans but also from actors who portrayed the characters in her books.

"Radcliffe, Harry Potter himself, was the first star from the franchise to release a statement (via the Trevor Project) about Rowling's comments.

"I realize that certain press outlets will probably want to paint this as in-fighting between J.K. Rowling and myself," he said, "but that is really not what this is about, nor is it what's important right now. While Jo is unquestionably responsible for the course my life has taken, as someone who has been honored to work with and continues to contribute to The Trevor Project for the last decade, and just as a human being, I feel compelled to say something at this moment. Transgender women are women. Any statement to the contrary erases the identity and dignity of transgender people and goes against all advice given by professional health care associations who have far more expertise on this subject matter than either Jo or I. According to The Trevor Project, 78% of transgender and nonbinary youth reported being the subject of discrimination due to their gender identity. It's clear that we need to do more to support transgender and nonbinary people, not invalidate their identities, and not cause further harm."

He continued, "To all the people who now feel that their experience of the books has been tarnished or diminished. I am deeply sorry for the pain these comments have caused you. I really hope that you don't entirely lose what was valuable in these stories to you…. And in my opinion, nobody can touch that. It means to you what it means to you and I hope that these comments will not taint that too much."

Watson, who played Hermione Granger, also spoke out in support of the trans community. "Trans people are who they say they are and deserve to live their lives without being constantly questioned or told they aren't who they say they are. I want my trans followers to know that I and so many other people around the world see you, respect you, and love you for who you are," she wrote in a series of tweets…Grint, who portrayed Ron Wesley, issued a statement in response to Rowling's essay as well.

"I firmly stand with the trans community and echo the sentiments expressed by many of my peers. Trans women are women. Trans men are men," Grint said, according to the Sunday Times on Friday, June 12. "We should all be entitled to live with love and without judgment."

Also, Bonnie Wright, the actor who played the onscreen sister of Grint's Ron, Ginny Weasley, spoke out via Twitter. "If Harry Potter was a source of love and belonging for you, that love is infinite and there to take without judgment or question. Transwomen are Women. I see and love you, Bonnie x," she wrote.

Redmayne, who appeared in Rowling's Fantastic Beasts franchise, released a lengthy statement to Variety.

"Respect for transgender people remains a cultural imperative, and over the years I have been trying to constantly educate myself. This is an ongoing process," he said. "As someone who has worked with both J.K. Rowling and members of the trans community, I wanted to make it absolutely clear where I stand. I disagree with Jo's comments. Trans women are women, trans men are men, and nonbinary identities are valid. I would never want to speak on behalf of the community but I do know that my dear transgender friends and colleagues are tired of this constant questioning of their identities, which all too often results in violence and abuse. They simply want to live their lives peacefully, and it's time to let them do so." [14]

The right to hold your own opinions if they differ from leftist agendas is vanishing at an alarming rate. What we are seeing now is a maturation of New Age countercultural values which are anti-God, anti-traditional values, and hyper-liberal. Disagreeing with liberal mindsets is now considered hate speech. Diversity is only for those who agree with them, and they demand tolerance from anyone who doesn't promote their ideologies while not tolerating any ideologies other than their own.

This suppression of the freedom of speech is part of a greater movement called the New Left. It is a term used in different countries to describe left-wing movements that occurred in the 1960s and 1970s which differed from earlier leftist movements that had been more oriented towards labor activism, and instead adopted social activism. It is associated with social justice organizations and has expanded into into identity politics or alternative lifestyles. Activism is not a bad thing, but it has become an effective vehicle for those preaching tolerance to be more intolerant. It is a form of free speech but only they are free to express themselves, and no one else is free to disagree with them. They want to be heard but do not want to listen to anyone else. You are forced to give in and compromise your beliefs or views, or they will shut you down if you maintain your position. Cancel culture is a term for it, and it was defined well in this excerpt from a New York Times article:

"Cancellation, properly understood, refers to an attack on someone's employment and reputation by a determined collective of critics, based on an opinion or an action that is alleged to be disgraceful and disqualifying. "Reputation" and "employment" are key terms here. You are not being canceled if you are merely being heckled or insulted — if somebody describes you as a moron or a fascist or some profane alternative to "Douthat" on the internet — no matter how vivid and threatening the heckling becomes. You are decidedly at risk of cancellation, however, if your critics are calling for you to be de-platformed or fired or put out of business, and especially if the call is coming from inside the house — from within your professional community, from co-workers or employees or potential customers or colleagues, on a professional message board or Slack or some interest-specific slice of social media." [15]

Chick-fil-A:

There are many examples of this and unfortunately, it has become the norm. A prominent example would be the protests against Chick-fil-A. In January 2011, it was reported in the media that fast-food chain was supporting anti-LGBT organizations by donations.

Chick-fil-A president and chief operating officer (COO) Dan Cathy had this to say on a 26 June 2012 interview on the Ken Coleman Show: "I think we are inviting God's judgment on our nation when we shake our fist at Him and say, 'We know better than you as to what constitutes a marriage,'" Cathy said. "I pray God's mercy on our generation that has such a prideful, arrogant attitude to think that we have the audacity to define what marriage is about." [16]

On July 2 when speaking to the Biblical Recorder, he said, "We know that it might not be popular with everyone, but thank the Lord, we live in a country where we can share our values and operate on biblical principles," [17]

To say there was a backlash in response to these statements would be an understatement. On August 15, 2012, a gunman carrying 15 Chick-fil-A sandwiches, a 9 mm handgun and a box of ammunition attempted to enter the Washington, D.C. headquarters of the Family Research Council. He shot a security guard in the left arm, and following his arrest he told police that he wanted to use the sandwiches to "make a statement against the people who work in that building ... and with their stance against gay rights and Chick-fil-A", and that he planned "to kill as many people as I could ... then smear a Chicken-fil-A [sic] sandwich on their face". [18]

Students at several colleges and universities launched efforts to ban or remove the company's restaurants from their campuses. On February 28, 2012, Northeastern University's Student Senate passed a resolution to cancel plans for a Chick-fil-A franchise on its campus, stating "Student concerns reflected CFA's history of donating to anti-gay organizations." The restaurant chain was finalizing a contract to bring it to NU when students protested. Many other campuses considered whether to retain or ban the restaurant on their campuses. [19]

Feminism

In 1963, US feminist Betty Friedan published The Feminine Mystique, giving momentum to the women's movement and influencing what many called Second-wave feminism. The 1970 pamphlet Women and Their Bodies, soon expanded into the 1971 book Our Bodies, Ourselves, which was particularly influential in bringing about the new feminist consciousness.

It started off good striving for basic rights such as equal pay and equal opportunity, but has become more than a political force with more than equality of sexes as its goals, even, matriarchy - the power or domination of women over men. Radical Feminism seeks to abolish patriarchy in any and all of its forms, and strives for a radical reordering of society in which male supremacy is eliminated in all social and economic contexts. Its ultimate goal is the rejection of Father God who is the ultimate Patriarch. It is interesting to note that with the rejection of God as Creator and sustainer of life that many consider Earth itself to be the Mother and sustainer of all life, and it is worshiped as such. This leads to the next point on environmentalism.

Environmentalism

The 1960s counterculture embraced a back-to-the-land ethic, being early adopters of practices such as recycling and organic farming long before they became mainstream. Communes of the era often relocated to the country from cities with some continuing to do so today. Thanks to books like Paul Ehrlich's The Population Bomb, counterculture environmentalists were quick to grasp his implications on over-population, pollution, nuclear energy, and many other things. The first Earth Day in 1970 was also significant in bringing environmental concerns to the forefront of youth culture, along with counterculture-oriented publications like the Whole Earth Catalog and The Mother Earth News. New Agers are known to be keen environmentalists who love nature even elevating it to the level of divinity, some of them literally worshiping it.

Nature worship

Environmentalism increasingly has the characteristics of a religion as outlined in the following excerpt from the article 'Environmentalism as Religion' in The New Atlantis:

"For some individuals and societies, the role of religion seems increasingly to be filled by environmentalism. It has become "the religion of choice for urban atheists," according to Michael Crichton, the late science fiction writer (and climate change skeptic). In a widely quoted 2003 speech, Crichton outlined the ways that environmentalism "remaps" Judeo-Christian beliefs:

"There's an initial Eden, a paradise, a state of grace and unity with nature, there's a fall from grace into a state of pollution as a result of eating from the tree of knowledge, and as a result of our actions there is a judgment coming for us all. We are all energy sinners, doomed to die, unless we seek salvation, which is now called sustainability. Sustainability is salvation in the church of the environment. Just as organic food is its communion, that pesticide-free wafer that the right people with the right beliefs, imbibe."

In parts of northern Europe, this new faith is now the mainstream... It is "quasi-religious in character," says Lugo. "It generates its own set of moral values." Freeman Dyson, the brilliant and contrarian octogenarian physicist... described environmentalism as "a worldwide secular religion" that has "replaced socialism as the leading secular religion." This religion holds "that we are stewards of the earth, that despoiling the planet with waste products of our luxurious living is a sin, and that the path of righteousness is to live as frugally as possible."

The ethics of this new religion, he continued, are being taught to children in kindergartens, schools, and colleges all over the world.... And the ethics of environmentalism are fundamentally sound. Scientists and economists can agree with Buddhist monks and Christian activists that ruthless destruction of natural habitats is evil and careful preservation of birds and butterflies is good. The worldwide community of environmentalists—most of whom are not scientists—holds the moral high ground, and is guiding human societies toward a hopeful future. Environmentalism, as a religion of hope and respect for nature, is here to stay. This is a religion that we can all share, whether or not we believe that global warming is harmful." [20]

The Gaia hypothesis

The Gaia hypothesis bridged the apparently religious nature of environmentalism with science to give it credibility. It was developed by atmospheric scientist and chemist Sir James Lovelock and is explained along with how environmentalism is affecting policies in this excerpt from a great article on the matter:

"the earth and its physical makeup, such as its geological and chemical properties are tied to the world's ecosystems, and their coexistence influences, if not governs completely, the geological, chemical, and biological circumstances, including the climate, of the earth. Many liken the Gaia theory to an understanding of the earth as a single organism. Originally referred to the Gaia hypothesis, Lovelock's idea has since been designated the Gaia theory, due to its ability to help predict some of the earth's behaviors.

Often referred to as Gaianism, or the Gaian religion, this spiritual aspect of the philosophy is very broad and inclusive, making it adaptable to other philosophies, such as Humanism, Taoism, Neo-Paganism, Pantheism, and others.

The beliefs of Gaianism are fairly open-ended:

1. Honor the Earth, who is often referred to as Gaia (sometimes spelled "Gaea").
2. Endeavor to soften or reduce the human impact on Gaia. Essentially, this means being mindful of one's actions and to be moderate with natural resources. Environmentalism and environmental education is strongly encouraged.
3. Be respectful of life in all its forms. Be respectful and courteous not only of human life, but also animal and plant life. Some Gaians are vegetarians and vegans because of this, but it is not a requirement.

Gaia philosophy and politics

Gaia worship is at the very heart of today's environmental policy. The Endangered Species Act, The United Nation's Biodiversity Treaty and the Presidents Council on Sustainable Development are all offspring of the Gaia hypothesis of saving "Mother Earth". This religious movement, with cult-like qualities, is being promoted by leading figures and organizations such as former Vice President Albert Gore, and the United Nations and its various NGO's. The United Nations has been extremely successful in infusing the "Green Religion" into an international governmental body that has increasing affect and control over all of our lives.

Gaia teaches that an "Earth spirit", goddess, or planetary brain must be protected; and it is this belief that fuels the environmental movement, sustainable development, and a global push for the return of industrialized nations to a more primitive way of life. Just as with the evolutionists, the humanists, and the other pagan religions of the world, Gaia has named Christianity as the obstacle to human evolution and our spiritual destiny. A document mandated by the U.N.-sponsored Convention on Biological Diversity, the Global Biodiversity Assessment, explicitly refers to Christianity as a faith that has set humans apart from nature and stripped nature of its sacred qualities. The document states:

"Conversion to Christianity has therefore meant an abandonment of an affinity with the natural world for many forest dwellers, peasants, fishers all over the world... The northeastern hilly states of India bordering China and Myanmar supported small scale, largely autonomous shifting cultivator societies until the 1950's. These people followed their own religious traditions that included setting apart between 10% and 30% of the landscape as sacred groves and ponds." (Global Biodiversity Assessment, Chapter 8.1 Introduction: Concepts of the Economic Value of Biodiversity, pp. 68, 69.)

Christianity, have gone farthest in setting humans apart from nature and in embracing a value system that has converted the world into a warehouse of commodities for human enjoyment. In the process, not only has nature lost its sacred qualities; conversion to Christianity has meant an abandonment of an affinity with the natural world for many forest dwellers, peasants, fishers all over the world.

"These people followed their own religious traditions which included setting apart between 10 and 30 percent of the landscape as sacred groves and ponds. Most of these people were drawn into the larger market economy and converted to Christianity by the late 1950s. On so converting to a religious belief system that rejects assignment of sacred qualities to elements of nature, they began to cut down the sacred groves to bring the land under cultivation...." (Ibid., p. 839.)

The Global Biodiversity Assessment concludes on page 863 that:

"the root causes of the loss of biodiversity are embedded in the way societies use resources. This world view is characteristic of large scale societies, heavily dependent on resources brought from considerable distances. It is a world view that is characterized by the denial of sacred attributes in nature, a characteristic that became firmly established about 2000 years ago with the Judeo-Christian-Islamic religious traditions."

While blaming especially Christianity as the root of "ecological evil", the document goes on to praise "Eastern cultures with religious traditions such as Buddhism, Jainism and Hinduism [as they] did not depart as drastically from the perspective of humans as members of a community of beings including other living and non-living elements." (Ibid, p. 863.) Non-Christian religions are definitely favored by the global government as good stewards of Mother Earth.

Gaianism and the Climate crisis

Members of this "Green Religion" will all agree that the Earth is in a crisis state and this ecological emergency is the result of Christian traditions. They believe that the Judeo-Christian belief that God assigned man to rule over the earth has caused us to exploit and abuse it. Monotheism, they assert, has separated humans from their ancient connection to the earth, and to reverse this trend governments, the media, our education system, artists, and other areas of influence must revive earth-centered myth and reconnect us to Earth's spirit. Al Gore, in his book "Earth in the Balance", expounds on this view:

"The richness and diversity of our religious tradition throughout history is a spiritual resource long ignored by people of faith, who are often afraid to open their minds to teachings first offered outside their own systems of belief. But the emergence of a civilization in which knowledge moves freely and almost instantaneously through the world has spurred a renewed investigation of the wisdom distilled by all faiths. This pan-religious perspective may prove especially important where our global civilization's responsibility for the earth is concerned." (Earth in the Balance, pp. 258-259.)

Gore praises the Eastern religions and new age spiritualism, while blaming Christianity for the elimination of the ancient goddess religion, and calls for a new spiritual relationship between man and earth.

"we feel increasingly distant from our roots in the earth....civilization itself has been on a journey from its foundations in the world of nature to an evermore contrived, controlled and manufactured world of our initiative and sometimes arrogant design.... At some point during this journey we lost our feeling of connectedness to the rest of nature.... We dare now to wonder: Are we so unique and powerful as to be essentially separate from the earth?" (Ibid, p. 1.)

"The spiritual sense of our place in nature predates Native American cultures; increasingly it can be traced to the origins of human civilization. A growing number of anthropologists and archaeomythologists, such as Marija Gimbutas and Riane Esler argue that the prevailing ideology of belief in prehistoric Europe and much of the world was based on the worship of a single earth goddess, (Gaia) who was assumed to be the fount of all life and who radiated harmony among all living things. Much of the evidence for the existence of this primitive religion comes from the many thousands of artifacts uncovered in ceremonial sites. These sites are so widespread that they seem to confirm the notion that a goddess religion was ubiquitous through much of the world until the antecedents of today's religions - most of which have a distinctly masculine orientation - swept out of India and the Near East, almost obliterating belief in the goddess. The last vestige of organized goddess worship was eliminated by Christianity as late as the fifteenth century in Lithuania." (Ibid, ch. 13, p. 260.)

"We are not used to seeing God in the world because we assume from the scientific and philosophical rules that govern us, that the physical world is made up of inanimate matter whirling in accordance to mathematical laws and bearing no relation to life, much less ourselves. Why does it feel faintly heretical to a Christian to suppose that God is in us as human beings? Why do our children believe that the Kingdom of God is up, somewhere in the ethereal reaches of space, far removed from this planet? By experiencing nature in its fullest...our own and that of all creation...with our senses and with our spiritual imagination, we can glimpse, "bright shining as the sun," an infinite image of God." (Ibid, p. 264.)" [21]

Suggested measures for tackling Climate crisis

We are seeing this movement gaining steam and the climate crisis will increasingly take center stage in how policies are going to be made. The California Governor, Gavin Newsom, just passed an executive order directing the state to require that, by 2035, all new cars and passenger trucks sold in California be zero-emission vehicles. The order also directs the state to take more actions to "tackle the dirtiest oil extraction and support workers and job retention and creation as we make a just transition away from fossil fuels." [22] It is more than likely that the other states are going to follow suit in the not so distant future.

A lockdown is even being suggested to tackle the Climate crisis by resetting how everything is done, as we see in a recent article "Avoiding a Climate Lockdown" by Mariana Mazzucato:

"In the near future, the world may need to resort to lockdowns again – this time to tackle a climate emergency. Shifting Arctic ice, raging wildfires in western US states and elsewhere, and methane leaks in the North Sea are all warning signs that we are approaching a tipping point on climate change, when protecting the future of civilization will require dramatic interventions. Under a "climate lockdown," governments would limit private-vehicle use, ban consumption of red meat, and impose extreme energy-saving measures, while fossil-fuel companies would have to stop drilling. To avoid such a scenario, we must overhaul our economic structures and do capitalism differently." [23]

Measures like cutting back on something as fundamental as farming by turning farmland into forests to reduce emissions sounds ridiculous, but it is seriously being proposed as one of the solutions to be implemented expediently in tackling the Climate crisis. This is pointed out in the following excerpt from a United Nations Panel on Climate Change report:

"The panel of scientists looked at the climate change effects of agriculture, deforestation and other land use, such as harvesting peat and managing grasslands and wetlands. Together, those activities generate about a third of human greenhouse gas emissions, including more than 40% of methane.

That's important because methane is particularly good at trapping heat in the atmosphere. And the problem is getting more severe…the panel broadly suggested that farmland would need to shrink and forests would need to grow to keep Earth from getting more than 1.5 degrees Celsius hotter than it was in the pre-industrial era. Global temperatures have already risen about 1 degree Celsius in the past 150 years.

To meet that temperature target, global greenhouse gas emissions will need to fall by 40% to 50% in the next decade.

Scientists say the only way to achieve that reduction is to significantly increase the amount of land that's covered in trees and other vegetation and significantly reduce the amount of methane and other greenhouse gases that come from raising livestock such as cows, sheep and goats...There's a growing consensus that a transition to a more plant-centered diet would help. Currently, about 50% of the globe's vegetated land is dedicated to agriculture — and about 30% of cropland is used to grow grain for animal feed. Given how much land it takes to grow food to feed livestock, meat production is a leading cause of deforestation." [24]

They are serious enough about tracking and limiting emissions that a Global Coalition of Tech, Climate Groups will combine AI and satellites to monitor GHG Emissions worldwide in Real Time. "The world has reached a tipping point on the climate crisis. In order to achieve a zero-carbon future, we need a comprehensive accounting of where pollution is coming from," said Vice President Al Gore. This unprecedented collaboration aims to track human-caused emissions to specific sources in real time—independently and publicly. The combined project will be known as Climate TRACE (Tracking Real-time Atmospheric Carbon Emissions). Tracking GHG emissions from nearly every major human-emitting activity worldwide—such as power plants, factories, large ships, and more—is an enormously difficult undertaking, but advanced AI and machine learning will now make it possible for the first time. [25]

As if drastic measures like locking down the whole world in addition to restrictions like limiting private vehicle usage or not eating beef to deal with this climate change crisis are not enough, they are perfecting this global emissions surveillance system which will likely monitor emissions being produced from an institutional down to an individual level. These measures are not science fiction but soon to be an uncomfortable reality for all of us, and it is all because this Gaia religion drives the United Nations and thus the world's policies on environmental issues.

A Sabbath for the earth

"Not long ago Sunday used to be a day of rest, a day of spiritual renewal, a day for families to come together, but we have changed Sunday from a day of rest to a day of shopping, flying and driving. However, in the context of excessive carbon dioxide emissions into the atmosphere, which are bringing catastrophic upheavals, we can and should restore Sunday to a day for Gaia, a day for the Earth. There will be no great hardship in cutting down all non-essential and non-urgent use of fossil fuels for one day a week. We can easily close supermarkets, department stores and petrol stations. We can reduce our mobility to the bare essentials and without harming the economy in any way." Satish Kumar suggested in a 2009 The Guardian article called "Slow Sunday: the simple solution to global warming". Interesting that he said this back in 2009. Fast forward to the present, and the push for a weekly Sabbath to give the Earth a rest is gaining momentum. At the World day of Prayer 2020, where the theme was 'Jubilee of the Earth' Pope Francis said the following in this excerpt from the article 'Pope Francis: the pandemic has given us a chance to develop new ways of living' in America The Jesuit Review magazine:

"The pope said the Covid-19 pandemic has "in some ways, given us a chance to develop new ways of living." Indeed, "already we can see how the earth can recover if we allow it to rest: the air becomes cleaner, the waters clearer, and animals have returned to many places from where they had previously disappeared."...He said: "The pandemic has brought us to a crossroads. We must use this decisive moment to end our superfluous and destructive goals and activities and to cultivate values, connections and activities that are lifegiving. We must examine our habits of energy usage, consumption, transportation and diet. We must eliminate the superfluous and destructive aspects of our economies and nurture life-giving ways to trade, produce and transport goods."

...He welcomed this year's theme (World day of Prayer Sep 1 2020) chosen by the ecumenical family, "Jubilee for the Earth," because 2020 marks the 50th anniversary of Earth Day, which began in the United States in 1969...He said we need constantly to remember that "everything is interconnected and that genuine care for our own lives and our relationships with nature is inseparable from fraternity, justice and faithfulness to others."...It is also a time "to listen" to "the voice of creation" and "remember that we are part of this interconnected web of life, not its masters." In this context, Francis said, "the disintegration of biodiversity, spiralling climate disasters, and unjust impact of the current pandemic on the poor and vulnerable: all these are a wakeup call in the face of our rampant greed and consumption."

A jubilee year is also "a time to rest," Francis said. He recalled that "God set aside the Sabbath so that the land and its inhabitants could rest and be renewed." But, he noted, "our constant demand for growth and an endless cycle of production and consumption are exhausting the natural world." He underlined the pressing need "to find just and sustainable ways of living...without destroying the ecosystems that sustain us."

Moreover, he said, a jubilee year is also "a time to restore the original harmony of creation" and "to re-establish equitable societal relationships, restoring their freedom and goods to all and forgiving one another's debts."

Pope Francis: "The pandemic has brought us to a crossroads. We must use this decisive moment to end our superfluous and destructive goals and activities and to cultivate values, connections and activities that are lifegiving."...He identified 2020 as "a time for restorative justice" and called again "for the cancellation of the debt of the most vulnerable countries, in recognition of the severe impacts of the medical, social and economic crises they face as a result of Covid-19." Moreover, he said, nations should ensure that the recovery packages "be focused on the common good and guarantee that global social and environmental goals are met."

Speaking of the "need to restore the land," Francis insisted that "climate restoration is of utmost importance, since we are in the midst of a climate emergency" and "are running out of time."

He said it's necessary "to do everything in our capacity to limit global average temperature rise under the threshold of 1.5°C enshrined in the Paris Climate Agreement, for going beyond that will prove catastrophic, especially for poor communities around the world."..."Biodiversity restoration" is also necessary, Francis said. He urged governments "to support the U.N. call to safeguard 30 percent of the earth as protected habitats by 2030 in order to stem the alarming rate of biodiversity loss."...Pope Francis concluded by recalling that in the biblical tradition a jubilee was also a cause for joy and said we, too, can rejoice as "we witness how the Holy Spirit is inspiring individuals and communities around the world to come together to rebuild our common home and defend the most vulnerable in our midst."

He is advocating for a change in how everything is done to address the climate crisis. This is the Great Reset that is meant by the World Economic Forum. Since we learned about the possibility of a global lockdown to address the climate crisis, it starts to make sense that they want a lockdown to reset how everything is done so that on the other side of the lockdown, life will be vastly different from what it is now.

He mentions that not only do we have to mend our relationship with the planet, but that we also have to mend the inequalities that exist in society. He is advocating for debt forgiveness to the poor countries as well as encouraging them to use funds they will receive in ensuring they reset how they do things as well. They are really serious about reseting how things are done, enough to forgive poor countries' debts and even fund the transformation of their societies through the recovery packages they will receive, which is unprecedented. Therefore these changes will be global and ideally they want the whole world to be on the same page. Poor countries will of course jump on board because they get their debts forgiven and even get funding to "modernise and green their societies".

The Pope is the most influential figure in the world, with his influence transcending religious differences. When he speaks, the world listens, so, whatever he says carries a lot of weight. In light of this, it is interesting that in his 2015 encyclical, Laudato si, he said:

"237. On Sunday, our participation in the Eucharist has special importance. Sunday, like the Jewish Sabbath, is meant to be a day which heals our relationships with God, with ourselves, with others and with the world. Sunday is the day of the Resurrection, the "first day" of the new creation, whose first fruits are the Lord's risen humanity, the pledge of the final transfiguration of all created reality. It also proclaims "man's eternal rest in God".[168] In this way, Christian spirituality incorporates the value of relaxation and festivity. We tend to demean contemplative rest as something unproductive and unnecessary, but this is to do away with the very thing which is most important about work: its meaning. We are called to include in our work a dimension of receptivity and gratuity, which is quite different from mere inactivity. Rather, it is another way of working, which forms part of our very essence. It protects human action from becoming empty activism; it also prevents that unfettered greed and sense of isolation which make us seek personal gain to the detriment of all else. The law of weekly rest forbade work on the seventh day, "so that your ox and your donkey may have rest, and the son of your maidservant, and the stranger, may be refreshed" (Ex 23:12). Rest opens our eyes to the larger picture and gives us renewed sensitivity to the rights of others. And so the day of rest, centred on the Eucharist, sheds it light on the whole week, and motivates us to greater concern for nature and the poor."

He is talking about Sunday as the Sabbath by differentiating it from what He calls the Jewish Sabbath, which is the Bible Sabbath for all humanity, not just the Jews. He is saying Sunday rest motivates us to greater concern for nature and the poor. It all sounds good but why not just keep Saturday which was sanctified by God as The Sabbath? Why keep a different day? It would make sense to keep the Lord's day which is Saturday because He already set it apart so that we would do no work, in the 4th commandment.

Considering that the Catholic Church is not shy about claiming to have authority to change the Sabbath from Saturday to Sunday, as we will learn in detail in the chapter on Rest, the Pope advocating for Sunday keeping starts to make sense. Sunday is the institution of the Catholic church, while Saturday is the Lord's day which He sanctified. By resting Sunday as Sabbath, Gaia would be honored as suggested by Satish Kumar's article, while resting Saturday would honor the Creator of the creation which is hoping to preserved by all these measures. Sunday is an institution of man and honors the creation, while Saturday as Sabbath was instituted by God when He set it apart as a Holy day to comemorate His work of creation. Given the Catholic church's history of persecuting Protestant Christians, Sunday keeping as a major part of the solution for addressing a global emergency such as the climate crisis means that it has the potential of becoming mandatory globally. Concerns about this are expressed best in the book, The Great Controversy by E. G. White:

"Fearful is the issue to which the world is to be brought. The powers of earth, uniting to war against the commandments of God, will decree that all, "both small and great, rich and poor, free and bond," [Revelation 13:16.] shall conform to the customs of the church by the observance of the false sabbath. All who refuse compliance will be visited with civil penalties, and it will finally be declared that they are deserving of death. On the other hand, the law of God enjoining the Creator's rest-day demands obedience, and threatens wrath against all who transgress its precepts.

With the issue thus clearly brought before him, whoever shall trample upon God's law to obey a human enactment, receives the mark of the beast; he accepts the sign of allegiance to the power which he chooses to obey instead of God. The warning from Heaven is, "If any man worship the beast and his image, and receive his mark in his forehead, or in his hand, the same shall drink of the wine of the wrath of God, which is poured out without mixture into the cup of his indignation." [Revelation 14:9, 10.]

But not one is made to suffer the wrath of God until the truth has been brought home to his mind and conscience, and has been rejected. There are many who have never had an opportunity to hear the special truths for this time. The obligation of the fourth commandment has never been set before them in its true light. He who reads every heart, and tries every motive, will leave none who desire a knowledge of the truth, to be deceived as to the issues of the controversy. The decree is not to be urged upon the people blindly. Every one is to have sufficient light to make his decision intelligently.

The Sabbath will be the great test of loyalty; for it is the point of truth especially controverted. When the final test shall be brought to bear upon men, then the line of distinction will be drawn between those who serve God and those who serve him not. While the observance of the false sabbath in compliance with the law of the State, contrary to the fourth commandment, will be an avowal of allegiance to a power that is in opposition to God, the keeping of the true Sabbath, in obedience to God's law, is an evidence of loyalty to the Creator. While one class, by accepting the sign of submission to earthly powers, receive the mark of the beast, the other, choosing the token of allegiance to divine authority, receive the seal of God. Pg 604-605.

This is the great test that is to come upon all of humanity shortly. All this talk of concern for the environment will lead to legislation for Sunday as the global day of rest, which will then put those loyal to God's commandments by keeping His Sabbath at odds with the law. May God help us to be loyal to Him when this time of trial comes.

Lifestyle

Marijuana, LSD, and other recreational drugs

During the counterculture, there was an increased experimentation and use of psychedelic drugs as their powerful effects encouraged an interest in mystical and religious symbolism, advocating their use as a method of raising consciousness. The personalities associated with the subculture, such as Dr. Timothy Leary and psychedelic rock musicians soon attracted a great deal of publicity, generating further interest in LSD. Aleister Crowley who was dubbed the "wickedest man in the world" by the paper of his time, a Black Magician and probably the most influential occultist, said in His book, Diary of a drug fiend, "Happiness lies within one's self, and the way to dig it out is cocaine." He was a great influence on Timothy Leary, as well as many musicians during the counterculture, who in turn influenced their fans. He continues to be a great influence on celebrities even today.

Experimentation with mushrooms, MDA, marijuana, LSD, peyote, psilocybin and other psychedelic drugs became a major component of 1960s counterculture, influencing philosophy, art, music and styles of dress. The popularization of drug use by musicians as well as personalities like Leary, has continued to this day as drug use is glamorized in pop culture.

Sexual revolution

Sexual liberation included increased acceptance of sex outside of traditional heterosexual, monogamous relationships and is one of the hallmarks of the counterculture. Contraception and the pill, public nudity, the normalization of premarital sex, casual sex, alternative forms of sexuality, and the legalization of abortion all followed as consequences of the sexual revolution. Premarital sex over time has become increasingly normal that it is odd and has become unusual for people to save themselves for marriage. With the explosion in sexual activity during this period, unfortunately most of it was unprotected. Referring to the famed 1967 Summer of Love in San Francisco,

"There was a price for all that free love. From 1964 through 1968, the rates of syphilis and gonorrhea in California rose 165 percent, according to published reports. "There was a lot of drug use, group sex, communal sex," says Dr. David Smith, who founded the Haight-Ashbury Free Clinic with $500 of his own money. "It would be an understatement to say there was a spike in STDs. That's like saying a hurricane is a strong wind." Abortion was another issue that erupted during Summer of Love. By the end of the summer, many women some of them young teenagers, needed treatment for botched abortions. Such experiences with abortions gone bad helped lead some states to further liberalize their abortion laws until 1973 when the U.S. Supreme Court decided Roe v. Wade, a ruling that still divides Americans." [27]

Abortion made it easier to terminate pregnancies made indulgence in fornication and adultery with reduced fear pregnancy. Pornography also became mainstream during the counterculture and has continued to increase its reach to this present day. It has been further boosted by the internet and mobile devices which have enabled private viewing and, and made it more accessible even to the young. Pornography in turn encourages risky sexual activity as some of those who watch it are more likely to be promiscuous. [28] It has become a mega industry with many actually aspiring to make it a full-time profession. It has become an acceptable and somewhat normal part of life today, although once-upon-a-time it was illegal and there were stiff penalties for its distribution and use.

Gay liberation

The Gay rights movement signaled the beginning of gay liberation as a sub-movement of the sexual revolution in the United States and around the world with the Stonewall riots. They were a reaction to a police raid that took place in the early morning hours of June 28, 1969, at the Stonewall Inn, a gay bar in the Greenwich Village neighborhood of New York City. Up to this point Homosexuality which up to the 1970s had been considered a mental disorder, began to be viewed as a healthy variation of human sexual orientation. It was declassified as a mental condition starting in 1973, by the American Psychiatric Association, and the American

Psychological Association Council of Representatives followed in 1975. Other major mental health organizations followed, including the World Health Organization.

Fast forward to 2015 and the U. S. Supreme Court on June 26th decided in a 5-4 vote that Gays and Lesbians have a constitutional right to marry which would essentially nullify and override any bans at state level. This Supreme Court decision was a landmark victory for the gay rights movement which would have been difficult to imagine just 10 years ago. It is the icing on the cake for a segment of the population which has become so powerful that there are consequences for not acknowledging them even if it's on a religious basis. They have rights but everyone else does not have rights to refuse acknowledging their marriages or lifestyles.

This is best illustrated by cases of bakeries, one in Oregon and the other in Colorado who faced the consequences for choosing not to make cakes for same-sex weddings. The first, Aaron and Melissa Klein from Oregon who owned Sweet cakes by Melissa faced a $135,000 fine for violating the state's non-discrimination law because they refused to bake a wedding cake for a lesbian couple in 2013. To add to this, GoFundMe removed a crowdfunding campaign on the couple's behalf less than a day after the effort was posted April 24 2015, following complaints from gay-marriage supporters. During that time, the campaign raised more than $109,000 on behalf of the Kleins.[29] Fortunately, a different fundraising platform stepped up to help. Continue to Give, an online crowdfunding platform aimed at helping raise money for churches, missionaries, non-profits and individual, allows the community to decide who and what they support."[30]

On the other hand The Civil Rights Commission in Colorado ruled that Jack Phillips had been discriminatory towards a same-sex couple after refusing to make a cake for their marriage and even offering to make it for any other reason as it would go against his beliefs. The same Commission not surprisingly ruled in favor of three other cake artists which had refused to make cakes with what would be deemed anti-gay messages. "The commission found that these three cake artists have the freedom to decline creating unique cake creations because the artists found the requests offensive, <u>but all Americans should be alarmed that the same commission determined that Jack doesn't have that same freedom.</u> Like the other bakers, Jack happily serves all people but declines to use his artistic talents to create cakes that violate his conscience." [31] Fortunately, the Supreme Court did end up ruling in his favor in 2018. [32]

It is clear that not endorsing or supporting them can lead to negative consequences, and that the system is less prone to uphold the religious freedom rights of Christians. Unfortunately, with time we will see more of such cases and they might not be victories as was Jack Phillips' case.

Divorce

Though divorce had been steadily increasing, there was a sharp increase in the 1970s, which may have been because no-fault divorce was first made available in the 70s. [33] It was the first time a spouse could also cite irreconcilable differences as a reason for divorce, making a divorce much easier to obtain. Prior to this point, anyone wanting to end their marriage had to prove adultery or cruelty in the marriage. Fast forward to 2015 and fortunately or unfortunately depending on how you look at it, fewer people are getting married altogether, and the divorce rate is declining as a result. Marriage is being viewed by a growing number of people as an old-fashioned institution that has become irrelevant in modern society. [34]

Religion, spirituality and the occult

The counterculture was marked by increased interest in expanded spiritual consciousness, yoga, occult practices and increased human potential which helped shift views on organized religion. Hippies rejected mainstream organized religion in favor of a more personal spiritual experience, often drawing on indigenous and folk beliefs, or they were likely to embrace mainstream faiths like Buddhism, Hinduism and Restorationist Christianity of the Jesus Movement. A significant number embraced neo-paganism, especially Wicca.

Aleister Crowley dubbed the "wickedest man in the world" by the press of his day, became an influential icon to the new alternative spiritual movements of the decade as well as for rock musicians. He once said "One would go mad if one took the Bible seriously; but to take it seriously one must be already mad...I was not content to believe in a personal devil and serve him, in the ordinary sense of the word. I wanted to get hold of him personally and become his chief of staff." [35] He was one of the many figures on the cover sleeve of the Beatles' 1967 album Sgt. Pepper's Lonely Hearts Club Band, which according to Ringo Starr, included people "we like and admire" [36] Paul McCartney said of Sgt. Pepper's cover, ". . . we were going to have photos on the wall of all our HEROES . . ." [37]. Ozzy Osbourne called Crowley "a phenomenon of his time." [38] Ozzy even had a song called "Mr. Crowley."

Kenneth Anger, a very influential underground experimental filmmaker whose films merged surrealism with homoeroticism and the occult, and was an inspiration for the birth of MTV among others, also had a fascination with Aleister Crowley. Openly gay at a time when it was quite controversial to be, he played an instrumental role in making homosexuality more visible through cinema. When asked about his belief that his films are invocations of magic spells in a March 18, 1976 interview by film critic Roger Ebert, he said, "Some movies can be the equivalent of mantras. They cause you to lose track of time you become disoriented magical things can happen…In commercial films, the occult is a subject for horror, but in my films, it's more friendly." In the interview when asked what the film, "Lucifer Rising" was about which celebrates the New Age or Age of Aquarius, he said, "Yes, the beginning of the pagan age and the end of Christianity. The forces of darkness and figures from mythology walk the streets." [39] He was friends with Satanist Anton LaVey, founder of the Church of Satan, who even appeared in his film, Invocation of my demon brother. Guitarist and co-founder of 1970s rock band Led Zeppelin, Jimmy Page who worked on a score for Kenneth Anger, was also fascinated by Crowley. He was such a fan he went as far as purchasing Boleskine House which was once owned by Crowley.

Timothy Leary openly acknowledged the inspiration of Crowley once saying in a TV interview, "I've been an admirer of Aleister Crowley. I think that I'm carrying on much of the work that he started over a hundred years ago…He was in favor of finding yourself, and 'Do what thou wilt shall be the whole of the law' under love. It was a very powerful statement. I'm sorry he isn't around now to appreciate the glories he started." [40] All these celebrities from the 70s had a great influence on what pop culture is today, and they were in turn greatly influenced by the openly satanic Aleister Crowley. His teachings live on, and are more influential than ever. [41]

Origins of New Age Spirituality

For something so commonly practiced, how did it start? According to Britannica, "In the late 19th century Helena Petrovna Blavatsky, cofounder of the Theosophical Society, announced a coming New Age. She believed that theosophists (who embraced Buddhist and Brahmanic notions such as reincarnation) should assist the evolution of the human race and prepare to cooperate with one of the Ascended Masters of the Great White Brotherhood whose arrival was imminent. Blavatsky believed that, as the world's hidden leaders, members of this mystical brotherhood guided the destiny of the planet. Her ideas contributed to expectation of a New Age among practitioners of Spiritualism and believers in astrology, for whom the coming of the New Aquarian Age promised a period of brotherhood and enlightenment. Blavatsky's successor, Annie Besant, predicted the coming of a messiah, or world savior, who she believed was the Indian teacher Jiddu Krishnamurti.

In the 1940s Alice A. Bailey, founder of the Arcane School (an organization that disseminated spiritual teachings), suggested that a new messiah, the Master Maitreya, would appear in the last quarter of the 20th century...In 1970 American theosophist David Spangler moved to the Findhorn Foundation, where he developed the fundamental idea of the New Age movement. He believed that the release of new waves of spiritual energy, signaled by certain astrological changes (e.g., the movement of the Earth into a new cycle known as the Age of Aquarius), had initiated the coming of the New Age. He further suggested that people use this new energy to make manifest the New Age. Spangler's view was in stark contrast to that of Bailey and her followers, who believed that the new era would arrive independent of human actions. Spangler's perspective demanded an active response and shifted the responsibility for the coming of the New Age to those who believed in it." [42]

The Father of the New Age movement is considered to be a Jesuit, Pierre Teilhard de Chardin, who played an important role in the awakening of this movement. "...Teilhard de Chardin, a French Jesuit priest[43]...eugenicist, Marxist[44]...pantheist[45], evolutionist (he "was heavily involved in the 1912 forgery that was called 'Piltdown Man'"[45]), humanist, and a proponent of a one-world government. He was also known as "The Father of the New Age."[46] "Teilhard dreamed of humanity merging into 'God' and each realizing his own godhood at the Omega point. This belief has inspired many of today's New Age leaders." In fact, Chardin is one of the most frequently quoted writers by leading New Age occultists."[47]

He was a major proponent of evolution and that the ultimate is to evolve spiritually into gods ourselves because: "It is a law of the universe that in all things there is prior existence. Before every form there is a prior, but lesser evolved form. Each one of us is evolving towards the godhead." …I can be saved only by becoming one with the universe." I believe that the Messiah whom we await, whom we we all without any doubt await, is the universal Christ; that is to say, the Christ of evolution."[48] "…a general convergence of religions upon a universal Christ who satisfies them all: that seems to me the only possible conversion of the world, and the only form in which a religion of the future can be conceived." [49] With the founders of this movement having these kind of beliefs, Aleister Crowley would be good company for them and it is no surprise that he influenced the New Age movement just as much as they did. It is self-evident from the things that have become the norm which resulted from the Counterculture that the source was not compatible with Judeo-Christian values.

New Age spirituality as inverted Christianity

It is most interesting that New Age spirituality talks about Christ consciousness and The Christ returning. We can even say they have an inverted form of Christianity. The end goal for both is a peaceful world which is brought on by, according to Alice A. Bailey, the return of the Maitreya or The Christ; but for us who believe, the return of Jesus Christ a second time, ushering in a world of everlasting peace with life eternal, a "new heaven and a new earth, for the first heaven and the first earth had passed away." Revelation 21:1. Both emphasize on a process of being transformed as one grows. The devil is a master of lies and wants to be like God so bad that he counterfeits a lot of things that God does or how God works.

Revelation of Wisdom

We see a counterfeit of how God revealed His will in how Helena Blavatzky and Alice Bailey got the foundational teachings for the New Age movement:

"The "Masters" concept has been employed by the theosophists and other "seers" for over 200 years. The Masters form a major portion of the occult mysteries of Blavatsky, Bailey, Olcott, Crowley, Leadbeater, Besant and hundreds of other occultists of lesser fame. The "theology" that the Masters "teach" is widespread. It is a major part of many large "religious" organizations. One such organization is the Church of Jesus Christ of Latter-day Saints. A Master can be defined basically as a perfected man or adept whose task it was (or is) to watch over and guide humanity along its path of spiritual and physical evolution - with concentration on the spiritual. Spiritual always refers to supernatural spirituality. Masters are godlike adepts with their "physical plane" headquarters in various mountain areas especially in the Himalayas and Tibet.

The Lucis Trust steadfastly claims that it is a fact that the Masters exist on this physical plane and even on the "dense physical plane" (i.e. the natural universe). (GI, p. 9). However, unbiased investigation, even after expeditions to Tibet, have failed to produce a modern manifestation of a Master in dense physical form. Bailey's second Master has the name Master Djwhal Khul or simply Master D. K. Moreover, "he" also is called by the more familiar name - The Tibetan. Bailey almost always writes as if she is taking dictation from her Master." [50]

The Masters do not appear in physical form because they are spirits. They are spiritual and not physical entities. Let us continue to identify what kind of spirits they are.

"A.A.B. takes down to my dictation an average of seven to twelve pages of typing (single-spaced) each time she writes for me; but owing to the exigencies of my work I cannot dictate to her every day, though I have found that she would gladly take my dictation daily if I so desired;. . . " (1, p. 251). [Master D. K.] ". . . is the latest of the adepts taking initiation, having taken the fifth initiation in 1875, and is therefore occupying the same body in which He took the initiation . . . . His body is not a young one, and He is a Tibetan."" [50]

The communication they did with these Masters is called mediumship or channeling, which is the process by which a medium can communicate information from nonphysical beings, such as spirits through entering a state of trance or some other form of altered consciousness. "Channeling, or spirit contact, is seen by some as possibly the single most important and definitive aspect of the New Age…New Age spirit contact is no different in form than that practiced in Spiritualism for the last 150 years. However, channeling distinguishes itself from Spiritualist mediumship in its purpose and content. In Spiritualism, the mediums have specialized in contact with the "spirits of the dead" for the purpose of demonstrating the continuance of individual life after death. Within the New Age movement, channeling has been accepted and redirected to the goal of facilitating the personal transformation of the channelers' clients."[51] This channeling is the devil's way of counterfeiting how God revealed His Word:

16 All Scripture is given by inspiration of God, and is profitable for doctrine, for reproof, for correction, for [c]instruction in righteousness,

17 that the man of God may be complete, thoroughly equipped for every good work...

20 knowing this first, that no prophecy of Scripture is of any private [j]interpretation,

21 for prophecy never came by the will of man, but [k]holy men of God spoke as they were moved by the Holy Spirit. 2 Timothy 3:16-17 and 2 Peter 1:20-21.

Revelation comes only from God by the Holy Spirit. Wisdom that God reveals brings forth good fruit, the fruit of righteousness. Wisdom from any other source other than from God is not True Wisdom and can only be from the source of all discord:

14 But if you have bitter envy and [h]self-seeking in your hearts, do not boast and lie against the truth.

15 This wisdom does not descend from above, but is earthly, sensual, demonic.

16 For where envy and self-seeking exist, confusion and every evil thing are there.

17 But the wisdom that is from above is first pure, then peaceable, gentle, willing to yield, full of mercy and good fruits, without partiality and without hypocrisy. James 3:14-17.

One of the devil's best lies is when he and his demons have to pretend being different "Masters" from the past to convince those who subscribe to this theology, that the Masters they will be revering were once human a long time ago, and through spiritual evolution by several reincarnations or "initiations", have become the Masters they are today but in truth, they are fallen angels whose mission is not to share knowledge and wisdom. They don't have humanity's best interests at heart, but in fact "the devil has come down to you, having great wrath, because he knows that he has a short time."Revelation 12:12.

The fact that he is a spirit entity means also that it is easier for his followers to buy into his lies because most of the world already believes in the immortality of the soul, his first lie in the garden of Eden; making it easier to believe that he whichever Master he says he is was a human once but has now evolved to a higher level of consciousness. When we die, we don't evolve to another level in spiritual evolution because:

5 ...the living know that they will die; But the dead know nothing,

And they have no more reward, For the memory of them is forgotten.

6 Also their love, their hatred, and their envy have now perished;

Nevermore will they have a share In anything done under the sun. Ecclesiastes 9:5-6.

The attention and devotion people give to these Masters, they are giving to the devil and his demons willfully or unawares. Most of them are doing it unawares because it is them behind all the different identities. This is how deceptive he is. He is the author of all lies, confusion, and every idea or philosophy which is anti-Christ, so he even gets reverence when people subscribe to philosophies that discourage them from believing in God as we are warned: "Beware lest any man spoil you through philosophy and vain deceit, after the tradition of men, after the rudiments of the world, and not after Christ. Colossians 2:8.

The devil and his demons are worshiped indirectly when any so-called deity is given reverence that is due only to God. This is one of the devil's greatest tricks, that by people worshiping anyone or anything but God, they are worshiping him and his demons as written:

16 They provoked Him to jealousy with foreign gods; With [e]abominations they provoked Him to anger.

17 They sacrificed to demons, not to God, To gods they did not know, To new gods, new arrivals that your fathers did not fear.

18 Of the Rock who begot you, you are unmindful, And have forgotten the God who fathered you. Deuteronomy 32:16-18.

Transformation

To achieve this New Age, those who believed in it would have to go through personal transformation, with enough transformed people leading to societal transformation according to the 100th monkey idea. The story has it that "a number of monkeys learned by example to wash their food. After the 100th monkey had absorbed the lesson, all monkeys jumped ahead in consciousness and started washing their food." [52] Traditional occult practices were integrated into the movement as tools to assist personal transformation. Transpersonal psychology encouraged the belief that consciousness-altering practices could be practiced apart from the particular contexts in which they originated. Let us examine these tools of transformation in more detail.

In The New Age and Biblical Worldview: Conflict and Dialogue by John Newport, he says the following about transformation: "From a New Age perspective, your problem, to begin with, is that you have an illusion that you are limited and finite. In the words of Eliade, a historian and philosopher who has written numerous books on world religions, "The wretchedness of human life is not owing to divine punishment or to an original sin, but to … metaphysical ignorance." The transformation from an ignorant state to an enlightened one releases the individual from the consequences (karma) of ignorance and brings forgiveness and/or understanding of the former experience of unpleasantness, what the mundane world calls evil. The enlightened being then lives beyond what this world calls good and evil.

In New Age, you are responsible to change your own consciousness. Humans are not depraved or dependent on any outside source for deliverance or strength. A person's blindness, which is the root of all his or her problems, can be eliminated by a change, or transformation, of consciousness. A person needs to have the experience of knowing the One and his or her own essential deity. This experience is brought about by psycho-spiritual techniques." [53]

Meditation

Meditation is one of the most important tools used to achieve transformation. Meditative techniques like yoga and martial arts both became popular during the counterculture, and seem harmless on the surface, but practicing them is in itself part of the process of realizing "godhood". One cannot practice them in their purity and not be "transformed". Some divorce yoga from its spiritual roots in Hinduism, and instead say it is just for stretching and to encourage flexibility along with other health benefits but according to the Hindu American website in the article, 'The Hindu roots of Yoga and the take back yoga campaign', their position is that it is a spiritual practice which is the whole point:

"The essence of yoga is to reach oneness with God....using it [yoga] for physical practice is no good, of no use - just a lot of sweating, pushing, and heavy breathing for nothing. The spiritual aspect, which is beyond the physical is the purpose of yoga. When the nervous system is purified, when your mind rests in the atman [the Self], then you can experience the true greatness of yoga... When the five fold qualities of yoga consisting of the earth, water, fire, air and ether are firmly established in the body, then in that body strengthened by the fire of yoga, there is no place for sickness, old age and death...Asanas are not meant for physical fitness, but for conquering the elements, energy, and so on. So, how to balance the energy in the body, how to control the five elements, how to balance the various aspect of the mind without mixing them all together, and how to be able to perceive the difference between the gunas, and to experience that there is something behind them, operating in the world of man - that is what asanas are for…" [54]

The yoga postures or asanas are used specifically with spiritual intent. Going into these postures in itself is supposed to be spiritual and nothing to do with the physical. Even for martial arts, the ultimate goal is spiritual with the movements all a part of achieving that goal. A good example of this is tai chi. An article, 'The Shamanic Origins of Tai Chi' expands on this:

"Tai Chi has often been described and written about as form of meditation, a moving meditation. The purpose of meditation is to alter one's consciousness in order to achieve a variety of goals from relaxation and healing, to extending one's lifespan and many believe, developing supernatural abilities. The picture that most often comes to mind when we consider meditation is that of the Yogi, the Buddhist, and the Taoist, sitting cross-legged in a temple. The key ingredients are silence, stillness, and solitude. Contrast this image with one of continually flowing, and sometimes explosive movements of Tai Chi, and it would appear to be the antithesis of the conditions needed for meditation. From where then did this unique concept, the linking of physical movement with an altered state of consciousness, originate? "The five elements and their associated heraldic animals represent an ancient knowledge of how heavenly forces could be manipulated to affect earthly destinies. The central ritual of Taoist magic consists in the ability to call up the forces of these Spirit-Generals and indicates that the heraldic Animals are indeed the essence of supernatural powers. -The Chinese PauKua, Ong Hean-Tatt"" [55]

The five elements spoken about in the above excerpts are fundamental to Eastern Religion and Philosophy and for example are known as Wu Xing in Chinese philosophy, Five elements (Japanese philosophy), Mahābhūta in Hinduism and Pancha Tattva (Vaishnavism). They are also spoken of in Babylonian mythology, in ancient Greek beliefs which influenced European culture throughout the middle ages and Renaissance; and ancient Egyptian beliefs. "The four elements of fire, water, air, and earth are the basis of many magical and spiritual systems: the native American medicine wheel, the four corners of pagan European ritual, the four elements of alchemical schools of ancient Egypt, and the four elements of astrology. Even the tarot deck and playing cards are based on these four elements whereby fire is wands (clubs), water is cups (hearts), air is words (spades), and earth is pentacles (diamonds)." [56] "

A fundamental aspect of Wiccan belief is the Elements of Nature. Some hold to the earlier Greek conception of the four classical elements (air, fire, water, earth), while others recognize five elements: earth, air, water, fire, and spirit (akasha). Some see the points of the pentagram symbol as representing the five elements. The elements are commonly invoked at the beginning of rituals or used in their physical forms...Each element has associated symbols, rituals and meanings" [57] The pentagram spoken of here is used as a symbol in Chinese tradition but in the West is mostly associated with Wicca and Satanism. You will find it in New Age stores on some of their merchandise; you find it, T-shirts, mugs, music videos, films, etc; it is everywhere and not hard to find. Some celebrities wear it proudly especially Rock musicians.

The star with two points upward is also called the "Goat of Mendes," because the inverted star is the same shape as a goat's head. When the upright star turns and the upper point falls to the bottom, it signifies the fall of the Morning Star. Remember that the Morning Star is referring to Lucifer or Satan. To sum it up, all these New Age psycho-spiritual techniques and practices with deep roots in the occult, originated from the devil and the founder of the Church of Satan, Anton LaVey said it best: "In the scores of books lining the shelves of New Age bookstores, there are instructions for guided meditation, creative visualizations, out of body experiences, getting in touch with your spirit guides, fortune telling by cards, crystal balls or the stars. What if Satanists reclaimed these for their own dark purposes and integrated them into rituals dedicated to the Devil, where they rightfully belong? New Agers have freely drawn upon all manner of Satanic material, adapting it to their own hypocritical purposes... But in truth, all 'New Age' labeling is, again, trying to play the Devil's game without using His Infernal name." [58]

The Human potential movement – Personal development seminars

The Human Potential Movement has become one of the most significant and influential forces in modern Western society. It started on the premise that people have a lot of potential that is largely untapped, and influenced heavily by idea that self-actualization is the supreme expression of life, according to

Maslow's theory. Self-actualization according to Abraham Maslow, is "the desire to accomplish everything that one can, to become the most that one can be" and initially it was at the top of the hierarchy of needs which are named after him. For example, an individual may have the strong desire to become a successful businessman. For someone else, the desire may be expressed academically. There are so many ways in which it can be expressed. In other words, self-actualization would be the fulfillment of what one would consider the ultimate purpose for their life or the highest goals they would have set for themselves. He later modified this hierarchy of needs to culminate in self-transcendence which was that the actualization takes place when one gives of themselves to spirituality or some higher goal like altruism. [59]

Along with the ten percent brain idea, that most humans are using ten percent or less of their brain capacity, pushed by the likes of George Leonard, these basic ideas gave fertile ground for the movement to develop. The Human Potential movement is more in tune with eastern mysticism and the occult, but the terminology has been changed to sound scientific and psychological. It has been especially packaged to be appealing to corporations, government, small businesses, and the educational system as motivational seminars and home training programs and such. Their goal is to help people become aware of or tap into this "infinite" potential that they have. Tapping into this potential is achieved by:

- rejecting traditional or any beliefs that are considered limiting and avoiding any negative thoughts.
- consciousness altering techniques that create a state of higher suggestibility, such as meditation, visualization, guided imagery, and other inward looking activities which help with the reprogramming process.
- Stress management is also pushed as a side benefit.
- reprogramming the subconscious through positive thinking, daily affirmations, and constant self-talk like "I am successful, I am a winner, I am wonderful, I will achieve!".
- taking responsibility to "create one's own reality and all these other things are done to tap into "self" which is the source of all success and wisdom.

The 2006 best-selling book by Rhonda Byrne, The Secret which focuses on the Law of Attraction, epitomizes what the Human Potential movement is all about with New Age teachings at the heart of it. Here are some examples of Human Potential Seminar organizations:

    Silva method
    Insight Seminars
    The Human Potential Project
    Hoffman Institute
    Landmark seminars
    Ascension Leadership Academy
    Next Level Trainings
    Leaders In Transformation
    Choice Center
    Wright Foundation
    Rebirthing Breathwork International

Alternative Healing therapies

So far we have learned that a lot of New Age practices have deep roots in Eastern Philosophy, religion and Paganism. The alternative healing practices all have certain things in common, even though they focus on different things. A few things to note about them:

- Deep roots in Eastern Philosophy, religion, occultic and pagan practices.
- Wholistic/Holistic – that is their focus is not just physical healing, but emotional and spiritual healing as well.
- Basic idea that everything in the universe vibrates, has color, sound, a number and a form attached to it.
- an intelligence, a cosmic force, or a vital force which pervades the universe, and that people become sick when they are not aligned or attuned to this force.
- This force has different names in the various disciplines but they all refer to the same thing. It can be called prana, mana, odic force, orgone energy, universal intelligence, holy spirit, the ch'i, mind, the healing force, and etc.
- Practitioners of the various New Age therapies focus on healing the entire person through the working of the vital

force and the restoration of the cosmic energy flow in patients.
• The source of healing is rarely if ever revealed – therefore it can be practiced under the name of any religion.

Some of the Therapies

Reiki
Aura reading
Reflexology
Iridology
Therapeutic touch
Polarity massage
Chiropractic
Acupuncture
Ayurveda
Yoga
Homeopathy
Emotional Freedom Technique (EFT)
Acupressure
Hypnotherapy
Healing with Crystals
Healing with color
Healing with sound
Astral/soul travel
Biofeedback
Rolfing
Shiatsu

Most if not all of these therapies are quite effective in helping people get well. However, we cannot ignore their occult and pagan roots. Can we still use them if we are aware of this? On one hand we are warned not to have anything to do with the works of darkness. "Walk as children of light (for the fruit of the Spirit is in all goodness, righteousness, and truth), finding out what is acceptable to the Lord. And have no fellowship with the unfruitful works of darkness, but rather expose them." Ephesians 5:8-11. Not only are we supposed to shun any works of darkness once we know them, we are also encouraged to expose them by warning others of their possible dangers. On the other hand, we are implored to:

21 Test all things; hold fast what is good.

22 Abstain from every form of evil...

8 Finally, brethren, whatever things are true, whatever things are noble, whatever things are just, whatever things are pure, whatever things are lovely, whatever things are of good report, if there is any virtue and if there is anything praiseworthy—meditate on these things. 1 Thessalonians 5:21-22 and Philippians 4:8.

My part is to be honest with you and tell you the Truth about these things. We learned about how something like taking care of the environment, though quite noble, is being used used as a trojan horse for an anti-Christ agenda. It is something that is dear to many, regardless of religious belief, and one can do the best one can to take care of the environment, while remaining separate from the pagan nature of environmentalism as we learned about earlier. The same goes for holidays, of which many are pagan but were Christianized by the Catholic church. Examples are Easter, which supposedly celebrates the death and ressurection of Christ, while Christmas celebrates His birth, but the essence of these two holidays are anything but Christian, as they are undoubtedly pagan in origin and substitute their true pagan symbols and meanings with those that are Christian, Can these holidays be a way to reach those who are unbelievers? Yes. These sort of holidays might be the only opportunity for some to ever go to a church, and God may use such an occasion to reach them. In any of these things, there is some good and some bad. Just as with environmetalism and any of these holidays, I would say for you to pray about anything you need guidance on so that God reveals to you individually whether to keep using these therapies or not; whether to hold on to some or none. If you sincerely ask for wisdom regarding this matter or anything for which you will be needing wisdom, the promise is given:

5 If any of you lacks wisdom, let him ask of God, who gives to all liberally and without reproach, and it will be given to him. James 1:5.

The goal of transformation: Realizing your godhood

Using all these transformation tools leads to transformation or godhood. "This is the path to self-realization, cosmic consciousness, and enlightenment. Your self is a cosmic treasure of wisdom, power, and delight. Realization of oneness and divinity leads to spiritual power and well-being. Transcendental Meditation even promises that advanced students can achieve the ability to levitate, fly, and become invisible… There are many names for this transformation, such as God-realization, enlightenment, illumination, nirvana, satori, and "at-one-ment."" [60]

The transformation is dependent on effort on the part of the New Ager through the utilization of these tools. The tools are all rooted in practices that are forbidden by God because they involve contact with demons in some form as written:

10 There shall not be found among you anyone who makes his son or his daughter pass[e] through the fire, or one who practices witchcraft, or a soothsayer, or one who interprets omens, or a sorcerer,

11 or one who conjures spells, or a medium, or a spiritist, or one who calls up the dead.

12 For all who do these things are [f]an abomination to the Lord…

14 …the Lord your God has not [h]appointed such for you. Deuteronomy 18:11-14.

Transformation for the better is good, but not when it involves the use of practices forbidden by God. All these things are of the devil and God would want us to have no part with such practices. The fact that a person has to engage in all this activity is righteousness by works. The tools themselves are not rooted in righteousness, but the end goal is to be more righteous or to be a better person in the world's eyes and according to the world's understanding or standards. However, we are told in scripture:

5 not by works of righteousness which we have done, but according to His mercy He saved us, through the washing of regeneration and renewing of the Holy Spirit…

2 And do not be conformed to this world, but be transformed by the renewing of your mind, that you may prove what is that good and acceptable and perfect will of God;

8 For by grace you have been saved through faith, and that not of yourselves; it is the gift of God,

9 not of works, lest anyone should boast.

10 For we are His workmanship, created in Christ Jesus for good works, which God prepared beforehand that we should walk in them. Titus 3:5, Romans 12:2 and Ephesians 2:8-10.

Transformation is a gift by God's Grace through faith and is the work of the Holy Spirit who renews and transforms us. We will look at how the Holy Spirit accomplishes this in detail in the Air chapter. Transformation is a gift that we don't deserve nor earn. The work of the Holy Spirit of transforming our lives culminates in the transformation even of our bodies from being mortal to being immortal:

50 Now this I say, brethren, that flesh and blood cannot inherit the kingdom of God; nor does corruption inherit incorruption.

51 Behold, I tell you a [m]mystery: We shall not all sleep, but we shall all be changed—

52 in a moment, in the twinkling of an eye, at the last trumpet. For the trumpet will sound, and the dead will be raised incorruptible, and we shall be changed.

53 For this corruptible must put on incorruption, and this mortal must put on immortality.

54 So when this corruptible has put on incorruption, and this mortal has put on immortality, then shall be brought to pass the saying that is written: "Death is swallowed up in victory."

55 "O[n] Death, where is your sting? O Hades, where is your victory?" 1 Corinthians 15:50-55.

Homo Noeticus

God transforms His people to put on immortality, and the devil transforms his to have higher consciousness. In the book Hidden Dangers of the Rainbow, author Constance Cumbey writes:

"In fact, the New Agers claim they are a "new species." They have "evolved" into homo noeticus. They "evolved" by employing mind-expansion techniques such as meditation and the "other disciplines.""[61]

Upon looking this up because I had never heard of it before, I found that it is somewhat a common term in New Age circles. The following is an excerpt from an article 'About the Homo Sapiens ethicus (aka Homo noeticus) by Dr. Cesidio Tallini which is a good explanation of what it is:

"Blumenbach's 19th-century classification roughly corresponds with the five different groups of people Noah A. Rosenberg and Jonathan K. Pritchard discovered, whose ancestors were typically isolated by oceans, deserts or mountains:

1. Europeans and Asians west of the Himalayas;
2. Sub-Saharan Africans;
3. East Asians;
4. Native Americans; and
5. Inhabitants of New Guinea and Melanesia.

Today, because of the developing Fifth World paradigm, one can speak of a fifth-sixth race as well, the Indigo race, which is:

1. A global, not a continental race;
2. A phenotype, not a genotype;
3. Not just a new race, but also a genuine new human subspecies.

The great leap from Homo sapiens neandertalensis to Homo sapiens sapiens actually occurred more recently in time, and is actually recorded in historic, not prehistoric times. Diogenes of Sinope (412–323 BC) is credited with the first known use of the word 'cosmopolitan'. When he was asked where he came from, he replied, "I am a citizen of the world". This was an extremely original concept at the time, because the broadest basis of social identity in Greece was either the city-state to which the individual Greek belonged, or the Greeks themselves as a group.

The term 'cosmopolitan' derives from the Greek (cosmos) meaning 'world', plus the Greek (polis) meaning 'city', 'people', or 'citizenry'. Many people think that 'cosmopolitan' means 'world city'. It is for this reason that cities like New York or London are called 'cosmopolitan' cities (or worldly and sophisticated). Yet Diogenes used the Greek word (kosmopolítis), which means 'citizen of the world', not 'world city'. Cosmopolitanism is the idea that all kinds of human beings belong to a single community based on a shared morality. This is contrasted with communitarian and particularistic theories, especially the ideas of patriotism and nationalism. Cosmopolitanism is the idea that human beings are essentially one, and they are not citizens of Sinope like Diogenes, or even Greeks, but citizens of planet Earth...

Very recently another quantum leap has occurred. There are signs that at least one Homo sapiens sapiens is already a new subspecies called Homo sapiens ethicus...This New Man who has come into being is not a New Yorker, an American, an Italian-American, and he is not a 'citizen of the world' either. No, this New Man, to use Modern Greek, is a (kyverpolítis) or 'cybercitizen', and if we go to the original meaning of the English root word 'cyber', this actually means that he is a (politikó kyvernítis) or 'political master'. This New Man is not a citizen of some place he was accidentally born to, the citizen of some place he moved to, or the citizen of some planetary community he feels connected with, but a master, governor, or steersman of his citizenry or entourage.

According to consciousness researcher John White, the next step in human evolution is the Homo noeticus. Is the Homo sapiens ethicus I mention, and John White's Homo noeticus the same thing? You be the judge. I state that Homo sapiens ethicus is a new phenotype, not a new genotype. According to John White, Homo noeticus is characterised by noetic changes, not by genetic changes. A phenotype is any observable characteristic or trait of an organism, such as its morphology, development, biochemical or physiological properties, and includes behavior, and the tangible outcomes of specific behaviors. White's noetic changes, on the other hand, are based on a radical transformation of consciousness, and consciousness is anything that we are aware of at a given moment. So basically White and I are talking about the same thing, except

I'm viewing the difference in the New Man from the outside, i.e. exoterically, while White is viewing the difference from the inside, i.e. esoterically. White, on the other hand, states that Homo noeticus is characterised by a radical transformation of consciousness, a movement from self-centredness to God-centredness — God-centredness, in reality, is consciousness of that which is both outside and within oneself, since a portion of the external God is correctly perceived as being within oneself (a holistic, rather than the typically religious atomistic perspective)." [62]

Combining my understanding of what Constance Cumbey and Dr. Tallini said, the belief is that when one utilizes the New Age tools of transformation, they end up transitioning from being an ordinary human being (homo sapiens sapiens) to being one with a radically transformed consciousness from self-centredness to God-centredness. In other words, one reaches the level of finding God within oneself. The ultimate goal for New Agers is to transform from being ordinary humans to those having higher consciousness which will mean transformed actions transcending attachment to nationality or religion. This transformation is a prerequisite to being proud global citizens of the New World Order. It is to be the kingdom of god here on earth, when the majority of the world has been prepared for and is expecting his appearance. The god is of course Satan as we have already determined. We learn all this in the following Bailey quotes:

"It is of importance that you realize that today something new is happening. There is the emergence of a new kingdom in nature, the fifth kingdom; this is the Kingdom of God on earth, or the kingdom, of souls. It is precipitating on earth and will be composed of those who are becoming group-conscious, and who can work in group formation. This will be possible, because people will have achieved a self-initiated perfection (even if relative in nature) and will be identified with certain group expansions in consciousness. It will also be because they have arrived at love of their fellow men, just as they have loved themselves in the past. Think on this with clarity, my brothers, and grasp if you can, the full significance of this last sentence." [63]

"That Kingdom has ever been with us, composed of all those who down the ages, have sought spiritual goals, liberated themselves from the limitations of the physical body, emotional controls and the obstructive mind. Its citizens are those who today (unknown to the majority) live in physical bodies, work for the welfare of humanity, use love instead of emotion as their general technique, and compose that great body of "illumined Minds" which guides the destiny of the world. The Kingdom of God is not something which will descend on Earth when man is good enough! It is something which is functioning efficiently today and demanding recognition. It is an organized body which is already evoking recognition from those who do seek first the Kingdom of God, and discover thereby that the

Kingdom they seek is already here. Christ and His disciples are known to be physically present on Earth, and the Kingdom which they rule, with its laws and modes of activity, is familiar to many and has been throughout the centuries." [64]

For Christians, we ultimately hope to be with God for Eternity. Confessing that you are a sinner and that Jesus Christ died for your sins as well as allowing the Holy Spirit to work in transforming you, is the prerequisite to being with Him forever. He will change everything. Heaven and earth will be made new, and our bodies will put on immortality so we can be citizens in God's Kingdom forever, a place where there is no more death and all the other problems we have come to associate with sin, as written:

1 Now I saw a new heaven and a new earth, for the first heaven and the first earth had passed away...

3 ...He will dwell with them, and they shall be His people. God Himself will be with them and be their God.

4 And God will wipe away every tear from their eyes; there shall be no more death, nor sorrow, nor crying. There shall be no more pain, for the former things have passed away." Revelation 21:1, 3-4.

New Age of Peace

The New Age movement united a body of diverse believers on the idea that a New Age of heightened spiritual consciousness and international peace would arrive and bring an end to racism, poverty, sickness, hunger, and war. This social transformation would result from the massive spiritual awakening of the general population, and individuals could obtain a foretaste of the New Age through their own spiritual transformation.

New Age spirituality is big on getting along and coexisting regardless of religious differences or lifestyle preferences. Exclusiveness and separateness are in fact discouraged. All should unite and disregard differences. The United Nations whose links to Alice Bailey's teachings are not a secret and a subject in itself for an entire book; in The United Nations Educational, Scientific and

Cultural Organization (UNESCO)'s Declaration of the Principles of Tolerance says:

"Tolerance is the responsibility that upholds human rights, pluralism (including cultural pluralism), democracy and the rule of law. It involves the rejection of dogmatism and absolutism and affirms the standards set out in international human rights instruments...It also means that one's views are not be be imposed on others" [65]

The U.N.'s definition of tolerance involves rejecting absolutism and discourages one's views being imposed on others. The Truth as it is in the Word of God is Absolute, and if we love our fellow brothers and sisters, it is imperative to let them know that God loves them and desires to save them. The nature of the Truth as it is in the Word of God sets the Christian at odds with New Age spirituality which would require setting aside Truth in order to get along with others. The interesting thing is that it preaches tolerance but is in fact intolerant of those who do not conform. New Age spirituality is the heartbeat of the U.N. so it is no surprise that they desire to unite all religions under one banner as in the following quote:

"Thus the expressed aims and efforts of the United Nations will be eventually brought to fruition and a new church of God, gathered out of all religions and spiritual groups, will unitedly bring to an end the great heresy of separateness. Love, unity, and the Risen Christ will be present, and He will demonstrate to us the perfect life. [66]

Belief in God as He is presented in the Word is the Truth, while religion or philosophy from any other source, if it is anti-Christ all comes from the same source which is the devil. By anti-Christ, I mean it does not lift up Jesus Christ, refuses to confess that He is Lord and He is the Only Way, denies who He is or His mission in reconciling us back to God by saving us. That is why Christianity in its purity as presented in the Word of God is incompatible with this One World religion that they desire to bring to reality and they know this. A form of Christianity which compromises the Truth as it is in the Word of God is anything but Christianity, "having a form of godliness but denying its power." 2 Timothy 3:5. The unity must be based on "educated goodwill and right human relations" as seen in the following quotes:

"The New Age is upon us and we are witnessing the birth pangs of the new culture and the new civilization. That which is old and undesirable must go, and of these undesirable things, hatred and the spirit of separateness must be first to disappear." [67]

"That the major required preparation is a world at peace; however that peace must be based on an educated goodwill, which will lead inevitably to right human relations, and, therefore, to the establishment (figuratively speaking) of lines of light between nation and nation, religion and religion, group and group, man and man."[68]

In the first quote, she mentions that the old and undesirable must go, with hatred and the spirit of separateness being the first ones to go. According to Alice Bailey, all of the undesirable elements will not be part of the new culture and civilization. Interesting that she uses the word hatred. Today with political correctness as the order of the day, anything that one can say which is considered not politically correct is called hate speech.

The most prominent example of this is when Christians who speak against all sin, including homosexuality which God has said is an abomination. God hates the sin but loves the sinner, and desires to deliver from all sin and to reconcile us back to Him. The Truth is spoken so that by chance, those who might not know that it is an abomination to God, can be delivered, but how will people know unless the Truth is spoken to them? Unfortunately because of trying to be politically correct, nothing is said and in fact people are being encouraged to continue in such activities who need deliverance:

22 You shall not lie with a male as with a woman. It is an abomination...

14 Also I have seen a horrible thing in the prophets of Jerusalem: They commit adultery and walk in lies; They also strengthen the hands of evildoers, So that no one turns back from his wickedness. All of them are like Sodom to Me, And her inhabitants like Gomorrah.

20 Woe to those who call evil good, and good evil; Who put darkness for light, and light for darkness; Who put bitter for sweet, and sweet for bitter!

21 Woe to those who are wise in their own eyes, And prudent in their own sight!Leviticus 18:22, Jeremiah 23:14 and Isaiah 5:20-21.

Instead of encouraging people to continue engaging in all activities that God considers abominable, we should discourage them and lead them to deliverance from such in Christ. We are quite guilty of this as Christians because we ourselves have been living sinful lives rendering us useless in correcting others lest we be hypocrites, as the Jeremiah verse above mentions. In this chapter I am writing about how occult activities are also an abomination.

This could also be considered hate speech but it is truth and must be said so that someone out there who might be unaware can seek the Lord and be delivered when they realize their error. Such is the case for all sin, not just homosexuality or engaging in occult activities, but all sin which Jesus Christ died for. If we are to help people in their need of deliverance from sin so God can save them, it unfortunately requires speaking the truth about sin and also living a life that is blameless by His help (1 Timothy 6:14).

It is this nature of Christianity that makes it foremost of the undesirable elements which should disappear so that there can be peace in the new culture and civilization? Inclusiveness is necessary to bring about this unity. To be included, in this unity, identity and unique beliefs essentially have to be set aside to enable a coming together of people from vastly different and even, normally conflicting viewpoints and ways of life. This is highlighted in the following Alice Bailey quote:

"The major effect of his appearance will surely be to demonstrate in every land the effects of a spirit of inclusiveness – an inclusiveness which will be channeled or expressed through him. All who seek right human relations will be gathered automatically to him, whether they are in one of the great world religions or not;...all who see no true or basic difference between religion and religion or between man and man or nation and nation will rally around him; those who embody the spirit of exclusiveness and separateness will stand automatically and equally revealed and all men will know them for what they are." [69]

The New Age Peace they hope to achieve is based on inclusiveness and right human relations. Emphasis is put on right human relations which in itself is not a bad thing if observed superficially, but for a Christian who is trying to live life according to God's definition of love in the Bible which is the fulfilling of the

Ten Commandments, it is clear that God is entirely omitted from the picture leaving no standard from which to measure what the right human relations are. For Christians, the standard for "right human relations" is the Ten Commandments of which the first 4 are about how to love or relate to God. The way to relate to others is put in context by our love for God, which is why the first 4 are about God, before we get to how to relate to others in the last 6.

How does love for God put into context our love for others you may ask? We can use the first commandment as an example, "You shall have no other gods before Me." Exodus 20:3. How can a believer who believes in the One and Only Living God; fellowship with those who might be worshiping idols, the devil himself, or agreeing with them that all religions are true or lead to the same outcome, which means the believer is acknowledging the other gods, and yet they are not gods because there is only One God. Right human relations as set forth in the Ten Commandments are defined by how we relate to God and cannot stand alone but have to take God into consideration. Without taking God into consideration, there is no context in which to define the relations. That means fellowship with a child molester or a murderer is alright. By fellowship, I mean to get along with those engaging in such activities knowing full well that they are engaging in them, in a sense being complicit in their activities by endorsing their behavior with the continued friendship. In the Word we are told:

14 Do not be unequally yoked together with unbelievers. For what [d]fellowship has righteousness with lawlessness? And what [e]communion has light with darkness?

15 And what accord has Christ with Belial? Or what part has a believer with an unbeliever?

16 And what agreement has the temple of God with idols? For you[f] are the temple of the living God. As God has said: "I will dwell in them And walk among them. I will be their God, And they shall be My people."

17 Therefore "Come out from among them And be separate, says the Lord. Do not touch what is unclean, And I will receive you."2 Corinthians 6:14-17.

Jesus Christ is the "Prince of Peace", but not of the New Age kind of Peace. In fact He says:

34 "Do not think that I came to bring peace on earth. I did not come to bring peace but a sword.

35 For I have come to 'set[j] a man against his father, a daughter against her mother, and a daughter-in-law against her mother-in-law';

36 and 'a man's enemies will be those of his own household.' Matthew 10:34-36.

The Truth actually sets at variance and can be dividing and not uniting in nature because "the natural man does not receive the things of the Spirit of God, for they are foolishness to him; nor can he know them, because they are spiritually discerned." 1 Corinthians 2:14. The things of God cannot be understood in the way we understand everything else like Academic disciplines. It is spiritual and so the ones who accept the call out of sin into a new life empowered by the Holy Spirit, can be hard to understand if one tries to understand them as they understand temporal matters.

Family and friends end up at odds with the one who chooses life in Christ. The Gospel causes division because it takes one on a path less trodden which those who do not understand will not agree with.

13 Enter by the narrow gate; for wide is the gate and broad is the way that leads to destruction, and there are many who go in by it.

14 [c]Because narrow is the gate and [d]difficult is the way which leads to life, and there are few who find it.

5 They are of the world. Therefore they speak as of the world, and the world hears them.

6 We are of God. He who knows God hears us; he who is not of God does not hear us. By this we know the spirit of truth and the spirit of error. Matthew 7:13-14 and 1 John 4:5-6.

The Gospel causes division and does not bring peace in the New Age spirituality sense of peace. Real peace and unity can be achieved between and among people whose lives are directed by the Holy Spirit who helps them to follow the Ten Commandments, doing to others as they want done to themselves. We have an example of this in the book of Acts:

32 Now the multitude of those who believed were of one heart and one soul; neither did anyone say that any of the things he possessed was his own, but they had all things in common…

34 Nor was there anyone among them who lacked; for all who were possessors of lands or houses sold them, and brought the proceeds of the things that were sold,

35 and laid them at the apostles' feet; and they distributed to each as anyone had need. Acts 4:32, 34-35.

True peace is found only in Christ, because it is a peace that is not determined by circumstance but by His presence:

33 These things I have spoken to you, that in Me you may have peace. In the world you will have tribulation; but be of good cheer, I have overcome the world...

27 Peace I leave with you, My peace I give to you; not as the world gives do I give to you. Let not your heart be troubled, neither let it be afraid. John 16:33 and 14:27.

Jesus Christ can give us peace not only now in this present world of ours with its troubles and uncertainty, but is coming again to take us with Him to a world of Eternal life with peace as one of the perks as written:

4 And God will wipe away every tear from their eyes; there shall be no more death, nor sorrow, nor crying. There shall be no more pain, for the former things have passed away." Revelation 21:4.

Christ's return

As we learned earlier, the Cosmic Christ or Bailey's Christ will appear before Jesus Christ's return. Speaking of how overpowering the delusion of Satan's appearance will be, E. G. White says the following in the book The Great Controversy:

"As the crowning act in the great drama of deception, Satan himself will personate Christ. The church has long professed to look to the Savior's advent as the consummation of her hopes. Now the great deceiver will make it appear that Christ has come. In different parts of the earth, Satan will manifest himself among men as a majestic being of dazzling brightness, resembling the description of the Son of God given by John in the Revelation. Revelation 1:13-15. The glory that surrounds him is unsurpassed by anything that mortal eyes have yet beheld. The shout of triumph rings out upon the air: 'Christ has come! Christ has come!' The people prostrate themselves in adoration before him, while he lifts up his hands and pronounces a blessing upon them, as Christ blessed His disciples when He was upon the earth. His voice is soft and subdued, yet full of melody. In gentle, compassionate tones he presents some of the same gracious, heavenly truths which the Savior uttered; he heals the diseases of the people...This is the strong, almost overmastering delusion." [70]

The father and master of deceit will crown his work of deceiving humanity with the impersonation of Jesus Christ our Savior. This return of Satan is what the New Age believers are looking forward to as seen in the following Alice Bailey quotes:

"It is not for us yet to know the date or hour of the reappearance of the Christ. His coming is dependent upon the appeal (the often voiceless appeal) of all who stand with massed intent; it is dependent also upon the better establishment of right human relations & upon certain work being done at this time by senior Members of the Kingdom of God, the Church Invisible, the spiritual Hierarchy of our planet; it is dependent also upon the steadfastness of the Christ's disciples in the world at this time and His initiate-workers---all working in the many groups: religious, political & economic. To the above must be added what Christians like to call "the inscrutable Will of God," that unrecognized purpose of the Lord of the World, the Ancient of Days (as He is called in the Old Testament) Who "knows His own Mind, radiates the highest quality of love & focuses His Will in His Own high Place within the center where the Will of God is known.

He has been for two thousand years the supreme Head of the Church Invisible, the Spiritual Hierarchy, composed of disciples of all faiths. He recognizes and loves those who are not Christian but who retain their allegiance to Their Founders--the Buddha, Mohammed and others. He cares not what the faith is if the objective is love of God and of humanity. If men look for the Christ Who left His disciples centuries ago, they will fail to recognize the Christ Who is in process of returning. The Christ has no religious barriers in His consciousness. It matters not to Him of what faith a man may call himself...So a peace will come again on earth, but a peace unlike aught known before. Then will the will-to-good flower forth as understanding, & understanding blossom as goodwill in men...When He comes...to inaugurate the New Age and so complete the work He began in Palestine two thousand years ago, He will bring with Him some of the great Angels, as well as certain of the Masters. [71]

We have already learned that a lot of terminology Alice Bailey uses is inverted in how we understand it. Her Christ is actually Satan as we learned. She mentions that his appearance "is dependent upon the appeal (the often voiceless appeal) of all who stand with massed intent; it is dependent also upon the better establishment of right human relations". In other words, he will appear when there are enough people who are intently waiting for his appearance, when the majority of the world is waiting for him so that he can solve the world's problems and usher in a peaceful world. Once again, the love she mentions here is a misguided love which excludes God from the picture. It is this misguided love which she means by right human relations; people setting aside their differences for the greater good of coexisting and letting others be. The following quotes clearly show that this is not Jesus Christ that they are waiting for:

"His reappearance will knit and bind together all men and women of goodwill throughout the world, irrespective of religion or nationality. <u>The work and the teaching of the Christ will be hard for the Christian world to accept, though easier of assimilation in the East.</u> Nevertheless, some hard blow or some difficult presentation of the truth is badly needed if the Christian world is to be awakened, and if Christian people are to recognise their place within a worldwide divine revelation and see the Christ as representing all the faiths and taking His rightful place as World Teacher. He is the World Teacher and not a Christian teacher. He Himself told us that He had other folds and to them He has meant as much as He has meant to the orthodox Christian. They may not call Him Christ, but they have their own name for Him and follow Him as truly and faithfully as their Western brethren..."[72]

The work and teaching of Bailey's Christ will be hard for true Christians to accept because it will have no compatibility with the truth as it is presented in God's Word, the only safeguard against the powerful delusion Satan will perform in his impersonation of Christ. One has to know the fashion in which Jesus Christ returns as well as understanding His teaching, because Satan will mix some truth with error to reinforce some of his false doctrines to further deceive those already deceived by his appearance. We see just how powerful his deception will be in this following Alice Bailey quote:

"The major effect of his appearance will surely be to demonstrate in every land the effects of a spirit of inclusiveness – an inclusiveness which will be channeled or expressed through him. All who seek right human relations will be gathered automatically to him, whether they are in one of the great world religions or not;...all who see no true or basic difference between religion and religion or between man and man or nation and nation will rally around him; those who embody the spirit of exclusiveness and separateness will stand automatically and equally revealed and all men will know them for what they are." [73]

All who will seek for people to just get along regardless of differences will be automatically drawn to him whether they are religious or not. Considering all religions as being truth and leading to the same outcome will set people up for this master delusion. Global citizens who see themselves as citizens of the world and not of their nation will be drawn to him. He will say things that sound good to those who look at things in this way. Those who "embody the spirit of exclusiveness and separateness" will stand out because they will be the minority, and there will be a clear distinction between the two classes, of which there will only be two. All of humanity will fall into one of these two groups. The ones who will cling to Jesus Christ, "the ones who follow the Lamb wherever He goes" will be on one end and everyone else will be on the other. (Revelation 14:4). This is what is meant in the following scriptures:

2 ...The dragon (the devil – see Revelation 12:9) gave him his power, his throne, and great authority.

3 ...And <u>all the world marveled and followed the beast</u>.

4 So they worshiped the dragon who gave authority to the beast; and they worshiped the beast, saying, "Who is like the beast? Who is able to make war with him?"

8 <u>All who dwell on the earth will worship him, whose names have not been written in the Book of Life of the Lamb</u> slain from the foundation of the world...

11 Then I saw another beast coming up out of the earth, and he had two horns like a lamb and spoke like a dragon.

12 And he exercises all the authority of the first beast in his presence, and causes the earth and those who dwell in it to worship the first beast, whose deadly wound was healed...

14 And he deceives [f]those who dwell on the earth by those signs which he was granted to do in the sight of the beast, telling those who dwell on the earth to make an image to the beast who was wounded by the sword and lived.

15 He was granted power to give breath to the image of the beast, that the image of the beast should both speak and cause as many as would not worship the image of the beast to be killed.

16 He causes all, both small and great, rich and poor, free and slave, to receive a mark on their right hand or on their foreheads,

17 and that no one may buy or sell except one who has [g]the mark or the name of the beast, or the number of his name.

8 ...<u>And those who dwell on the earth will marvel, whose names are not written in the Book of Life</u> from the foundation of the world, when they see the beast that was, and is not, and [e]yet is.

15 And anyone not found written in the Book of Life was cast into the lake of fire. Revelation 13:2-4, 8, 11-12, 14-17; 17:8 and 20:15

The subject of the mark of the beast is a subject for a book all by itself, but the most important thing to understand about it is that the ones who follow and marvel after the beasts and get the mark of the beast are the ones who are not written in the Lamb's Book of Life. In other words, everyone follows and marvels after the beast except for those in the Book of Life. The ones who get the mark of the beast are the same ones who marvel and follow the beast. The source of power for these beasts is the dragon or the devil himself as we see in Revelation 13:4. The source of this New Age Spirituality is in the devil as you have figured out by now. Here are some quotes from the originators of the New Age movement in case you are still not convinced:

Alice Bailey
"Around Him—in that High Place on Earth where He has His abiding place—are gathered today all His great Disciples, the Masters of the Wisdom, and all Those liberated Sons of God Who, down the ages, have passed from darkness to Light, from the unreal

to the Real, and from death to Immortality; They stand ready to carry out His bidding and to obey the Master of all the Masters and the Teacher alike of Angels and of men. The Exponents and the Representatives of all the world faiths are there waiting—under His guidance—to reveal to all those who today struggle in the maelstrom of world affairs, and who seek to solve the world crisis, that they are not alone. God Transcendent is working through the Christ and the Spiritual Hierarchy to bring relief; God Immanent in all men is standing on the verge of certain stupendous Recognitions...

He is now waiting to descend. This descent into our unhappy world of men can present Him with no alluring picture. From the quiet mountain retreat where He has waited, guided and watched over humanity, and where He has trained His disciples, initiates and the New Group of World Servers, He must come forth and take His place prominently on the world stage, and take His part in the great drama which is there being played. This time, He will play His part, not in obscurity as He previously did, but before the eyes of the entire world. Because of the smallness of our little planet, and because of the prevalence of the radio, television and the rapidity of communication, His part will be watched by all, and the prospect must surely, for Him, hold certain horror, must present its tests and major adjustments, plus painful and unavoidable experience. He does not come as the omnipotent God of man's ignorant creation, but as the Christ, the Founder of the Kingdom of God on Earth, to complete the work He started, and again to demonstrate divinity in far more difficult circumstances." [74]

"His activity is necessarily a mass activity, for He can only channel His energies through the mass consciousness or through a group conscious entity, such as the Hierarchy, the United Nations or Humanity. The focal point of His effort and the Agent through which distribution of His energy can be made is the New Group of World Servers; ...Their task is to usher in the New Age; in that New Age, the five Kingdoms in Nature will begin to function as one creative whole. Their work falls into the following parts, functions or activities:

    a. The production of a human synthesis or unity which will lead to an universal recognition of the one humanity, brought about through right human relations.

b. The establishing of right relations with the subhuman kingdoms in nature, leading to the universal recognition that there is One World.

c. The anchoring of the Kingdom of God, the spiritual Hierarchy of our planet, in open expression on Earth, thus leading to the universal recognition that the sons of men are one." [75]

"The vision in men's minds today is that of the Aquarian Age, even if they recognise it not. The future will see right relationships, true communion, a sharing of all things (wine, the blood, the life and bread, economic satisfaction) and goodwill; we have also a picture of the future of humanity when all nations are united in complete understanding and the diversity of languages — symbolic of differing traditions, cultures, civilisations and points of view — will provide no barrier to right human relations. At the centre of each of these pictures is to be found the Christ. Thus the expressed aims and efforts of the United Nations will be eventually brought to fruition and a new church of God, gathered out of all religions and spiritual groups, will unitedly bring to an end the great heresy of separateness. Love, unity, and the Risen Christ will be present, and He will demonstrate to us the perfect life." [76]

Helena Petrovna Blavatzky
"Lucifer represents... Life... Thought... Progress... Civilization... Liberty... Independence... Lucifer is the Logos... the Serpent, the Savior." [76] It is Satan who is the God of our planet and the only God." [77] The Celestial Virgin which thus becomes the Mother of Gods and Devils at one and the same time; for she is the ever-loving beneficient Deity...but in antiquity and reality Lucifer or Luciferius is the name. Lucifer is divine and terrestrial Light, 'the Holy Ghost' and "Satan' at one and the same time."[78]

David Spangler
"The true light of Lucifer cannot be seen through sorrow, through darkness, through rejection. The true light of this great being can only be recognized when one's own eyes can see with the light of the Christ, the light of the inner sun. LUCIFER works within each of us to bring us to wholeness, and as we move into a NEW AGE, which is the age of man's wholeness, each of us in some way is

brought to that point which I term the LUCIFERIC INITIATION, the particular doorway through which the individual MUST PASS IF he is to come "fully" into the presence of his light and his wholeness…Lucifer comes to give us the final gift of wholeness…

Lucifer prepares man in all ways for the experience of Christhood and the Christ prepares man for the experience of God… But the light that reveals to us the presence of the Christ, the light that reveals to us the path to the Christ comes from Lucifer. He is the light giver. He is aptly named the Morning Star because it is his light that heralds for man the dawn of a greater consciousness. He is present when that dawn of a greater consciousness. He is present when that dawn is realized. He stands no longer as the tester or the tempter but as the great initiator, the one who hands the soul over to the Christ and from the Christ on into ever greater realms."[79]

"We can take all the scriptures and all the teachings and all the tablets and all the laws, and all the marshmallows and have a jolly good bonfire and marshmallow roast, because that is all they are worth."[80]

These are just a few of the quotes in their own words that Satan is the power behind this movement. Without going into the topic any deeper, the most important thing we learn is that to be safe from worshiping the dragon, the beast or its image, and from getting the mark of the beast, your name has to be written in the Book of Life. The end result of not being in the Book of Life is to end up in the lake of fire. Being a good person, being charitable and being nice is not enough in itself. We do not get into the Book of life by being nice and generous. We do not get into the Book by sacrificing principle to get along with others. The only prescribed way of getting your name in the Book of Life is:

9 ...if you confess with your mouth the Lord Jesus and believe in your heart that God has raised Him from the dead, you will be saved.

13 For "whoever calls on the name of the Lord shall be saved." Romans 10:9 and 13.

All those who are going to be deceived by the false Christ will not have their names written in the Book of Life. Our Savior knows those that belong to Him:

27 My sheep hear My voice, and I know them, and they follow Me.

28 And I give them eternal life, and they shall never perish; neither shall anyone snatch them out of My hand.

29 My Father, who has given them to Me, is greater than all; and no one is able to snatch them out of My Father's hand.

30 I and My Father are one." John 10:27-30.

How will the Second Coming be like?

Since Satan is going to impersonate Christ, it is critical to understand how Jesus Christ's Second Coming. The Second Coming will be a spectacle for all to behold and not something to be reported on the news or an event for which convincing will be needed. In scripture we are told it will be spectacular:

26 "Therefore if they say to you, 'Look, He is in the desert!' do not go out; or 'Look, He is in the inner rooms!' do not believe it.

27 For as the lightning comes from the east and flashes to the west, so also will the coming of the Son of Man be…

14 Then the sky [i]receded as a scroll when it is rolled up, and every mountain and island was moved out of its place.

15 And the kings of the earth, the great men, [j]the rich men, the commanders, the mighty men, every slave and every free man, hid themselves in the caves and in the rocks of the mountains,

16 and said to the mountains and rocks, "Fall on us and hide us from the face of Him who sits on the throne and from the wrath of the Lamb!

17 For the great day of His wrath has come, and who is able to stand?"

10 But the day of the Lord will come as a thief in the night, in which the heavens will pass away with a great noise, and the elements will melt with fervent heat; both the earth and the works that are in it will be [d]burned up.

7 Behold, He is coming with clouds, and every eye will see Him, even they who pierced Him. And all the tribes of the earth will

mourn because of Him. Even so, Amen. Matthew 24:26-27, Revelation 6:14-17, 2 Peter 3:10 and Revelation 1:7.

May you accept Him so your name is written in the Book of Life and that you can joyfully expect His spectacular return instead of crying and hiding from Him.

References

1. https://www.pewresearch.org/fact-tank/2019/12/06/10-facts-about-atheists/
2. https://news.gallup.com/poll/248837/church-membership-down-sharply-past-two-decades.aspx
3. https://www.pewresearch.org/fact-tank/2018/10/01/new-age-beliefs-common-among-both-religious-and-nonreligious-americans/
4. https://www.encyclopedia.com/philosophy-and-religion/other-religious-beliefs-and-general-terms/miscellaneous-religion/new-age-movement
5. Thomas Frank (December 1, 1998). The Conquest of Cool: Business Culture, Counterculture, and the Rise of Hip Consumerism. University of Chicago Press. pp. 132–.
6. https://www.aacap.org/AACAP/Families_and_Youth/Facts_for_Families/FFF-Guide/The-Influence-Of-Music-And-Music-Videos-040.aspx
7. Parker, Kim; Horowitz, Juliana Menasce; Anderson, Monica (June 12, 2020). "Majorities Across Racial, Ethnic Groups Express Support for the Black Lives Matter Movement". Pew Research Center's Social & Demographic Trends Project.
8. https://tristatevoice.com/2020/09/01/are-black-lives-matter-leaders-calling-on-the-spirits-of-the-dead/
9. https://en.wikipedia.org/wiki/United_States_abortion-rights_movement
10. https://www.psychologytoday.com/us/blog/hide-and-seek/201509/when-homosexuality-stopped-being-mental-disorder
11. https://www.washingtonpost.com/opinions/free-speech-is-flunking-out-on-college-campuses/2015/10/22/124e7cd2-78f5-11e5-b9c1-f03c48c96ac2_story.html
12. http://www1.cbn.com/cbnnews/us/2015/December/Students-Call-for-Terrifying-Wave-of-Censorship/
13. http://www.cbn.com/cbnnews/us/2011/september/nrb-study-social-sites-censoring-christians-/?mobile=false
14. https://www.glamour.com/story/a-complete-breakdown-of-the-jk-rowling-transgender-comments-controversy
15. https://www.nytimes.com/2020/07/14/opinion/cancel-culture-.html
16. http://www.christianpost.com/news/chick-fil-a-president-says-gods-judgment-coming-because-of-same-sex-marriage-78485/#YjWy8Z6AmkUXQ53D.99
17. http://www.brnow.org/News/July-2012/Guilty-as-charged-Dan-Cathy-says-of-Chick-fil-A-s
18. http://www.cbsnews.com/news/floyd-lee-corkins-pleads-guilty-in-family-research-council-shooting/
19. http://www.boston.com/yourtown/news/roxbury/2012/02/chick-fil-a_move_to_northeaste.html?camp=pm
20. https://www.thenewatlantis.com/publications/environmentalism-as-religion
21. http://www.catholic-saints.net/gaia-and-gaianism/
22. https://www.gov.ca.gov/2020/09/23/governor-newsom-announces-california-will-phase-out-gasoline-powered-cars-drastically-reduce-demand-for-fossil-fuel-in-californias-fight-against-climate-change/
23. https://www.project-syndicate.org/commentary/radical-green-overhaul-to-avoid-climate-lockdown-by-mariana-mazzucato-2020-09

24. https://www.npr.org/sections/thesalt/2019/08/08/748416223/to-slow-global-warming-u-n-warns-agriculture-must-change
25. https://carbontracker.org/climatetrace
26. Aleister Crowley. The Diary of a drug fiend. pp. 71.
27. http://www.nbcnews.com/id/19053382/ns/health-sexual_health/t/free-love-was-there-price-pay/#.VW4gqtJViko
28. https://www.bbc.com/future/article/20170926-is-porn-harmful-the-evidence-the-myths-and-the-unknowns
29. http://www.washingtontimes.com/news/2015/may/5/sweetcakes-melissa-snubbed-gofundme-gets-new-crowd/#ixzz3eCL5XKpv
30. https://www.kgw.com/article/news/local/sweet-cakes-by-melissa-breaks-record-on-crowdfunding-site/283-67340282
31. https://www.adflegal.org/press-release/colo-civil-rights-commission-issues-inconsistent-cake-artist-decisions
32. http://www.adfmedia.org/News/PRDetail/8700
33. https://www.hg.org/legal-articles/forty-years-on-no-fault-divorce-faces-scrutiny-18784
34. http://www.nytimes.com/2014/12/02/upshot/the-divorce-surge-is-over-but-the-myth-lives-on.html
35. Magick: Liber ABA: Book 4
36. Hit Parade, Oct. 1976, p.14
37. Musician, Special Collectors Edition, - Beatles and Rolling Stones, 1988, p.12
38. Circus, Aug. 26, 1980, p. 26
39. http://www.rogerebert.com/interviews/interview-with-kenneth-anger
40. Stephen Gaskin (2005). Monday Night Class.
41. https://www.theguardian.com/books/2004/jul/10/society
42. https://www.britannica.com/topic/New-Age-movement
43. Alan Morrison, The Serpent and the Cross: Religious Corruption in an Evil Age (Birmingham, England: K & M Books, 1994), p. 175.
44. Alan Morrison, The Serpent and the Cross: Religious Corruption in an Evil Age (Birmingham, England: K & M Books, 1994), p. 584
45. Now is the dawning of the New Age New World Order (Oklahoma City, OK: Hearthstone Publishing, Ltd., 1991), p. 137.
46. "News Alert," The Berean Call (October 1992), p. 4.
47. Dave Hunt and T.A. McMahon, The Seduction of Christianity: Spiritual discernment in the Last Days (Eugene, OR: Harvest House Publishers, 1985), p. 80.
48. Gary Kah, En route to Global Occupation (Lafayette, LA: Huntington House Publishers, 1992), p. 41
49. "Teilhard de Chardin: Christianity and Evolution," SCP Journal (19:2/3), p. 56.
50. http://www.raherrmann.com/bailey.htm
51. The New Age and the Biblical worldview: Conflict and Dialogue. John P. Newport. Pg 6.
52. https://www.britannica.com/topic/New-Age-movement
53. The New Age and the Biblical worldview: Conflict and Dialogue. John P. Newport. Pg 6-7.
54. https://www.hinduamerican.org/projects/hindu-roots-of-yoga
55. https://www.streetdirectory.com/travel_guide/45495/martial_arts/the_shamanic_origins_of_tai_chi.html
56. https://susanlevitt.com/about/writers-resume/the-five-taoist-elements-fire-earth-metal-water-and-wood/
57. http://www.religionfacts.com/five-elements
58. Anton LaVey, quoted in Church of Satan, B. Barton, p.107
59. https://ieet.org/index.php/IEET2/more/Messerly20170204
60. The New Age and the Biblical worldview: Conflict and Dialogue. John P. Newport. Pg 9.
61. Hidden Dangers of the Rainbow, pp. 63.
62. https://www.academia.edu/3449174/About_the_Homo_sapiens_ethicus_aka_Homo_noeticus_
63. Alice Bailey. Discipleship in the New Age, Vol. I. pp. 3.
64. Alice Bailey. The Reappearance of the Christ. pp. 50.
65. http://portal.unesco.org/en/ev.php-URL_ID=13175&URL_DO=DO_TOPIC&URL_SECTION=201.html

66. Alice A. Bailey, Destiny of the Nations (Jersey City, NJ: Aquarian Age Community): pp. 152.
67. Alice A. Bailey, Discipleship in the New Age, Vol. I: 74
68. Alice A. Bailey, The Reappearance of the Christ, pp. 58.
69. Alice A. Bailey, The Reappearance of the Christ. Pp. 110.
70. Ellen. G. White, The Great Controversy. pp. 624.
71. Alice A. Bailey, The Externalisation of the Hierarchy, pp. 508.
72. Alice A. Bailey, The Rays & the Initiations, pp. 615.
73. Alice Bailey. Externalization of the Hierarchy. pp. 593 and 607.
74. Alice Bailey. The work of the Christ today and in the future. pp. 77-78.
75. Alice Bailey. Christ and the coming New Age. pp. 152.
76. Helena Petrovna Blavatsky. The Secret Doctrine. Volume 2. pp. 171, 225, 255
77. Helena Petrovna Blavatsky. The Secret Doctrine. Volume 6. pp. 215, 216, 220, 245, 255, 533.
78. Helena Petrovna Blavatsky. The Secret Doctrine. pp. 539.
79. David Spangler, Reflections on the Christ (Scotland: Findhorn Publications, 1977), pp. 43-44.
80. David Spangler, Reflections on the Christ (Scotland: Findhorn Publications, 1977), pp. 73.

17
BREAD OF LIFE: WHO ARE WE?

Who we are is another point upon which the devil has caused a lot of confusion. We have been given an idea of who we are in the following scriptures:

26 Then God said, "Let Us make man in Our image, according to Our likeness; let them have dominion over the fish of the sea, over the birds of the air, and over the cattle, over [g]all the earth and over every creeping thing that creeps on the earth."

27 So God created man in His own image; in the image of God He created him; male and female He created them. Genesis 1:26-27.

We were created in God's image and were meant to have dominion over the earth and creatures upon it. Earth being our domain, we were supposed to be a reflection of His having dominion over everything by having dominion over the earth, which is why it is written: "You have put all things in subjection under his feet." For in that He put all in subjection under him, He left nothing that is not put under him. But now we do not yet see all things put under him."" Hebrews 2:8. As we learned earlier, not only did we lose the dominion that was meant for us, but went from having the dominion to being dominated as subjects through sin which is, "...the snare of the devil, having been taken captive by him to do his will." 2 Timothy 2:26.

The devil has made it one of his prime areas of focus to distort this fact that we are made in God's image, and this identity crisis manifests in the form of the myriad of theories to explain who we are by how we came to be. These theories serve to devalue who we are because we were "fearfully and wonderfully made", and our Creator God is diminished in the process. What are some of these theories?

The Origin of the Universe

Understanding how we came to be can help us to understand who we are. There are many theories that attempt to explain our origins. We cannot begin to understand who we are if God is not in the picture because as we learned earlier, we came from Him because He created us. Excluding Him from our origins is like attempting to put a puzzle together without using the most important piece which would complete it, as it is written, "The stone which the builders rejected Has become the chief cornerstone." Psalms 118:22. The theories fall short in many respects which is why it is surprising that they are taught in school as fact. Dr. Walter Veith, in his book The Genesis Conflict, touches on some of their flaws:

"Briefly put, the naturalistic theory states that: In the beginning there was the 'cosmic egg' (a very dense compressed object into which was compressed all the matter of the universe and according to various speculations could have been smaller than a pinhead or some claim that it could have been a few kilometers in diameter).

This primordial egg exploded some 15 thousand million years ago and produced some atoms of hydrogen and helium, which together with photons came shooting out of the explosion with great speed. As it cooled, it clumped together to form stars, and nuclear reactions within the stars produced the heavier elements such as oxygen and iron. When these stars in turn exploded, they scattered these elements. Enriched by these elements, the gas clouds eventually spawned other objects including our sun and planets, which contain all the elements necessary for life to evolve. The evolutionary process then continued until by chance molecules arose which gave rise to life. Eventually, all the plants and animals, including man, came into existence through these naturalistic processes.

This scenario also requires a substantive leap in faith, since the very essence of the theory violates the laws of thermodynamics. The First Law of Thermodynamics tells us that matter cannot be created or destroyed. Since the world is here, this leaves us with two choices, either somebody made it, or it made itself.

Of course it does not answer the question: where did the initial material, or for that matter God, come from? The Second Law of Thermodynamics says: everything tends toward disorder. This phenomenon is known as entropy. The first law is one of conservation and implies that the substance of the universe (matter and energy) is a constant. No matter or energy is thus being added to the universe, or one could say that the 'creation' of all matter is thereof complete. The second law states that all processes in the universe will result in an increase in the entropy or movement toward a final equilibrium where all processes cease and this will lead to what has been described as heat-death of the universe. According to this law, order will tend to decrease rather than increase, but because there is so much order in the universe today this law of necessity must be violated by all theories that postulate the development of order out of chaos. This applies both to the physical and to the biological world, but in spite of these constraints, naturalistic theories of origins, with their implied long ages, are the accepted paradigms within which the educational systems of the world operate. Dr. Isaac Asimov stated in the Smithsonian Institute Journal, 1970:

"The universe is constantly becoming more disorderly. Viewed that way, we can see the second law all about us. We have to work hard to straighten a room; but left to itself it becomes a mess again – very quickly and very easily; even if we never enter it – it becomes dusty and musty. How difficult to maintain houses and machinery and our own bodies in perfect working order… How easy to let them deteriorate – in fact, all we have to do is nothing – and everything deteriorates, collapses, breaks down, wears out – all by itself – and that is what the second law of Thermodynamics is all about.""[1]

The Big bang theory

The Big Bang theory states that a cosmic explosion occurred billions of years ago, and the universe rapidly inflated and then cooled, and that it is still expanding at an increasing rate and mostly made up of unknown dark matter and dark energy. This well-known story is usually taken as a self-evident scientific fact just like the theory of Evolution, despite the relative lack of empirical evidence and despite discrepancies arising from observations of the distant universe. The following are some of the problems with this theory in an article by Bjorn Ekeberg based on edited excerpts from the book

Metaphysical Experiments: Physics and the Invention of the Universe:

1. Recently, new measurements of the Hubble constant, the rate of universal expansion, suggested major differences between two independent methods of calculation. Discrepancies on the expansion rate have huge implications not simply for calculation but for the validity of cosmology's current standard model at the extreme scales of the cosmos.

2. Another recent probe found galaxies inconsistent with the theory of dark matter, which posits this hypothetical substance to be everywhere.

3. A crucial function of theories such as dark matter, dark energy and inflation—each in its own way tied to the big bang paradigm—is not to describe known empirical phenomena but rather to maintain the mathematical coherence of the framework itself while accounting for discrepant observations. Fundamentally, they are names for something that must exist insofar as the framework is assumed to be universally valid.

4. Each new discrepancy between observation and theory can, of course, in and of itself be considered an exciting promise of more research, a progressive refinement toward the truth, but they continue adding up, suggesting a bigger problem not resolved by tweaking parameters or adding new variables.

5. The cosmos is unlike any scientific subject matter on earth so a theory of the entire universe, based on our own tiny neighborhood as the only known sample of it, requires a lot of simplifying assumptions. When these assumptions are multiplied and stretched across vast distances, the potential for error increases, and this is further compounded by our very limited means of testing.

6. Most observations of the universe occur experimentally and indirectly. Today's space telescopes provide no direct view of anything—they produce measurements through an interplay of theoretical predictions and pliable parameters, in which the model is involved every step of the way. The framework literally frames the problem; it determines where and how to observe. And so, despite the advanced technologies and methods involved, the profound limitations to the endeavor also increase the risk of being led astray by the kind of assumptions that cannot be calculated.

7. When Hubble observed that the universe was expanding and Einstein's solution no longer seemed to make sense, some mathematical physicists tried to change a fundamental assumption of the model: that the universe was the same in all spatial directions but variant in time.

8. The crux of today's cosmological paradigm is that in order to maintain a mathematically unified theory valid for the entire universe, we must accept that 95 percent of our cosmos is furnished by completely unknown elements and forces for which we have no empirical evidence whatsoever. For a scientist to be confident of this picture requires an exceptional faith in the power of mathematical unification.[2]

The Theory of Evolution

The theory of evolution by natural selection, first formulated in Darwin's book "On the Origin of Species" in 1859, is the process by which organisms change over time as a result of changes in heritable physical or behavioral traits. The changes allow an organism to better adapt to its environment helping it survive and have more offspring. It is taught from Primary school all the way through College as fact. In the following excerpt, Walter Veith points out flaws with this theory:

"The evidence for man's evolution is extremely scant, and the main role players are Australopithecines, which are small to medium sized ape-like creatures, which some researchers believe to have walked upright. Remains of these creatures have been found in eastern and southern Africa and the famous Lucy belongs to this group. Then there are the so-called archaic Homo sapiens, which include forms such as the Neanderthals. It is noteworthy that all the forms on which human evolution is based were contemporaneous, which means that they lived at the same time. In fact, all the primates existed at the same time, and the evolutionary tree is once again a morphological sequence pieced together by the scientists according to their perceptions. Australopithecines thus existed side by side with humans and are thus regarded as a side branch from which information can be inferred but that could not have been on the ancestral line of modern humans...

In his book 'Bones of Contention: controversies in the search for human origins', Roger Lewin, research news editor of the journal Science at the time, sums up the main issues of contention in the saga of human origins. He sites competition amongst researchers and their passions as some of the reasons for the confusion in the field of hominid evolution. The main controversies in his report revolve around:

1) the Taung child found in South Africa and originally rejected but now accepted as an intermediary ancestor in man's evolution;

2) the Piltdown Hoax where a human skull and an Orangutan's jaw were 'doctored' to lend credence to the naturalistic origin of man and which was unchallenged for almost four decades;

3) Nebraska man who was based on a tooth which turned out to be a pig's tooth;

4) the distortions towards primitiveness in the original description of Neanderthals;

5) the battle over the dethroning of Ramapithecus from the level of human ancestor to a relative of the orangutan;

6) the heated controversy over the dating of the volcanic layer associated with the hominid fossils in East Africa;

7) the controversy between Richard Leakey and Donald Johanson over the position of the newer australopithecine finds;

8) the conflicts about what constituted the force that brought about human evolutionary change (was it predation, hunting, or cooperation). Lewin's own feelings are revealed in the following statement:

In the physical realm, any theory of human evolution must explain how it was that an apelike ancestor, equipped with powerful jaws and long, dagger-like canine teeth and able to run at speed on four limbs, became transformed into a slow, bipedal animal whose natural means of defense were at best puny. Add to this the power of intellect, speech, and morality, upon which we 'stand raised as upon a mountain top' as Huxley put it, and one has the complete challenge to evolutionary theory." [1]

Problems with theory of evolution

1. Lack of a viable mechanism for producing high levels of complex and specified information. Related to this are problems with the Darwinian mechanism producing irreducibly complex features,

and the problems of non-functional or deleterious intermediate stages.

2. The failure of the fossil record to provide support for Darwinian evolution.

3. The failure of molecular biology to provide evidence for a grand "tree of life."

4. Natural selection is an extremely inefficient method of spreading traits in populations unless a trait has an extremely high selection coefficient;

5. The problem that convergent evolution appears rampant — at both the genetic and morphological levels, even though under Darwinian theory this is highly unlikely.

6. The failure of chemistry to explain the origin of the genetic code.

7. The failure of developmental biology to explain why vertebrate embryos diverge from the beginning of development.

8. The failure of Neo-Darwinian evolution to explain the bio-geographical distribution of many species.

9. A long history of inaccurate predictions inspired by Neo-Darwinism regarding vestigial organs or so-called "junk" DNA.

10. Humans show many behavioral and cognitive traits and abilities that offer no apparent survival advantage (e.g. music, art, religion, ability to ponder the nature of the universe).[3]

Author Roger Mourner before his conversion to Christianity, was given insight into the source of this theory. The following is an excerpt from his book A Trip into the Supernatural:

"…'The spirits decided when the two children [Charles Darwin and Henry Huxley] became adults they would be instruments to advance the religion that we know as the theory of evolution. By tying it in with the scientific revolution breaking across the world, most people wouldn't even recognize that it is a religion – a religion that crossed all denominational boundaries and even caught up the non-religious.'

"To my shock and amazement the priest then explained that 'The spirits consider anyone who teaches the theory of evolution to be a minister of that great religious system, and the individual will receive a special unction from Satan himself. Satan gives him great power to induce spiritual blindness, to convince and to convert. In fact, he holds such people in such high regards that he assigns a special retinue of angels to accompany him or her all of his or her life. It is the greatest honor that Satan can bestow upon a person in the presence of the galaxy.'

"The priest explained that Satan and his counselors had concluded that they could use the theory of evolution to destroy the very foundation of the Bible. 'They could turn it against the creation week, the fall, and the plan of redemption. The stakes were so high here that the spirits tell us that Satan himself tutored Charles Darwin in setting up the principles of his scientific concept.'" [4]

Radiometric Dating

A radioactive element is capable of changing into a new element by the emission of a charged particle. The parent isotope is thus transformed into a daughter product. This process will continue until a stable element is produced. The rates of decay vary from element to element and the rate is measured in half-lives. For example, if an element has a half-life of 5730 years, as is the case for carbon-14, then after 5730 years, only half the original amount of carbon-14 will be left in any non-living carbon-containing object after this time period. In order to determine the age of a substance, it is vital that the amount of parent element and its daughter product in the sample be known.

The ratio of daughter to parent together with the half-life criteria then enables one to calculate the age of the sample. Of course, one can only determine the quantity of the parent element in the present sample; the quantity of the parent element in the past must be estimated. Knowing the decay rates and using the assumption that these decay rates have remained constant over time, the age of the material can then be determined. In other words, all methods of radioactive dating rely on some a priori assumptions, which may not necessarily be true. These are:

1) The rate of radioactive decay and half-lives has remained constant over time. This assumption has the backing of numerous scientific studies and is relatively sound; however, conditions may have been different in the past and could have influenced the rate of decay or formation of radioactive elements.

2) The assumption that the clock was set to zero when the study material was formed. This requires that only the parent isotope be initially present or that the amount of daughter isotope present at the beginning is known so that it can be subtracted.

3) The assumption that we are dealing with a closed system. No loss of either parent or daughter elements has occurred since the study material formed.

4) Even if the rate of decay is constant, without knowledge of the exact ratio of carbon-12 to carbon-14 in the initial sample, the dating technique is subject to question. It is thus quite an extrapolation to assume that the decay of radioisotopes with high half lives is exponential, when experimental data is only available for short lived isotopes with half-lives of less than 100 years." [5]

5) The Flood of Noah's time would have buried large amounts of carbon from living organisms (plant and animal) to form today's fossil fuels (coal, oil, etc.). The amount of fossil fuels indicates there must have been a vastly larger quantity of vegetation in existence prior to the Flood than exists today. This means that the biosphere just prior to the Flood might have had 500 times more carbon in living organisms than today. This would further dilute the amount of 14C and cause the 14C/12C ratio to be much smaller than today.

6) The earth has a magnetic field around it which helps protect us from harmful radiation from outer space. This magnetic field is decaying (getting weaker). The stronger the field is around the earth, the fewer the number of cosmic rays that are able to reach the atmosphere which would result in a smaller production of 14C in the atmosphere in earth's past.

7) In 1997 an eight-year research project was started to investigate the age of the earth. The group was called the RATE group (Radioisotopes and the Age of The Earth) and they took samples from ten different coal layers that, according to evolutionists, represent different time periods in the geologic column (Cenozoic, Mesozoic, and Paleozoic). Samples, in all three "time periods", displayed significant amounts of 14C. This is a significant discovery since the half-life of 14C is relatively short (5,730 years), there should be no detectable 14C left after about 100,000 years. The average 14C estimated age for all the layers from these three time periods was approximately 50,000 years. However, using a more

realistic pre-Flood 14C /12C ratio reduces that age to about 5,000 years. [6]

The Bible's account of Creation

Attempts at explaining our origins which do not take into account that God made us fall short because they are not true. If they were true, they would be able to prove that is the case, but they evolve as they try to address the obvious discrepancies. It takes faith to believe that we came to be through evolution, or that gases whose origins we do not know exploded which eventually led to the diverse complex life forms we find on this earth. Believing in these theories make them spiritual and not scientific which is yet another masterpiece of the devil's deceptions, as written:

4 Now the Spirit [a]expressly says that in latter times some will depart from the faith, giving heed to deceiving spirits and doctrines of demons…

3 For the time will come when they will not endure sound doctrine, but according to their own desires, because they have itching ears, they will heap up for themselves teachers;

4 and they will turn their ears away from the truth, and be turned aside to fables.

1 Timothy 4:1 and 2 Timothy 4:3-4.

People buy into them because they are promoted by science as fact yet there is no proof. Had they been religious theories without the science veil, less of those who profess to be learned would subscribe to them. They are spiritual because they are intended to deny the fact that God is the Creator, countering the Biblical account in Genesis chapter 1 of who we are and how we came to be. Faith is needed to believe the Biblical account just as much as in evolution or the Big Bang theory. The Biblical account is more believable because it simply identifies the Creator and how He created everything. Unfortunately many believe the flawed theories instead of believing a more believable account of a Living God creating the world and everything in it.

References

1. Walter Veith, The Genesis Conflict. pp. 40.
2. https://evolutionnews.org/2012/07/what_are_the_to_1/
3. https://blogs.scientificamerican.com/ observations/cosmology-has-some-big-problems/
4. Roger Mourner, A Trip into the Supernatural, 46-47.
5. Walter Veith, The Genesis Conflict. pp. 40.
6. https://answersingenesis.org/geology/carbon-14/doesnt-carbon-14-dating-disprove-the-bible/

18
BREAD OF LIFE:
WHY ARE WE HERE?

    Having the desire to treat others as we want to be treated and being able to do it is what pleases God and why we are here,"for it is God who works in you both to will and to do for His good pleasure." Philippians 2:13.

    The deeper we get into a relationship with God, the more His Power works in us and through us to love Him and to love our neighbor. His Power working in us is because of how much we allow His Holy Spirit to work in us (Ephesians 3:20.) We learned earlier in the book that for us to be able to love others as ourselves and to love God whom we we have not seen takes a power outside of ourselves because on our own we cannot do it.

    The most important reason for God's power to work in our lives is to transform our lives so they come in to conformity with His will, which is to love our neighbor and to love Him. That is why the greatest manifestation of God's Power is a transformed life, going from having selfish desires being the motivation for selfish actions, to loving God not seen who empowers to consider others in deed. A transformed life goes from being in bondage to sin to being free from sin.

    Those who allow the Holy Spirit to work in them to do His will can also be enabled to manifest this Power in helping God's cause namely in delivering those bound by illness and demonic bondage. The miracles performed are never for the glory of the performer but rather for the glory God who would have enabled them. They also help in making known who He is and about His mission of saving souls from sin. Christ gave his disciples the Power to do these things:

    10 After these things the Lord appointed [a]seventy others also, and sent them two by two before His face into every city and place where He Himself was about to go...

16 He who hears you hears Me, he who rejects you rejects Me, and he who rejects Me rejects Him who sent Me."

17 Then the [e]seventy returned with joy, saying, "Lord, even the demons are subject to us in Your name."

18 And He said to them, "I saw Satan fall like lightning from heaven.

19 Behold, I give you the authority to trample on serpents and scorpions, and over all the power of the enemy, and nothing shall by any means hurt you.

20 Nevertheless do not rejoice in this, that the spirits are subject to you, but [f]rather rejoice because your names are written in heaven."

The disciples were able to do these things by the Holy Spirit working through them, for the sake of helping in Jesus' mission of setting people from sin and from any form of bondage they might have been in. Jesus Himself even made mention of His disciples being able to do greater things than He did:

12 "Most assuredly, I say to you, he who believes in Me, the works that I do he will do also; and greater works than these he will do, because I go to My Father.

13 And whatever you ask in My name, that I will do, that the Father may be glorified in the Son.

14 If you [c]ask anything in My name, I will do it. John 14:12-14.

Later on we see that after Jesus' Resurrection and upon His return to Heaven, the Holy Spirit was poured out on His Disciples on the Day of Pentecost. The Holy Spirit came upon them in large measure once they were of one accord or had settled any differences or misunderstandings among them, and in essence, they loved one another as well as now fully understanding Christ and loving Him.

1 When the Day of Pentecost had fully come, they were all [a]with one accord in one place.

2 And suddenly there came a sound from heaven, as of a rushing mighty wind, and it filled the whole house where they were sitting.

3 Then there appeared to them [b]divided tongues, as of fire, and one sat upon each of them.

4 And they were all filled with the Holy Spirit...Acts 2:1-4.

This outpouring of the Holy Spirit in large measure is what empowered the early Christians to preach, and do great miracles:

46 So continuing daily with one accord in the temple, and breaking bread from house to house, they ate their food with gladness and simplicity of heart,

47 praising God and having favor with all the people. And the Lord added [q]to the church daily those who were being saved. Acts 2:46-47.

You could call it the fuel for the initial growth of the church, the manifestation of the Power of God through this great outpouring of the Holy Spirit. It was meant for those witnessing the miracles and wonders to inquire who these people were and about the God they worshiped. It was for the Glory to be given to God, the source of the Power, and that the people would know that He came to set them free from sin and any form of bondage to the devil.

More would then believe and be saved from sin, which was the ultimate goal, which is why the early church grew in leaps and bounds as more were added to the believers. As long as they were of one accord, the Holy Spirit was at work through them in a great way. As Christ had foretold, they were able to do great things like raising the dead, healing the sick, casting out demons; and He was not just talking about believers in that day only but throughout the ages including believers today.

To know God and help others know Him

Just as God empowers us to do His will, he also reveals knowledge which aids us in the same. He doesn't reveal knowledge for knowledge's sake, but always has a reason. The most basic reason is for us to believe and to help us grow in our faith in Him so: "the genuineness of your faith, being much more precious than gold that perishes, though it is tested by fire, may be found to praise, honor, and glory at the revelation of Jesus Christ." 1 Peter 1:7.

Faith is so important to God because "6 without faith it is impossible to please Him, for he who comes to God must believe that He is, and that He is a rewarder of those who diligently seek

Him." Hebrews 11:6. Believing is how we are saved which is why it is so important to God. It pleases Him to save us, that is why it is impossible to please God without faith. He reveals this knowledge through His Word and His messengers who speak or write about His love and desire to save us as Paul says:

14 How then shall they call on Him in whom they have not believed? And how shall they believe in Him of whom they have not heard? And how shall they hear without a preacher?

15 And how shall they preach unless they are sent? As it is written:"How beautiful are the feet of those who [b]preach the gospel of peace, Who bring glad tidings of good things!"" Romans 10:14-15.

It is important to note that just as the manifestation of Power in a believer's life is because of the Holy Spirit, to hear, understand and apply knowledge is only by the Holy Spirit. Revelation is by the Holy Spirit as written:

17 that the God of our Lord Jesus Christ, the Father of glory, may give to you the spirit of wisdom and revelation in the knowledge of Him,

18 the eyes of your [f]understanding being enlightened; that you may know what is the hope of His calling, what are the riches of the glory of His inheritance in the saints,

19 and what is the exceeding greatness of His power toward us who believe, according to the working of His mighty power...Ephesians 1:17-19.

Revelation can come through a Preacher, directly to the person while studying the Word, and it can come through other ways such as dreams and visions. (Joel 2:28)

19
BREAD OF LIFE: WHERE ARE WE GOING?

The devil is the father of lies, and he told Eve what is possibly the greatest lie he ever told, when he said: "You will not surely die. Genesis 3:4.

It is the foundational belief of New Age spirituality. It is not surprising because all the religions and philosophies which gave rise to New Age Spirituality believe in immortality of the soul. God is the only one who has immortality as seen in the following scriptures:

17 Now to the King eternal, immortal, invisible, to [e]God who alone is wise…

16 who alone has immortality, dwelling in unapproachable light, whom no man has seen or can see, to whom be honor and everlasting power. Amen. 1 Timothy 1:17; 6:16.

God is the Source of all life, therefore He is immortal and has life in Himself. No life can exist unless God allows it be so. To live is to be in God as we see in the following scriptures:

4 Abide in Me, and I in you. As the branch cannot bear fruit of itself, unless it abides in the vine, neither can you, unless you abide in Me.

5 "I am the vine, you are the branches. He who abides in Me, and I in him, bears much fruit; for without Me you can do nothing.

6 If anyone does not abide in Me, he is cast out as a branch and is withered; and they gather them and throw them into the fire, and they are burned. John 15:4-6.

In these scriptures is illustrated the principle that He is the Source of life, and that life is found in staying connected to Him. Maintaining a connection or relationship with God is life, while being disconnected from Him is death. A branch has no life in itself, unless it stays connected to the Vine. Disconnecting from the Vine means it dies and though it might still appear green with leaves on it for a while, it is surely dead and starts to wither. It summarizes what happens to all intelligent life whether human or angels. We will learn later that even angels are mortal, therefore they can also die. Adam and Eve when they sinned did not die right away, but eventually died. Death was not meant to exist, but came into existence because of sin. Eternal life is a gift, meaning you can only have it if He gives it to you.

23 For the wages of sin is death, but the [h]gift of God is eternal life in Christ Jesus our Lord. Romans 6:23.

The Tree of Life

If death was not meant to exist, does that then mean we would have been immortal, you may ask? God is the Source of Life and only He has immortality! No other life form, angel or not, has life within itself and so cannot be immortal, unlike God who is immortal because He is the source of life. He is life! Even the angels whether loyal to God or fallen, all have their life in God. How then does He allow or enable a life which cannot live forever within itself, to live forever you may ask? The Tree of Life! When Adam and Eve sinned, they were banished from the garden and restricted access to the tree of life:

22 Then the Lord God said, "Behold, the man has become like one of Us, to know good and evil. And now, lest he put out his hand and take also of the tree of life, and eat, and live forever." Genesis 3:22.

To live forever is a gift from God, because we cannot live forever within ourselves. The only way to access this gift is through Christ as your Savior. Those who accept Christ as their Savior and are saved go from certain death apart from God, to life forever with Him. Adam and Eve's banishment from the Tree was to ensure they would not live forever in sin. On the other hand those who accept Christ as their Savior will regain access to the Tree of Life, including Adam and Eve if they repented from their sin as written:

24 "Most assuredly, I say to you, he who hears My word and believes in Him who sent Me has everlasting life, and shall not come into judgment, but has passed from death into life…

7 "He who has an ear, let him hear what the Spirit says to the churches. To him who overcomes I will give to eat from the tree of life, which is in the midst of the Paradise of God." '

14 Blessed are those who [g]do His commandments, that they may have the right to the tree of life, and may enter through the gates into the city. John 5:24; Revelation 2:7 and 22:14.

The living dead

Adam and Eve did not die right away after the fall but eventually died. Death came into existence because of their sin but thankfully, even death has a remedy which is Christ. Apart from God we can be alive in human eyes, but to God, there is no life apart from Him and we are like the branches which appear green for a time until they dry up. We are dead people walking until we accept Christ, which is when we begin to live in God's eyes. Those who died in Christ are dead to us but alive in God's eyes because they passed from death due to sin, to life in Christ. The physically dead to us who died in sin, are no different from the ones who are physically alive in sin as we see in God's eyes, as we see in the following exchange when he was calling someone to follow Him:

59 Then He said to another, "Follow Me." But he said, "Lord, let me first go and bury my father."

60 Jesus said to him, "Let the dead bury their own dead, but you go and preach the kingdom of God." Luke 9:59-60.

Life and death in God's eyes is determined by whether we are reconciled to Him through Christ or not. Sin reigns in our lives when we are not reconciled to Him. This is why it is written:

31 But concerning the resurrection of the dead, have you not read what was spoken to you by God, saying,

32 'I am the God of Abraham, the God of Isaac, and the God of Jacob'? God is not the God of the dead, but of the living..."

21 For as the Father raises the dead and gives life to them, even so the Son gives life to whom He will…

25 Most assuredly, I say to you, the hour is coming, and now is, when the dead will hear the voice of the Son of God; and those who hear will live. Matthew 22:31-32 and John 5:21, 25.

Death as sleep?

When our physical bodies die, God considers it to be sleep. After death, life and death in His eyes are the ultimate outcomes depending on whether or not we chose to be reconciled back to Him or not while still alive. First, let us look at how what He considers to be sleep is physical death to us:

18 While He spoke these things to them, behold, a ruler came and worshiped Him, saying, "My daughter has just died, but come and lay Your hand on her and she will live."

19 So Jesus arose and followed him, and so did His disciples…

23 When Jesus came into the ruler's house, and saw the flute players and the noisy crowd wailing,

24 He said to them, "Make room, for the girl is not dead, but sleeping." And they ridiculed Him.

25 But when the crowd was put outside, He went in and took her by the hand, and the girl arose...Matthew 9:18-19, 23-25.

Powerful how He just held her hand and she resurrected from death or to Him, rose from her sleep.

The death and resurrection of Lazarus

Understanding what sleep is versus death in God's eyes, is very important to understand because misunderstanding this is how the devil has convinced many of the false teaching of immortality of the soul. The following is an extensive look into the resurrection of Lazarus:

1 Now a certain man was sick, Lazarus of Bethany, the town of Mary and her sister Martha.

2 It was that Mary who anointed the Lord with fragrant oil and wiped His feet with her hair, whose brother Lazarus was sick.

3 Therefore the sisters sent to Him, saying, "Lord, behold, he whom You love is sick."

4 When Jesus heard that, He said, "This sickness is not unto death, but for the glory of God, that the Son of God may be glorified through it."

5 Now Jesus loved Martha and her sister and Lazarus.

6 So, when He heard that he was sick, He stayed two more days in the place where He was.

7 Then after this He said to the disciples, "Let us go to Judea again."

11..He said to them, "Our friend Lazarus sleeps, but I go that I may wake him up."

12 Then His disciples said, "Lord, if he sleeps he will get well."

13 However, Jesus spoke of his death, but they thought that He was speaking about taking rest in sleep.

14 Then Jesus said to them plainly, "Lazarus is dead.

15 And I am glad for your sakes that I was not there, that you may believe. Nevertheless let us go to him."

17 So when Jesus came, He found that he had already been in the tomb four days.

18 Now Bethany was near Jerusalem, about [a]two miles away.

19 And many of the Jews had joined the women around Martha and Mary, to comfort them concerning their brother.

20 Then Martha, as soon as she heard that Jesus was coming, went and met Him, but Mary was sitting in the house.

21 Now Martha said to Jesus, "Lord, if You had been here, my brother would not have died.

22 But even now I know that whatever You ask of God, God will give You."

23 Jesus said to her, "Your brother will rise again."

24 Martha said to Him, "I know that he will rise again in the resurrection at the last day."

25 Jesus said to her, "I am the resurrection and the life. He who believes in Me, though he may die, he shall live.

26 And whoever lives and believes in Me shall never die. Do you believe this?"

27 She said to Him, "Yes, Lord, I believe that You are the Christ, the Son of God, who is to come into the world."

.38 Then Jesus, again groaning in Himself, came to the tomb. It was a cave, and a stone lay against it.

39 Jesus said, "Take away the stone." Martha, the sister of him who was dead, said to Him, "Lord, by this time there is a stench, for he has been dead four days."

40 Jesus said to her, "Did I not say to you that if you would believe you would see the glory of God?"

41 Then they took away the stone [d]from the place where the dead man was lying. And Jesus lifted up His eyes and said, "Father, I thank You that You have heard Me.

42 And I know that You always hear Me, but because of the people who are standing by I said this, that they may believe that You sent Me."

43 Now when He had said these things, He cried with a loud voice, "Lazarus, come forth!"

44 And he who had died came out bound hand and foot with grave clothes, and his face was wrapped with a cloth. Jesus said to them, "Loose him, and let him go." John 11:1-7, 11-15, 17-27 and 38-44.

Jesus delayed so long that Lazarus had been dead 4 days and his body had started to decompose. He was late to them and in no hurry, but what they did not understand was that Jesus has Power over even death itself. Martha thought He referred to raising Lazarus up at the last day which would be His second coming, but to prove that death has no power to hold those He desires to loose from its grip, He resurrected him right then. We are promised that on the last day when:

54 ...this corruptible has put on incorruption, and this mortal has put on immortality, then shall be brought to pass the saying that is written: "Death is swallowed up in victory."

55 "O[n] Death, where is your sting? O Hades, where is your victory?" 1 Corinthians 15:54-55.

All the dead are sleeping and are not involved in any of the affairs of the living because:

4 ...for him who is joined to all the living there is hope, for a living dog is better than a dead lion.

5 For the living know that they will die; But the dead know nothing, And they have no more reward, For the memory of them is forgotten.

6 Also their love, their hatred, and their envy have now perished; Nevermore will they have a share in anything done under the sun. Ecclesiastes 9:4-6.

This is very important to understand because there are many who believe that their dead loved ones are watching over them and follow the affairs of their lives. The following is an excerpt from the book the Great Controversy by E.G. White in which this point is eloquently made:

"The doctrine of natural immortality, first borrowed from the pagan philosophy, and in the darkness of the great apostasy incorporated into the Christian faith, has supplanted the truth, so plainly taught in Scripture, that "the dead know not anything." Multitudes have come to believe that it is the spirits of the dead who are the "ministering spirits sent forth to minister for them who shall be heirs of salvation." And this notwithstanding the testimony of Scripture to the existence of heavenly angels, and their connection with the history of man, before the death of a human being.

The doctrine of man's consciousness in death, especially the belief that the spirits of the dead return to minister to the living, has prepared the way for modern Spiritualism. If the dead are admitted to the presence of God and holy angels, and privileged with knowledge far exceeding what they before possessed, why should they not return to the earth to enlighten and instruct the living? If, as taught by popular theologians, the spirits of the dead are hovering about their friends on earth, why should they not be permitted to communicate with them, to warn them against evil, or to comfort them in sorrow? How can those who believe in man's consciousness in death reject what comes to them as divine light communicated by glorified spirits? Here is a channel regarded as sacred, through which Satan works for the accomplishment of his purposes. The fallen angels who do his bidding appear as messengers from the spirit world. While professing to bring the living into communication with the dead, the prince of evil exercises his bewitching influence upon their minds.

He has power to bring before men the appearance of their departed friends. The counterfeit is perfect; the familiar look, the words, the tone, are reproduced with marvelous distinctness. Many are comforted with the assurance that their loved ones are enjoying the bliss of Heaven; and without suspicion of danger, they give ear to "seducing spirits, and doctrines of devils."

When they have been led to believe that the dead actually return to communicate with them, Satan causes those to appear who went into the grave unprepared. They claim to be happy in Heaven, and even to occupy exalted positions there; and thus the error is widely taught, that no difference is made between the righteous and the wicked. The pretended visitants from the world of spirits sometimes utter cautions and warnings which prove to be correct. Then, as confidence is gained, they present doctrines that directly undermine faith in the Scriptures.

With an appearance of deep interest in the well-being of their friends on earth, they insinuate the most dangerous errors. The fact that they state some truths, and are able at times to foretell future events, gives to their statements an appearance of reliability; and their false teachings are accepted by the multitudes as readily, and believed as implicitly, as if they were the most sacred truths of the Bible. The law of God is set aside, the Spirit of grace despised, the blood of the covenant counted an unholy thing. The spirits deny the divinity of Christ, and place even the Creator on a level with themselves. Thus under a new disguise the great rebel still carries forward his warfare against God, begun in Heaven, and for nearly six thousand years continued upon the earth." [1]

Angels are not immortal

As we have learned, only God is Immortal. All other life forms live because He allows it be so. The angels that are loyal to God will continue to live forever because they stayed in communion with Him and did not rebel like the devil and the other fallen angels. The rebels, though alive now will not continue to live forever. Angels are not immortal because the devil and his fallen angels are going to die in "the everlasting fire prepared for the devil and his angels..." Matthew 25:41. The fact that they are going to die means they are not immortal because being immortal would mean they cannot die. They are going to die because they brought sin upon humanity and are the driving force behind it in our world. Death results from sin.

(Romans 6:23.) Everlasting fire implies that the fire does not stop burning, but we will learn later what it means.

Doctrine of the Immortality of the soul

As alluded to in the Great Controversy excerpt earlier, this idea that souls are immortal started in the ancient religions of Egypt, China and Greece. In fact, it exists in the many different cultures of the world in one form or the other, especially in the form of ancestor worship, as well as in the practice of divination when the dead are consulted. Let us look at some of the major forms in which this belief exists.

Reincarnation

According to Britannica, Reincarnation, also called transmigration or metempsychosis, is the rebirth of the aspect of an individual that persists after bodily death—whether it be consciousness, mind, the soul, or some other entity—in one or more successive existences. Depending upon the tradition, these existences may be human, animal, spiritual, or, in some instances, vegetable. While belief in reincarnation is most characteristic of South Asian and East Asian traditions, it also appears in the religious and philosophical thought of local religions, in some ancient Middle Eastern religions (e.g., the Greek Orphic mystery, or salvation, religion), Manichaeism, and gnosticism, as well as in such modern religious movements as theosophy.

The major religions that hold a belief in reincarnation, however, are Asian religions, especially Hinduism, Jainism, Buddhism, and Sikhism, all of which arose in India. They all hold in common a doctrine of karma (karman; "act"), the law of cause and effect, which states that what one does in this present life will have its effect in the next life. In Hinduism the process of birth and rebirth—i.e., transmigration of souls—is endless until one achieves moksha, or liberation (literally "release") from that process. Moksha is achieved when one realizes that the eternal core of the individual (atman) and the Absolute reality (brahman) are one. Thus, one can escape from the process of death and rebirth (samsara). [2]

Purgatory

Purgatory, the condition, process, or place of purification or temporary punishment in which, according to medieval Christian and Roman Catholic belief, the souls of those who die in a state of grace are made ready for heaven. [3]

The Catechism of the Catholic Church defines purgatory as a "purification, so as to achieve the holiness necessary to enter the joy of heaven," which is experienced by those "who die in God's grace and friendship, but still imperfectly purified" (CCC 1030). It notes that "this final purification of the elect . . . is entirely different from the punishment of the damned" (CCC 1031)...

Augustine said in The City of God that "temporary punishments are suffered by some in this life only, by others after death, by others both now and then; but all of them before that last and strictest judgment"...It is between the particular and general judgments, then, that the soul is purified of the remaining consequences of sin..." [4]

Eternal hell fire

There is no doctrine that has caused more harm to God's cause, than the doctrine of Eternal hell fire. Many Christians believe that those who die without being forgiven of their sins end up in a place of Eternal torment called Hell. Many who do not know God cannot reconcile Him being the embodiment of love with tormenting people for eternity, regardless of their sin. It has served to misrepresent God effectively. "In his sermon 'Sinners in the Hands of an Angry God', Jonathan Edwards an 18th century preacher, taught the doctrine of an eternal burning hell.

In the second volume of 'Sermons' by Jonathan Edwards, he also says: 'Those wicked men who died many years ago, their souls went to hell, and there they are still; those who went to hell in former ages of the world have been in hell ever since, all the while suffering torment. They have nothing else to spend their time in there, but to suffer torment; they are kept in being for no other purpose.' ..." [5]

Many of the preachers of the time started preaching this and it has carried over into modern preaching. It is accepted as doctrine, but is this what the Bible teaches? The following is an excerpt from helltruth.com which goes much deeper on this subject.

What is hell?
"In the Old Testament, hell is mentioned 31 times, which is derived from the Hebrew "Sheol," which means "the grave." In the New Testament, it is mentioned 10 times from the Greek "Hades," which means "the grave"; 12 times from the Greek "Gehenna," which means "a place of burning", and 1 time from the Greek "Tartarus," which means "a place of darkness."

The basis for this teaching
The story of the rich man and Lazarus in Luke 16:19–31 is for many who believe this, the basis for this teaching...Many facts make it clear that this is a parable. A few are as follows:
- Abraham's bosom is not heaven (Hebrews 11:8–10, 16).
- People in hell can't talk to those in heaven (Isaiah 65:17).
- The dead are in their graves (Job 17:13; John 5:28, 29). The rich man was in bodily form, with eyes, a tongue, etc., yet we know that the body does not go to hell immediately at death. The body remains in the grave, as the Bible says.
- People are rewarded at Christ's second coming, not at death (Revelation 22:12).

The lost are punished in hell at the end of the world, not when they die (Matthew 13:40–42). Luke 16:31, the last verse of the story, contains a spiritual lesson, showing that the story is actually a parable. Parables cannot be taken literally. If we took parables literally, then we must believe that trees talk! (See this parable in Judges 9:8–15). By representing the beggar as being in heaven and the rich man as lost, Jesus taught His hearers that, contrary to the prevailing view, wealth was not necessarily an indicator of divine favor, just as poverty was not a sign of God's judgment upon a person.

Also, Jesus was seeking to educate the Jews that salvation would not be theirs by birthright. The rich man in torments calls out to "father Abraham," just as the Jews of Jesus' day were mistakenly pointing to heritage as assurance of salvation. Furthermore, Jesus was seeking to lead His hearers to understand that only faithfulness to God's Word would prepare them to enter into eternal life. He told them, "If they do not hear Moses and the prophets, neither will they be persuaded though one rise from the dead" (Luke 16:31).

To use the parable of the rich man and Lazarus to promote the false doctrine of an eternally burning hell is to misuse God's Word and to misrepresent His character.

Angels cast down to hell

In the Old Testament, "hell" is always translated from the Hebrew word sheol, which means simply "the unseen state." (See Young's Analytical Concordance.) The idea of fire or punishment is not found in the word. We read, "Jonah prayed unto the LORD his God out of the fish's belly. ... Out of the belly of hell cried I" (Jonah 2:1, 2 KJV). It would be difficult to imagine anything akin to fire in connection with a cold sea monster. The margin of this text translates hell, or sheol, as "the grave."

Sheol is frequently translated "grave." Both good and bad go there. "What man can live and not see death? Can he deliver his life from the power of the grave [sheol]?" (Psalm 89:48). The godly man Job said, "If I wait, the grave [sheol] is mine house" (Job 17:13 KJV). The psalmist wrote, "The wicked shall be turned into hell [sheol]" (Psalm 9:17). In the New Testament, the word "hell" is translated from the three following Greek words:

1. Once from the root tartaros, which means "a dark abyss." (See Liddell and Scott's Greek Lexicon.) This word is used in connection with the casting out of the evil angels from heaven down "into chains of darkness." There is no idea of fire or torment in the word. The passage specifically declares that these angels were "reserved for judgment." It is a future event. (See 2 Peter 2:4; Revelation 12:7–10.) Following are the New Testament references in which the word "hell" is used:

a. From tartaros (2 Peter 2:4).

b. From hades (Matthew 11:23; 16:18; Luke 10:15; 16:23; Acts 2:27, 31; Revelation 1:18; 6:13; 20:13, 14.

c. From gehenna, or as it is sometimes transliterated, geenna (Matthew 5:22, 29, 30; 10:28; 18:9; 23:15, 33; Mark 9:43, 45, 47; Luke 12:5; James 3:6.

2. Ten times from hades, which means "the nether world, the grave, death." (See Liddell and Scott's Greek Lexicon.) Hades

describes the same place as sheol. This is evident from these two facts:

a. The Septuagint, the ancient Greek translation of the Old Testament, translates sheol as hades almost without exception.

b. In quoting the Old Testament prophecy regarding Christ: "Thou wilt not leave my soul in hell [sheol]," the New Testament writer wrote, "hell [hades]." (See Psalm 16:10; Acts 2:27.)

When the word "hell" translated from hades appears in the New Testament, the reader should not understand it to mean the exclusive abode of the wicked or a place of fire and brimstone, because:

a. The primary definition of hades, as already noted, does not demand such an understanding of the word.

b. The Old Testament speaks of the righteous as well as the wicked going down to sheol. We have also shown that hades describes the same place or state. Did the ancient patriarchs go down into a place of flames?

c. The New Testament speaks of Christ being in hades. (See Acts 2:27.) In order to be consistent, most of those who believe in the doctrine of disembodied souls and present-burning hell-fire, feel forced to interpret this text in Acts to mean that Christ's disembodied soul went down into hellfire when He died on the cross, though at other times they endeavor to prove from Luke 23:43, 46 that Christ went up to God when He died. Both positions certainly cannot be right. The fact is that neither is correct...

We may view Acts 2:27 as showing that hades means simply the abode of the dead and thus in no way connected with fire or torment. We conclude this also from 1 Corinthians 15:55 KJV, in which the word "grave" is a translation of hades and describes that over which the righteous are finally victorious at the resurrection. Incidentally, 1 Corinthians 15:55 is a quotation from the Old Testament (Hosea 13:14), where we find the equivalent word sheol employed. Also, in Revelation 20:13, the translators of the King James Version indicated that "hell" may be properly translated "grave;" where hell is given in the text, the margin reads, "the grave."

- Twelve times from gehenna, or geenna. This is the Greek equivalent of the Hebrew word hinnom, the name of a valley near Jerusalem "used as a place to cast carcasses of animals and malefactors, which were consumed by fire constantly kept up." (See Liddell and Scott's Greek Lexicon.) Thus, gehenna is the only one of those words translated "hell" in the Bible, that has any idea of fire or torment resident in it. Now, in connection with the twelve times gehenna is used, two facts stand out:

1. The body as well as the soul is said to be "cast into hell." Twice is the phrase used, "the whole body." (See Matt. 5:29, 30.)

2. In not one of the twelve instances does the text tell when the wicked will be "cast into hell." The fiery judgment is described only as a future event.

However, these two facts contain evidence that this future event does not follow immediately after death. The "whole body" is not cast into the flames at death, and there is no suggestion in the texts that the soul is cast in at one time and the body at another. The immortal soul doctrine, by defining "soul" as the real person and the body as but a fleshly prison house, asks us to believe that the real person goes immediately at death to hellfire, and then at some distant future date God raises his body, which has turned to dust, and consigns it to the fires. We reject such an irrational and unscriptural conclusion by understanding the reference to soul and body to mean the whole person, viewed physically and mentally in his entirety —"the whole body." But when are persons cast bodily into the judgment fires? At the last great judgment day, when the wicked dead have been raised, judged guilty, and "cast into the lake of fire" (Revelation 20:11–15).

The only place in the Bible where fire or torment is coupled with hades is in Luke 16:23. This is in the parable of the rich man and Lazarus. It is an accepted rule in theology that doctrines should not be based upon parables. It is even more questionable to attempt to discover the real meaning of a word by its setting in a parable or allegory. Note that in Revelation 20:15, the wicked are "cast into" the fire, describing the act of hurling an object into the flames. Further, the very same word "cast" (even in the original Greek) is repeatedly used in the various gehenna texts. In no less than six of these texts we read, "Cast into hell [gehenna]." (See also Matthew 25:31, 41 regarding the time when the wicked are consigned to the judgment flames.)

We conclude that the Bible does not support the idea that the wicked go into the flames of hell at death, but that this day is still in the future.

What does Everlasting fire mean?

Matthew 25:41 speaks of "everlasting fire" for the wicked. Does it go out? According to the Bible, it does. We must let the Bible explain itself. Sodom and Gomorrah were destroyed with everlasting, or eternal, fire (Jude 7), and that fire turned these ancient cities "into ashes" as a warning to "those who afterward would live ungodly" (2 Peter 2:6). These cities are not burning today. The fire went out after everything was burned up. Likewise, everlasting fire will go out after it has turned the wicked to ashes (Malachi 4:3). The effect of the fire is everlasting, but not the burning itself.

Doesn't Matthew 25:46 say the wicked will receive "everlasting punishment"?

Notice the word is punishment, not punishing. Punishing would be continuous, while punishment is one act. The punishment of the wicked is death, and this death is everlasting. The Bible speaks of the wicked being tormented "forever"—doesn't it? The term "forever," as used in the Bible, means simply a period of time, limited or unlimited. It is used 56 times in the Bible in connection with things that have already ended. It is like the word "tall," which means something different when describing people, trees, or mountains. In Jonah 2:6, "forever" means "three days and nights." (See also Jonah 1:17.) In Deuteronomy 23:3, "forever" means 10 generations. It can also mean "as long as he lives," or "to death." (See 1 Samuel 1:22, 28; Exodus 21:6; Psalm 48:14.) So, the wicked will burn in the fire as long as they live, or until death. This fiery consequence of sin will vary according to the degree of sins for each individual, but after the punishment, the fire will go out.

The teaching of eternal torment has done more to drive people to atheism and insanity than any other invention of the devil. It is slander upon the loving character of a tender, gracious heavenly Father and has done untold harm to the Christian cause.

Death, Not Eternal Torment

The Bible tells us that "the wages of sin is"—not eternal life in hellfire—but "death" (Romans 6:23), the same result God assured Adam and Eve would be theirs if they ate the forbidden fruit. The prophet Ezekiel stated clearly that "the soul who sins shall die" (Ezekiel 18:4), and a plethora of other Bible passages endorse this position. The prophet Malachi wrote that sinners would burn up as "stubble" and become "ashes under the soles" of the feet of the redeemed (Malachi 4:1, 3). Even the final fate of Satan is explicitly pronounced in Ezekiel 28:18, where the Bible says that the enemy of souls will be reduced to "ashes upon the earth."

Compare that with Psalm 37:10 ("For yet a little while and the wicked shall be no more"); Psalm 68:2 ("as wax melts before the fire, so let the wicked perish at the presence of God"); and other similar verses. Soon you get a clear picture that the purpose of the fires of hell is to eradicate sin and to expunge the universe of its lethal presence. Interestingly, it was the devil who was first to suggest that sinners would not die (Genesis 3:4). A hell where sinners never perish would prove the devil right and make God a liar, who told Eve she would "surely die" as a result of transgression (Genesis 2:17).

Unquenchable fire

The Bible says hellfire will not be quenched and "their worm does not die." (See Mark 9:43–48 and Isaiah 66:24.) Doesn't this show that the soul is immortal? Even if we should agree that "unquenched" means endlessly burning, we would not find it necessary to accept the doctrine that at death an immortal soul is freed from man and lives apart from the body. These texts do not speak of disembodied souls, or spirits, burning. The Bible paints a picture of literal, wicked people at the judgment day being "cast into the lake of fire" (Revelation 20:15).

Christ spoke of the "whole body" being "cast into hell" (Matthew 5:29, 30.) If someone replies that the body would be destroyed by the flames and that the spirit would be left, we ask for the Bible evidence that spirits, or souls, are impervious to fire. Christ declared we should "fear him who is able to destroy both soul and body in hell" (Matthew 10:28). If "destroy" means consumed regarding the body, is it logical to believe that "destroy" means to leave unconsumed regarding the soul?

In Mark 9:43–48, Christ evidently referred to the same judgment fires as those described in Isaiah 66:24, where we read: "They [the righteous] shall go forth and look upon the corpses of the men who have transgressed against Me. For their worm does not die, and their fire is not quenched." We are told in so many words that the agencies of "worm" and "fire" are working, not upon disembodied spirits, but upon bodies—dead bodies.

The word "hell" used in Mark 9:43–48 is from the Greek word gehenna, or geenna. This term is the Greek equivalent of the Hebrew word hinnom, the name of a valley near Jerusalem, "used as a place to cast carcasses of animals and malefactors, which were consumed by fire constantly kept up." (See Liddell and Scott's Greek Lexicon.)

Christ used this valley of Hinnom to teach His hearers the fate awaiting the wicked. Certainly the Jews who heard His words could not possibly have obtained any idea of wicked, disembodied souls suffering endlessly. They saw in Hinnom dead bodies being devoured by flames, or if the flames did not reach them, then by worms, those ever-present agents of destruction and disintegration. The fact that the fires of Hinnom were always kept burning—were "not quenched"—was the surest proof that whatever was cast into them would be consumed. To declare that a fire is kept ever burning and that whatever is cast into it keeps ever living, is to go contrary to the evidence of our senses and of Scripture.

You may ask, If whatever is cast into this fire is completely consumed, why will the fire always be kept burning? The answer is, It will not. A city-wide conflagration once enveloped Chicago. If we should describe that fire by saying that the flames could not be quenched, would you conclude that Chicago is still burning? No—you would understand that the fire raged until it ran out of fuel. Common knowledge makes unnecessary the statement that the fire died down of itself.

It is this natural sense of the word "quench" that the Bible uses. Through the prophet Jeremiah, the Lord declared to the ancient Jews, "I will kindle a fire ... and it shall not be quenched" (Jeremiah 17:27). (The Septuagint, the ancient Greek translation of the Old Testament, uses the same Greek root for "quenched" as is used in Mark 9:43–48.) In 2 Chronicles 36:19–21, we read of this prophecy's literal fulfillment when the Babylonians put the torch to the city. Is that fire still burning? Are those Jewish "palaces" ever consuming, but never quite consumed? Preposterous, you say. Then why should anyone wish to take Christ's statement in Mark 9 and force from it the conclusion that the judgment fire will never end, and then build upon this conclusion that the wicked will be ever consuming but never quite consumed, and then finally perch upon this the conclusion that therefore the wicked have immortal souls?

Each and every one of these conclusions is unwarranted by logic and is contrary to Scripture. The Bible nowhere says that souls are immortal but declares that "the soul who sins shall die" (Ezekiel 18:4). Nowhere does the Bible say that the wicked will be ever consuming; instead it declares that they will become "ashes" (Malachi 4:3).

The Bible does not say that the judgment fires will burn endlessly, for we read that these fires are due to God's setting ablaze this wicked earth, and that following this conflagration He creates "a new earth." (See 2 Peter 3:7–13; Revelation 20:15; 21:1.) There must therefore be an end to the fire, else this earth could not be recreated. The very promise of God to give us a new earth "in which righteousness dwells" is contingent upon there being an end to the judgment fires." [6]

The Rapture

There is a popular belief among Christians that believers will disappear as they are taken to Heaven; with many believing that it happens before the Great Tribulation, some during and others after. Belief in the Rapture is often connected with a belief in the literal coming of the millennium, the 1,000-year rule of Jesus Christ after his return, as mentioned in chapter 20 of The Revelation to John, although there are also amillennial interpretations of the belief that reject that notion...Finally, dispensationalism, the notion that God periodically enters into a new covenant with his people, has had some influence on the belief, insofar as some believers in the Rapture consider themselves to be dispensationalists. [7] The "Left Behind" series of books by Tim LaHaye is the most well known proponent of the Pre-tribulation Rapture.

What does the Bible say?

Just as the doctrine of hell fire has caused great misrepresentation of God, this teaching of people being raptured secretly before the tribulation might be a source of false security that there will be a way of escape from what is coming if the Bible does not support it. As I write this, I come across many believers who seeing the signs of the times are saying they are glad they will be gone before the Tribulation. This teaching causes many to have a false security leading to lukewarm Christians without the need for great search of heart, which would be required to be able to endure an impending great Tribulation soon to be upon us. I will quote extensively from the book The Secret Rapture by Joe Crews who explains it well.

"The secret rapture doctrine contradicts the words of Christ in Matthew chapter 13 when He said that the wheat and tares would grow together until the "end of the world" and then would be separated. According to the two-stage teaching of His coming, both groups would not grow together until the end of the world. The righteous would be separated from the wicked seven years before the end. And what about the promise of the resurrection? Christ said, concerning the righteous, "And I will raise him up at the last day" (John 6:40). No one denies that this means the last day of the world. Yet Paul declares that the saints are caught up to meet the Lord at the same time the dead in Christ are raised. He says, "For the Lord himself shall descend from heaven with a shout, with the voice of the archangel, and with the trump of God: and the dead in Christ shall rise first: Then we which are alive and remain shall be caught up together with them in the clouds to meet the Lord in the air" (1 Thessalonians 4:16, 17).

Please keep in mind that Jesus called this resurrection the "last day." But how could it be the "last day" if this gathering of the saints takes place seven years before the end of the world? And how could the "last trump" sound if it really wasn't the very last moment of time?

Can you imagine the graves opening and the righteous rising and no one knowing that it had occurred? And consider this additional testimony of the Word of God:

Revelation 6:16,17 When the wicked see Christ come, they cry out to the rocks and mountains, "Fall on us, and hide us from the face of him that sitteth on the throne, and from the wrath of the Lamb: For the great day of his wrath is come; and who shall be able to stand?"

Matthew 24:27 "For as the lightning cometh out of the east, and shineth even unto the west; so shall also the coming of the Son of man be."

1 Corinthians 15:52 "For the trumpet shall sound, and the dead shall be raised."

Psalm 50:3 "Our God shall come, and shall not keep silence."

Revelation 1:7 "Every eye shall see him. "

Matthew 24:30 "Then shall all the tribes of the earth mourn, and they shall see the Son of man coming in the clouds of heaven with power and great glory."

Matthew 24:31 "He shall send his angels with a great sound of a trumpet, and they shall gather together his elect from the four winds, from one end of heaven to the other." (This is clearly the time when Christ comes to gather His saints.)

To say that the second coming of Christ to gather His saints will be secret, in view of these clear texts of Scripture, and in the absence of any text that even hints at His coming being secret, is to deny the Bible as the Word of God. In an attempt to uphold their contrived theory, the rapturists quote Matthew 24:40, 41 out of context. Notice this entire passage:

"But as the days of Noe were, so shall also the coming of the Son of man be. For as in the days that were before the flood they were eating and drinking, marrying and giving in marriage, until the day that Noe entered into the ark, And knew not until the flood came, and took them all away; so shall also the coming of the Son of man be. Then shall two be in the field; the one shall be taken, and the other left. Two women shall be grinding at the mill; the one shall be taken, and the other left" (Matthew 24:37-41).

Jesus is clearly drawing a parallel between the second coming and the days of Noah. Those who entered the ark in Noah's day were saved, and those who refused to enter the ark were left outside. But what were they left for? For another chance? No, obviously they were left to be destroyed by the Flood. So, says Jesus, will it be when He comes at the end of the world. One will be taken to heaven with Jesus, and the other will be left for destruction. Verse 51 makes clear what will happen to those who are left: "And shall cut him asunder, and appoint him his portion with the hypocrites: there shall be weeping and gnashing of teeth." Read Luke 17:26-37 for Luke's parallel account of these same words of Jesus. In verse 36, this statement is made: "Two men shall be in the field; the one shall be taken, and the other left." Now notice verse 37 and the question the disciples asked: "And they answered and said unto him, Where, Lord?" They wanted to know where those who didn't go to heaven were going to be left. Notice Jesus' clear answer: "And he said unto them, Wheresoever the body is, thither will the eagles be gathered together."

Take note how Jesus taught that the bodies of the wicked are going to be left on the ground for the eagles to consume. Scripture is too plain to be misunderstood. Only as we accept all that the Bible says can we be safe from such deceptive teachings that are confusing millions of sincere Christians today concerning this most glorious event of all ages, the second coming of Jesus Christ.

Now, I realize that the rapturists hang onto the texts that liken the Lord's coming to "a thief in the night." They assume that this must be a quiet, secret coming. But does it really mean that? Let's show that it definitely does not. Here is one of those texts in 2 Peter 3: 10: "The day of the Lord will come as a thief in the night; in the which the heavens shall pass away with a great noise, and the elements shall melt with fervent heat." Obviously the "thief" part has nothing to do with secrecy because the heavens will pass away with a great noise! And if coming "as a thief" is the secret rapture which takes place seven years before the end of the world, how can the heavens and earth "pass away," as Peter describes it? The heavens and earth could not pass away seven years before the world ends – that is the end!

The fact is that Jesus Himself explained clearly just how a thief's coming could be related to His coming: "Watch therefore: for ye know not what hour your Lord doth come. But know this, that if the goodman of the house had known in what watch the thief would come, he would have watched, and would not have suffered his house to be broken up" (Matthew 24:42, 43). There it is, so plain and simple! The thief would come unexpectedly when the owners were not looking for a thief. In the same way, His coming would take people by surprise. They would not be watching or looking for it.

Will Christ Return in Two Phases?

The dispensationalists teach that the two separate stages of Christ's coming are indicated "in the Greek." They argue that there will first be the rapture (parousia), a secret coming; then seven years later will be the revelation (apokalupsis), His coming in power and glory. But, actually, instead of teaching two separate events, the Greek terms are used interchangeably in the Bible. They give no indication of a seven-year interval.

For example, Paul uses the word "parousia" in the famous rapture chapter of 1 Thessalonians 4 in speaking of the coming of our Lord and our gathering together unto Him. He then goes right on to show that this "parousia" will destroy the man of sin. Speaking of the Antichrist, Paul says, "whom the Lord shall ... destroy with the brightness of his coming [parousia]" (2 Thessalonians 2:8). These texts clearly describe the coming (parousia) of Christ as taking place after the reign of the man of sin, not as an escape rapture before the reign of the Antichrist begins.

The other Greek word "apokalupsis" (revelation) is used in a way that indicates it is not a separate coming from the time the believers are gathered up. Peter said to "be sober, and hope to the end for the grace that is to be brought unto you at the revelation [apokalupsis] of Jesus Christ" (1 Peter 1:13). Why would Christians be exhorted to keep hoping to the very end of the world for the grace brought through the revelation of Christ if their real hope was a secret rapture seven years before the revelation?

Now look at some verses that prove beyond a doubt that the two words "parousia" and "apokalupsis" refer to the same event. In Matthew 24:37 we read, "But as the days of Noe were, so shall also the coming [parousia] of the Son of man be." Luke's account of the same passage says "As it was in the days of Noe ... Even thus shall it be in the day when the Son of man is revealed [apokalupsis]" (Luke 17:26, 30). This shows that the coming (parousia) of Christ and the revelation (apokalupsis) of Christ are the same event. There is absolutely no basis for placing seven years in between.

Many dispensationalist teachers actually claim that the rapture is not really the "coming" of Jesus at all. They say His coming is when Christ returns in power seven years after the rapture. But what a contradictory, confusing explanation that is! The fact is that there are many Scriptures that admonish Christians to wait and watch for the coming of the Lord. For example, James 5:7 says, "Be patient therefore, brethren, unto the coming of the Lord." But why should Christians need to be patient unto the coming of the Lord if there is to be a secret rapture to take them to heaven seven years before His coming?

Strange as it may seem, this whole counterfeit secret rapture is built upon a constant repetition of words and ideas that are not found in the Bible at all. But they have been repeated so often that millions have assumed that they must be soundly biblical. Let's take a look at some of the texts that have been used to support the doctrine of a two-phase coming of Christ. And please notice that none of the verses actually say what some try to read into them. In fact, it is only after a person has already assumed that Christ will return in two separate comings that these verses could even suggest the idea.

Revelation 3:10 is often quoted to try to prove that the righteous will be taken out of the world before the tribulation. "Because thou hast kept the word of my patience, I also will keep thee from the hour of temptation, which shall come upon all the world, to try them that dwell upon the earth." It is immediately obvious that this text does not speak of the righteous leaving this world at all. Jesus completely clarified the meaning by something He said in John 17:6, 15 which sounds very similar. "They have kept thy word. O I pray not that thou shouldest take them out of the world but that thou shouldest keep them from the evil." Don't miss the significance of the term "kept the word" in both these texts. Both statements are talking about the same group of people - the faithful ones.

Now if those who "kept the word" can be "kept from the evil" of the world without being taken out of the world, why should we suppose that a special coming and secret rapture is required for those who "kept the word" to be "kept from the hour of temptation"? Whatever else may be taught in Revelation 3:10, it is evident that no extra coming of Christ is indicated.

True biblical doctrine must be based upon clear statements of what the entire Bible teaches on a subject and not upon verses that offer only veiled inferences. Luke 21:36 is an example of that very thing. Jesus said to His disciples, "Pray always, that ye may be accounted worthy to escape all these things that shall come to pass." How? By a secret rapture to take them to heaven seven years before the end of the world? Definitely not, for in the prayer of Jesus we read, "I pray not that thou shouldest take them out of the world, but that thou shouldest keep them from the evil." When He told them to "pray ... to escape," He must have meant the same as when He prayed, "I pray not ... take them out of the world but ... keep them." This rules out a secret rapture entirely. The text that is used to prove the rapture is seen actually to forbid the saints being taken out of this world during the time of trouble.

The Seven-Year Tribulation

Since so much rapturist theology revolves around the seven-year period, one would assume that the Bible must speak frequently of such a time period. But not so. There is not one single scriptural reference that ties the seven years to the end of the world or the coming of Christ. Most rapturist literature mentions the seven-year tribulation period without offering any Bible proof or explanation. Millions have assumed that it must be so well documented that no proof is needed. In fact, the opposite is true. There just isn't any evidence to give.

Most Bible students are amazed to learn that the rapturists try to justify their seven years by lifting a prophecy of Daniel completely out of its context. In Daniel 9:24-27 God made a daring prophecy concerning the probation of the nation of Israel. He said to Daniel, "Seventy weeks ['weeks of years' RSV] are determined upon thy people ... to finish the transgression, and to make an end of sins" (v. 24). Please notice that God was going to allow Daniel's people seventy weeks to see what they would do with the Messiah when He appeared. The seventy weeks are prophetic time, and each day represents a literal year (Ezekiel 4:6). So the seventy weeks would be a literal period of 490 years, after which the Israelites would no longer be God's people. They would be rejected as a nation because of their rejection of the Messiah.

Don't miss the point in Daniel 9:25 that the prophecy of the seventy weeks was to begin with the decree to restore and build Jerusalem. That well-known date is 457 B.C., when Artaxerxes sent out the decree (Ezra 7:13). From that date, 457 B.C., the Jews would have exactly 490 years to finish filling up their cup of iniquity by rejecting the Messiah. That 490-year probation ended in A.D. 34, and the Jews ceased to be God's chosen people. Daniel 9:25 says that the Messiah would be anointed after sixty-nine of those prophetic weeks had passed by. That would be 483 years from the decree date of 457

B.C. It takes no mathematician to figure the end of that prediction. It brings us to the year A.D. 27, the very year that Jesus was baptized by John and the Holy Spirit anointed Him for His ministry. Since "Messiah" means" Anointed One," this had to be the fulfillment of Daniel's prophecy that the Messiah would appear in A.D 27.

Now mark this fact: seventy weeks were assigned to the Jewish probation, but Christ appeared as the Messiah after sixty-nine weeks. That leaves the seventieth week for Christ to minister before the Jews' probation ended. What was to happen in the seventieth week? Daniel 9:27 tells us, "And he shall confirm the covenant with many for one week: and in the midst of the week he shall cause the sacrifice and the oblation to cease."

The midst of the week would be three and a half prophetic days (literal years) from His baptism. And according to the Bible, the ministry of Jesus lasted for three and a half years. In the spring of A.D. 31 He was crucified. The veil of the temple was rent (Matthew 27:51), signifying the end of sacrifices. By His death He caused them to cease. Another three and a half years would lead up to the end of the seventy weeks and the end of Jewish probation. During that three and a half years the disciples labored largely for the Jews. But in A.D. 34 the seventy weeks ended; Stephen was stoned and the gospel began to go to the Gentiles (Acts 8:4). The Jews had rejected the gospel message and were no longer God's people - just as Daniel had predicted. Henceforth they could be saved only as individuals, in exactly the same way as the Gentiles. As a nation, they had been rejected as the chosen people. Here is the way the Bible describes that rejection:

Matthew21:43 "The kingdom of God shall be taken from you."

Matthew 21:19 "And when he saw a fig tree in the way, he came to it, and found nothing thereon, but leaves only, and said unto it, Let no fruit grow on thee henceforward for ever. And presently the fig tree withered away." (The fig tree was a symbol of the Jewish nation.)

Matthew 23:38 "Behold, your house is left unto you desolate."

Galatians 3:28 "There is neither Jew nor Greek, there is neither bond nor free, there is neither male nor female: for ye are all one in Christ Jesus."

Galatians 3:29 "And if ye be Christ's, then are ye Abraham's seed, and heirs according to the promise."

Romans 10:12 "For there is no difference between the Jew and the Greek: for the same Lord over all is rich unto all that call upon him."

Romans 9:6-8 "For they are not all Israel, which are of Israel: Neither, because they are the seed of Abraham, are they all children; but, In Isaac shall thy seed be called. That is, They which are ... the children of the promise are counted for the seed." (The New Testament teaches the acceptance of spiritual Israel, and the rejection of physical Israel and the children of the flesh.)

Romans 2:28, 29 "For he is not a Jew, which is one outwardly; neither is that circumcision, which is outward in the flesh: But he is a Jew, which is one inwardly; and circumcision is that of the heart, in the spirit, and not in the letter."

Acts 13:46 "It was necessary that the word of God should first have been spoken to you: but seeing ye put it from you, and judge yourselves unworthy of everlasting life, lo, we turn to the Gentiles."

The rapturists get their seven years' tribulation by lifting that seventieth week of Daniel's prophecy completely out of its context and shoving it far into the future. They claim it will be fulfilled after Christ comes to snatch away the righteous secretly. Incredible? Absolutely! But they must grasp desperately for some text to support their seven years. They agree that the sixty-nine weeks of Daniel 9:25 refer to the period before Christ's first advent, but then they insert a 2,000-year gap before the seventieth week is fulfilled. They allot 69 weeks plus 2,000 years plus one week, or a total of 2,490 years. By this devious manipulation of God's Word, the rapturists believe they have extended the Jewish probation; and based upon this, they teach that all the fleshly Jews will be saved in a great second chance after the "secret rapture" takes place.

The tragedy of the rapture theory is that it takes these beautiful verses of Daniel 9:24-27 that predict the coming of Jesus, His baptism and crucifixion, and apply them to Antichrist. They do this by stating that it is Antichrist that causes the sacrifice and oblation to cease after three and one-half years. But Daniel states that it is Jesus who caused the sacrificial system of the Jews to cease when He died on the cross. A misinterpretation that confuses something Christ has done, and applies it to the devil instead, is certainly a tragic occurrence. And yet this is the only way one can arrive at a seven-year tribulation period. How sad!

When Does the Antichrist Appear?

Now we are brought to focus on the most glaring inconsistency of the rapture theory, and that is that the Antichrist will not appear until after the saints are caught away - seven years before the end of the world. Paul settles the entire matter for us in the first few verses of 2 Thessalonians chapter 2. "Now we beseech you, brethren, by the coming of our Lord Jesus Christ, and by our gathering together unto him, That ye be not soon shaken in mind, or be troubled, neither by spirit, nor by word, nor by letter as from us, as that the day of Christ is at hand. Let no man deceive you by any means: for that day [of our gathering together unto Him] shall not come, except there come a falling away first, and that man of sin [Antichrist] be revealed, the son of perdition; Who opposeth and exalteth himself above all that is called God, or that is worshipped; so that he as God sitteth in the temple of God, shewing himself that he is God" (vs. 1-4).

The words of Paul are so plain that it is difficult to comment on them. How can they be plainer? Christ's coming will not take place "except there come a falling away first, and that man of sin be revealed." Show these words to any child who has learned to read; show them to anyone not prejudiced by "private" interpretations, and he will say, "These verses say that the man of sin (Antichrist) is going to be revealed before Jesus comes."

Paul is not referring to some superman suddenly to appear 2,000 years after his epistles. He wrote, "For the mystery of iniquity doth already work" (v. 7). While Paul lived, he combated the emerging spirit of the Antichrist. By the sixth century A.D., Antichrist had matured. The crowning act in the great drama of deception, however, occurs just before the return of Christ: "And then shall that Wicked be revealed, whom the Lord shall consume with the spirit of his mouth, and shall destroy with the brightness of his coming.'" Verse 8. This clearly states that Antichrist will be destroyed when Christ comes. He does not arrive after the Second Advent.

And here's the crowning clarification in this whole thing. Revelation 20:4 assures us that some of those who are raised in the first resurrection will be those who refused to worship the beast and receive his mark! How completely this demolishes the futuristic school of prophetic interpretation is evident, for they claim that the emergence of the Antichrist and the imposition of his mark are to be looked for after the first resurrection and what they call the secret rapture. But these verses declare that some of those who come up in the "first resurrection," when Christ comes the second time, have already refused to worship the Antichrist or receive his mark! Thus, the Antichrist must have already been on the stage of action carrying on his oppressive work before the "first resurrection" and well before the second coming of Jesus.

Without attempting to establish the identity of Antichrist at this point, let us notice how this teaching - that the Antichrist will come in the future - originated. At the time of the Reformation, most of the reformers understood the prophecy of the Antichrist to refer to the great apostate system of Romanism that developed during the Middle Ages. Of course, Rome did not appreciate this interpretation. Please notice Rome's course of action to nullify this interpretation:

"So great a hold did the conviction that the Papacy was the Antichrist gain upon the minds of men, that Rome at last saw she must bestir herself, and try, by putting forth other systems of interpretation, to counteract the identification of the Papacy with the Antichrist.

"Accordingly, toward the close of the century of the Reformation, two of the most learned doctors set themselves to the task, each endeavoring by different means to accomplish the same end, namely, that of diverting men's minds from perceiving the fulfillment of the prophecies of the Antichrist in the papal system. The Jesuit Alcazar devoted himself to bring into prominence the preterist method of interpretation, ... and thus endeavored to show that the prophecies of Antichrist were fulfilled before the popes ever ruled in Rome, and therefore could not apply to the Papacy.

"On the other hand, the Jesuit Ribera tried to set aside the application of these prophecies to the papal power by bringing out the futurist system, which asserts that these prophecies refer properly, not to the career of the Papacy, but to some future supernatural individual, who is yet to appear, and continue in power for three and a half years. Thus, as Alford says, the Jesuit Ribera, about A.D. 1580, may be regarded as the founder of the futurist system of modern times.

"It is a matter for deep regret that those who advocate the futurist system at the present day, Protestants as they are for the most part, are really playing into the hands of Rome, and helping to screen the Papacy from detection as the Antichrist."

Thus, the whole theory of the secret rapture with its future Antichrist had its origin with the Jesuits in an attempt to take the blame off the Papacy.

The origin of the two-phase coming of Christ has an equally unsavory history. It was not until around the year 1830 that this view began to be taught. In the Scottish church pastored by Edward Irving, a Miss Margaret McDonald gave what was believed at the time to be an inspired utterance. She spoke of the visible, open, and glorious second coming of Christ. But as the utterance continued, she spoke of another coming of Christ - a secret and special coming in which those who were truly ready would be raptured.

However, it was John Nelson Darby - Brethren preacher and diligent writer of the time in England - who was largely responsible for introducing this new teaching on a large scale. The teaching spread to the United States in the 1850s and 1860s, where it was to receive its biggest boost when Cyrus Ingerson Scofield, a strong believer in Darby's teachings, incorporated it into the notes of his Scofield Reference Bible, which was published in 1909. Since that time, this view has been widely accepted - often by people who are completely unaware that this was not the belief held by Christians over the centuries. Many fine Christians hold his view today who have never questioned its authority.

Oswald Smith, noted minister and author of Toronto, says in his booklet Tribulation or Rapture - Which? that he once held the two-stage teaching, but that when he began to search the Scriptures for himself, he discovered that there is not a single verse in the Bible to uphold this view. He confessed: "I had been taught that the Greek word 'parousia' always referred to the Rapture and that other words were used for the coming of Christ in glory ... but I found that this is not true. ... We might go through all the writers of the New Testament, and we would fail to discover any indication of the so-called 'two stages' of our Lord's coming ... That theory had to be invented by man. Search and see. There is no verse in the Bible that even mentions it."

The Second Chance

Finally, the secret rapturists claim that during the tribulation those not raptured will be given another chance to be saved. Let it be categorically stated that nowhere does Scripture speak of a second chance, nor does the Bible anywhere speak of people being saved after Jesus comes. This is just another manmade doctrine that is indeed pleasing to the carnal heart of man. Actually, the Bible teaches the opposite. Notice these clear texts of Scripture:

2 Corinthians 6:2 "Behold, now is the accepted time; behold, now is the day of salvation."

Revelation 22:11, 12 "He that is unjust, let him be unjust still: and he which is filthy, let him be filthy still: and he that is righteous, let him be righteous still: and he that is holy, let him be holy still. And, behold, I come quickly; and my reward is with me." (Evidently probation closes just prior to the Second Advent.)

Jeremiah 8:20 "The harvest (day of second coming) is past, the summer is ended, and we are not saved..."

When Jesus and His holy angels appear, then "before him shall be gathered all nations" (Matthew 25:32). There will only be two classes in that great company. The destiny of each has been set by what he did before the coming of Christ." [8]

How these beliefs become popular

The devil's agenda has been to be worshiped, starting with his rebellion in Heaven and continuing with the fall of our first parents and how we inherited the sinful nature from them. When we subscribe to his lies in the different forms they come, we give him attention which is due to God alone. That is why the devil lies because if he was open about his intentions, people would see him for who he is. He lies so he can be worshiped indirectly through the different philosophies, beliefs and practices, and strives to substitute lies for the truth in every way.

References

1. Ellen G. White, The Great Controversy (1888). pp. 551-2.
2. https://www.britannica.com/topic/reincarnation
3. https://www.britannica.com/topic/purgatory-Roman-Catholicism
4. https://www.catholic.com/tract/purgatory
5. https://www.helltruth.com/history/id/1857/t/sinners-in-the-hands-of-an-angry-god-

6. https://www.helltruth.com/
7. https://www.britannica.com/topic/Rapture-the
8. https: //www.amazingfacts.org/ media-library/ book/e/74/t/the-secret-rapture

20
COME OUT OF HER MY PEOPLE!

We have touched on so many things and you might be wondering if it is that important to know or understand these things. My goal in sharing all this is so that you understand what God expects of each and every one of us. He is calling all of us to repentance and if we heed the call, there are certain beliefs or practices that are not compatible with who He is. We get an idea of this in the following account of the two brothers, Cain and Abel:

2 ...Now Abel was a keeper of sheep, but Cain was a tiller of the ground.

3 And [c]in the process of time it came to pass that Cain brought an offering of the fruit of the ground to the Lord.

4 Abel also brought of the firstborn of his flock and of their fat. And the Lord respected Abel and his offering,

5 but He did not respect Cain and his offering. And Cain was very angry, and his countenance fell.

6 So the Lord said to Cain, "Why are you angry? And why has your countenance fallen?

7 If you do well, will you not be accepted? And if you do not do well, sin lies at the door. And its desire is [d]for you, but you should rule over it." Genesis 4:1-7.

In this account we learn that both of them made offerings to God but Cain's was not accepted. Not much detail is given, but we get the idea that God was not happy because Cain offered not according to God's expectation. On top of offering the wrong way, he was angry at God for not accepting his offering. We get an idea of Cain's character, that he wanted to do things his way; that he wanted God to conform to his way of doing things and not the other way around.

Cain and Abel as types

Cain is a type of those who are living today who have the same spirit and desire to do things their way and not God's, even when they know what He expects from them. Abel typifies those today who when they learn what He expects, strive to do it living obedient lives. In verse 7 above, God says "if you do not do well, sin lies at the door. And its desire is for you, but you should rule over it." Doing things any other way other than God's way leads to sin. The two brothers typify the two groups which will exist just before Christ's return. Those who live lives according to false teachings, doctrines and philosophies as we have learned about; get the mark of the beast because "all who dwell on the earth will worship him, whose names have not been written in the Book of Life of the Lamb" Revelation 13:8. They are "not found written in the Book of Life.."and "cast into the lake of fire". Revelation 20:15. Those on the other hand who live their lives according to God's Word avoid the mark of the beast and; "Blessed are those who do His commandments, that they may have the right to the tree of life, and may enter through the gates into the city." Revelation 22:14. Jesus alludes to there being only two groups in the end:

31 "When the Son of Man comes in His glory, and all the [c]holy angels with Him, then He will sit on the throne of His glory.

32 All the nations will be gathered before Him, and He will separate them one from another, as a shepherd divides his sheep from the goats.

33 And He will set the sheep on His right hand, but the goats on the left.

34 Then the King will say to those on His right hand, 'Come, you blessed of My Father, inherit the kingdom prepared for you from the foundation of the world…

41 "Then He will also say to those on the left hand, 'Depart from Me, you cursed, into the everlasting fire prepared for the devil and his angels. Matthew 25:31-33.

The mark of the beast is imminent and we are the generation more than likely to experience the enforcement of it. The only way to escape it is to have your name written in the Book of Life. Those who choose to be like Abel, will be overcomers and avoid the mark, finally inheriting the Kingdom of God and eternal life. The ones who live their own way will get the mark, and share the same fate as the devil and his demons, which is the lake of fire resulting in eternal death.

Importance of separating from all false teachings

In the book of Revelation chapter 14, we learn of the three Angels who proclaim the Truth:

6 Then I saw another angel flying in the midst of heaven, having the everlasting gospel to preach to those who dwell on the earth—to every nation, tribe, tongue, and people—

7 saying with a loud voice, "Fear God and give glory to Him, for the hour of His judgment has come; and worship Him who made heaven and earth, the sea and springs of water."

The first angel's message is one to fear God out of reverence for Him and His ways, giving glory to Him, because Judgement is upon us. He made everything as we know and we ought to revere Him and give glory to Him as our Creator. We have to stop believing in theories of evolution, Big Bang theory, etc, and to acknowledge Him as our Creator.

8 And another angel followed, saying, "Babylon[f] is fallen, is fallen, that great city, because she has made all nations drink of the wine of the wrath of her fornication."

Babylon encompasses all that is anti-Christ, past, present and future, whether it be religious systems like the Papacy, philosophies, false teachings, pagan practices and even economic and political systems like this imminent New World Order which is looking forward to the appearance of Satan as the false Christ. It is all encompassing because, "in her was found the blood of prophets and saints, and of all who were slain on the earth." Revelation 18:24. This Babylon system of false worship is and will be responsible for all who have been and will be slain, from Abel all the way down through time to the last believer who will be martyred before Christ returns.

9 Then a third angel followed them, saying with a loud voice, "If anyone worships the beast and his image, and receives his mark on his forehead or on his hand,

10 he himself shall also drink of the wine of the wrath of God, which is poured out full strength into the cup of His indignation. He shall be tormented with fire and brimstone in the presence of the holy angels and in the presence of the Lamb.

11 And the smoke of their torment ascends forever and ever; and they have no rest day or night, who worship the beast and his image, and whoever receives the mark of his name."

We are warned not to get the mark of the beast, which leads to ending up in the lake of fire. We learned in the chapter on New Age Spirituality that all who believe in just getting along with others will unite based on this principle which leads them to being susceptible to the overpowering delusion of Satan appearing as the false Christ. All those who fall prey to this lie will not see a problem of being global citizens in the New World Order with him as their leader, as they will be the enlightened ones according to New Age spirituality. We are to separate from the system entirely as we are warned:

4 ..."Come out of her (Babylon), my people, lest you share in her sins, and lest you receive of her plagues.

5 For her sins [c]have reached to heaven, and God has remembered her iniquities. Revelation 18:4-5.

Being a part of the New World Order, means one is a willing participant in a system deeply rooted in every manner of false worship, which will use economic and political power so "all, both small and great, rich and poor, free and slave, to receive a mark on their right hand or on their foreheads, and that no one may buy or sell except one who has [g]the mark or the name of the beast, or the number of his name." Revelation 13:16-17. Separate yourself from anything which is incompatible with God, and this can only be achieved by accepting Christ and living a new life by His strength as written:

20 I have been crucified with Christ; it is no longer I who live, but Christ lives in me; and the life which I now live in the flesh I live by faith in the Son of God, who loved me and gave Himself for me. Galatians 2:20.

19
FAITH

Exercise is one of the laws of health, just as much as it is a law of spiritual health. One of the benefits of exercise is endurance. Endurance builds up over time with consistent exercise. What might have seemed difficult in the beginning will not be as one continues to exercise and keeps up with it. The same thing happens with spiritual health. What is exercise for the soul? It is faith! Just as a baby can not eat solid food at first until older, "as newborn babes, desire the pure milk of the word, that you may grow [a]thereby..." 1 Peter 2:2. One has to start with milk of the Word and as they continue to exercise faith or to act upon and believe what the Word says, they grow, as we are encouraged:

13 (for not the hearers of the law are just in the sight of God, but the doers of the law will be justified;...

22 But be doers of the word, and not hearers only, deceiving yourselves.

23 For if anyone is a hearer of the word and not a doer, he is like a man observing his natural face in a mirror;

24 for he observes himself, goes away, and immediately forgets what kind of man he was.

25 But he who looks into the perfect law of liberty and continues in it, and is not a forgetful hearer but a doer of the work, this one will be blessed in what he does. Romans 2:13, James 1:22-25.

Growth comes by actually exercising or practicing what the Word says. Even if one reads, no growth takes place unless one acts on what they've read. Reading the Bible can be just like reading any other book if the reader does not believe what it says. Believing what it says requires an action that confirms the belief. Our actions show whether we have faith or not. If you believe something with your mind but your actions say otherwise, then you don't have faith. Faith can be defined as the actions that show someone's belief and trust in the Word. Only the actions will show if that person truly believes because our actions speak louder than our words.

We can talk about something all day but faith is shown by the actions which are a confirmation of belief in the Word as is written:

19 You believe that there is one God. You do well. Even the demons believe—and tremble!…

18 let us not love in word or in tongue, but in deed and in truth;…

14 What does it profit, my brethren, if someone says he has faith but does not have works? Can faith save him?

15 If a brother or sister is naked and destitute of daily food,

16 and one of you says to them, "Depart in peace, be warmed and filled," but you do not give them the things which are needed for the body, what does it profit?

17 Thus also faith by itself, if it does not have works, is dead.

18 But someone will say, "You have faith, and I have works." Show me your faith without [f]your works, and I will show you my faith by [g]my works. James 2:19; 1 John 3:18; James 2:14-18.

"Faith is the [a]substance of things hoped for, the [b]evidence of things not seen" (Hebrews 11:1) and when one is born-again, challenges come to test whether one will believe in, trust and hold on to an invisible God. There are times when certain things that He requires of us might put us between what seems like a rock and a hard place. Returning tithe and Sabbath keeping are good examples of that. The following verses give a more in-depth look at tithing which you can study later hopefully at your leisure but the quoted verse will help in clarifying the point on growth and faith.

Tithing by faith

8 "Will a man rob God? Yet you have robbed Me! But you say, 'In what way have we robbed You?' In tithes and offerings.

9 You are cursed with a curse, For you have robbed Me, Even this whole nation.

10 Bring all the tithes into the storehouse, That there may be food in My house, And try Me now in this," Says the Lord of hosts, "If I will not open for you the windows of heaven And pour out for you such blessing That there will not be room enough to receive it.

11 "And I will rebuke the devourer for your sakes, So that he will not destroy the fruit of your ground, Nor shall the vine fail to bear fruit for you in the field," Says the Lord of hosts;

12 "And all nations will call you blessed, For you will be a delightful land," Says the Lord of hosts. Malachi 3:8-12.

The tithing system was instituted by God to ensure that the Levites who were the priests (and that was their only work as they were set apart by God to minister in the Sanctuary) would be sustained since they did not have regular jobs or businesses like everyone else (See Numbers 18:21-28). Their sole purpose was to minister to everyone else in the Sanctuary or God's house. A tenth would be required from the increase or gain that all others who worked would have made and that would then be used to sustain the Levites so that they would be wholly devoted to ministering to the rest in God's work and not have to worry about their next meal was going to come from. Modern day Levites would be those who have dedicated their lives to Ministry. Unfortunately, we are not short of hearing stories of Ministries that abuse this system and enrich themselves at the expense of their faithful members. In God's system, the servants in ministry survive but do not get rich off people's tithes. When done right and in moderation, tithes support the employment of Pastors as well as supporting different church ministries that further the spreading of the Gospel.

It is a requirement (see also Malachi 3:6-11) to return tithe but it is one that has a promise full of blessings if obeyed. God indirectly has the rest to take part in His work by supporting it through sustaining those who would have to commit their lives completely to His service. By doing so, His work goes forth and the ones who partake are also blessed in the process. Now, let's put this into perspective in our own lives! You get a paycheck and it is not enough to cover your expenses! Even by withholding the tithe you still fall short of meeting your needs, would it not be a great temptation to doubt God's promise to "prove me now herewith, saith the LORD of hosts, if I will not open you the windows of heaven, and pour you out a blessing, that [there shall] not [be room] enough [to receive it]"?

An invisible God has made a requirement of you to return a portion of what He would have blessed you with and then you look at your circumstances which seem impossible to overcome especially if you subtract His portion. It not only takes faith to believe in God whom you have not seen, but even more to return a portion which He says belongs to Him, especially when you seem to be losing by doing so. Returning tithe in a crisis like this would therefore require more faith and this comes by trusting the promises in His Word and acting upon them. The more one returns tithe even in the face of crises, the more one grows because God somehow delivers as promised and they see that "The entirety of Your word is truth, And every one of Your righteous judgments endures forever." Psalms 119:160.

Sabbath keeping by faith

Another good example is Sabbath keeping. The Sabbath was instituted in Eden, long before the Law was proclaimed on Mt. Sinai. It is one of the Ten Commandments which are the whole law which Christ mentions when asked what the greatest commandments are in the following verses:

36 "Teacher, which is the great commandment in the law?"

37 Jesus said to him, "'You shall love the Lord your God with all your heart, with all your soul, and with all your mind.'

38 This is the first and great commandment.

39 And the second is like it: 'You shall love your neighbor as yourself.'

40 On these two commandments hang all the Law and the Prophets." Matthew 22:36-40.

The 2 greatest commandments are a summary of the Ten Commandments on which they hang. The first 4 commandments are about how we should relate to God and the last 6 to our fellow man. The Sabbath commandment is the fourth and is therefore one of those required in how we should relate to God. Now, to put things into perspective, we are living in hard times! It's hard to get work and anyone would be grateful to get a job in such an economy. What is one to do if they finally manage to get a job but work is mandatory on the Sabbath? Maybe there is a family to feed and bills to pay, you know, the sort of things that don't take vacation when you are unemployed. It would seem crazy for one to turn down a job in such an economy for any reason but especially because one wants to keep the Lord's Sabbath. For one in the situation who believes that keeping the Sabbath is not only a requirement in how we relate to God but a symbol in itself of rest in God's salvation and provisions spiritually and temporally, the promise is given in His Word:

31 Therefore do not worry, saying, 'What shall we eat?' or 'What shall we drink?' or 'What shall we wear?'

32 For after all these things the Gentiles seek. For your heavenly Father knows that you need all these things.

33 But seek first the kingdom of God and His righteousness, and all these things shall be added to you.

34 Therefore do not worry about tomorrow, for tomorrow will worry about its own things. Sufficient for the day is its own trouble. Matthew 6:26-34.

Faith is how we are transformed

Exercising faith in the Word, has a sanctifying effect on our lives in effect transforming us as "How can a young man cleanse his way? By taking heed according to Your word." Psalms 119:9.

An increase in knowledge of God and His will come by prayerfully studying the Word; and an understanding of it along with the desire to act upon that Word by faith, comes by the Spirit. The more we study, understand and practice what we read, the more we grow. Just as a baby grows and first feeds on milk, we also progress from newborns into adults by exercising faith:

13 For everyone who partakes only of milk is unskilled in the word of righteousness, for he is a babe.

14 But solid food belongs to those who are [c]of full age, that is, those who by reason of [d]use have their senses exercised to discern both good and evil. Hebrews 5:13-14.

22
HOLY SPIRIT

Earlier on we read about the Air we breathe as being crucial to our survival. Good air quality promotes good health, but if the air quality is poor, bad health can be the only result. In a Spiritual sense, the Holy Spirit is the Good Air which promotes good Spiritual health. To be alive to God, we have to be in fellowship with Him. We were meant to live forever, until sin came into existence which separated us from God as written,

22 For as in Adam all die, even so in Christ all shall be made alive…

17 For if by the one man's [g]offense death reigned through the one, much more those who receive abundance of grace and of the gift of righteousness will reign in life through the One, Jesus Christ.)

18 Therefore, as through [h]one man's offense judgment came to all men, resulting in condemnation, even so through one[i] Man's righteous act the free gift came to all men, resulting in justification of life.

19 For as by one man's disobedience many were made sinners, so also by one Man's obedience many will be made righteous. 1 Corinthians 15:22; Romans 5:17-19.

Life or living is only found in Jesus Christ as He is the Bridge that connects us to God, and there is no other way, as He said, "I am the way, the truth, and the life. No one comes to the Father except through Me." John 14:6. If Christ is the Bridge from sin back to God, the Holy Spirit guides us to the Bridge so that we can cross back to God, and helps us along the way to make it to this destination. In the absence of the Holy Spirit, we are lost and cannot find the Bridge. Comparing the Holy Spirit to the air we breathe, the Holy Spirit is vital to life and is the only way to live in God's eyes.

It is the only Spirit God intended for us to experience in our lives, just as air is meant to sustain us. We can not live on any other planet so far as we know, but earth was made with the perfect atmosphere to sustain us. In the same sense, the Holy Spirit is literally the only means to bring us to life, and to continue to live in God's eyes.

The Holy Spirit serves to draw us to God, maintain and deepen our relationship with Him. Our Spiritual health is totally dependent on the presence of the Holy Spirit in our lives. A lack in oxygen reaching cells can negatively affect body function, the same way a minimal presence of the Holy Spirit can negatively affect Spiritual health. Partaking more in the Holy Spirit encourages Spiritual growth and strength.

The spirit of disobedience

God created us to be responsive to the Holy Spirit whose work would be to draw us closer to God which pleases Him, "for it is God who works in you both to will and to do for His good pleasure." Philippians 2:13. When we discourage God's presence in our lives, we discourage the Holy Spirit's presence unawares and a different spirit reigns which serves to hinder us from revealing God's character through our lives:

2 in which you once walked according to the [a]course of this world, according to the prince of the power of the air, the spirit who now works in the sons of disobedience,

3 among whom also we all once conducted ourselves in the lusts of our flesh, fulfilling the desires of the flesh and of the mind, and were by nature children of wrath, just as the others. Ephesians 2:2-3.

The prince of the power of the air is the devil. He seizes any opportunity to take over our lives. The same way the Holy Spirit serves to draw us to God helping us to do His will, the spirit of disobedience serves to get us off track and to do his will which is bondage through sin. In general it is the Spirit of disobedience because the devil's motive is to destroy our relationship with God but more specifically, demons or foul spirits can enter and take over one's life to achieve this end because "The thief does not come except to steal, and to kill, and to destroy." John 10:10.

If the Holy Spirit guides us to the right way to take, guiding all the way to the final destination which is back to God as was intended, we find life and can live eternally. Part of the guidance on the right way is enabling us to respond to the wooing of God's love and to have the desire to please Him by obedience which is how we stay on the right way, "for it is God who works in you both to will and to do for His good pleasure." Philippians 2:13. The spirit of disobedience is manifest in the working of the devil and his demons through diverse means to cause us to lose our way back to God, and to actively cause us to stay lost preventing us from being reconciled back to God and from living forever.

If obedience is how we stay on the way back to God, disobedience is how the enemy keeps us lost from our way back to God. The Holy Spirit can be likened to good clean air which is good for Spiritual health, while the spirit of disobedience which is at the heart of the agenda of the devil and his demons in preventing as many as possible from being saved, it is polluted unhealthy air which is bad for spiritual health.

Understanding our true condition

How do we find the right Way, or even begin to recognize that we are lost? We see a world that is falling apart around us. It does not take much to recognize that the world is a very different place, and that things are definitely worsening with time, with the changes being rapid ones. Whether it is the economy, natural disasters, tension among nations, race relations; it is clear to most if not all of us that these are strange times we are living in because "there will be signs in the sun, in the moon, and in the stars; and on the earth distress of nations, with perplexity, the sea and the waves roaring; men's hearts failing them from fear and the expectation of those things which are coming on the earth, for the powers of the heavens will be shaken." Luke 21:25-26.

The Holy Spirit serves to open our eyes, and to help us to recognize all these symptoms around us of a world descending further and further into chaos. The other is to help us to recognize that we ourselves have symptoms that show us that some things are wrong with us individually, and that they may be things we seem to be inclined to do or cannot help but do as written:

18 For I know that in me (that is, in my flesh) nothing good dwells; for to will is present with me, but how to perform what is good I do not find.

19 For the good that I will to do, I do not do; but the evil I will not to do, that I practice.

20 Now if I do what I will not to do, it is no longer I who do it, but sin that dwells in me. Romans 7:18-20.

When we take a moment to notice that there is something off about us or the world around us, we are responding to the Holy Spirit unawares. For most, the moment might be fleeting, and it is back to life as usual. Some might even make attempts at silencing their recognition of themselves or the world around them by a distraction like alcohol or drugs or just deliberately ignoring this awareness in themselves. For those bothered enough by what they might have recognized about themselves, or the state of things around them them, they continue to respond to the working of the Holy Spirit.

The next step in how the Holy Spirit works is that the responsive ones then start to consider if there is a solution. They begin to question: is there anything beyond the present, anything to look forward to beyond the worsening state of things in this world? Jesus speaking of this critical role that the Holy Spirit is to play in our lives said:

7 It is to your advantage that I go away; for if I do not go away, the Helper will not come to you; but if I depart, I will send Him to you.

8 And when He has come, He will convict the world of sin, and of righteousness, and of judgment:

9 of sin, because they do not believe in Me;

10 of righteousness, because I go to My Father and you see Me no more;

11 of judgment, because the ruler of this world is judged. "I still have many things to say to you, but you cannot bear them now. However, when He, the Spirit of truth, has come, He will guide you into all truth; for He will not speak on His own authority, but

whatever He hears He will speak; and He will tell you things to come…

17 that the God of our Lord Jesus Christ, the Father of glory, may give to you the spirit of wisdom and revelation in the knowledge of Him

18 the eyes of your [f]understanding being enlightened; that you may know what is the hope of His calling, what are the riches of the glory of His inheritance in the saints,

19 and what is the exceeding greatness of His power toward us who believe, according to the working of His mighty power

20 which He worked in Christ when He raised Him from the dead and seated Him at His right hand in the heavenly places,

21 far above all principality[g] and [h]power and [i]might and dominion, and every name that is named, not only in this age but also in that which is to come…

13 In Him you also trusted, after you heard the word of truth, the gospel of your salvation; in whom also, having believed, you were sealed with the Holy Spirit of promise,

14 who[d] is the [e]guarantee of our inheritance until the redemption of the purchased possession, to the praise of His glory. John 16:7-13; Ephesians 1:17-21, 13-14.

The Holy Spirit is a guarantee of our inheritance in being reconciled to God through Christ, which is eternal life and all that comes with it like no more crying, sorrow, death and all the negative things we associate with our present lives as we learned in Revelation 20. The Holy Spirit is the Spiritual GPS that alerts us that we are lost, directs us to the Way, and keeps us on that Way until we get to our destination which is this inheritance found in reconciliation to God.

Communication

To keep the body alive, we have to breathe. Breathing is a ceaseless activity. For the soul, breathing is prayer! We are encouraged to pray as much and as often as possible likening it to breathing as written, "Pray without ceasing." 2 Thessalonians 5:17. What does prayer do for us? It serves many purposes.

For any relationship to thrive there has to be communication and the relationship with God is no exception. Prayer is how we communicate with God. God reveals His will for our lives primarily through His Word. We communicate with Him through prayer and let Him know about our anxieties and worries, as well as our thanks and praises as written:

6 Be anxious for nothing, but in everything by prayer and supplication, with thanksgiving, let your requests be made known to God;

7 and the peace of God, which surpasses all understanding, will guard your hearts and minds through Christ Jesus. Philippians 4:6-7.

The more time we spend communicating with Him through prayer, the closer we draw to Him. In fact, prayer is such a privilege considering that we have direct access to the Creator and Sustainer of all life as we know it. It can be done anytime and without an appointment! It is very difficult to get in touch with a president, not to mention a mayor or senator personally but here you have the Highest who can be reached anytime:

14…Lord of lords, and King of kings;…

15 the High and Lofty One Who inhabits eternity, whose name is Holy: "I dwell in the high and holy place, With him who has a contrite and humble spirit, To revive the spirit of the humble, And to revive the heart of the contrite ones." Revelation 17:14; Isaiah 57:15.

Though He is the King of kings, He loves to hear from the humble and lowly who realize that their very lives are dependent on Him, that they are nothing and can achieve nothing without His strength. They are not self-sufficient but realize that God is everything. On the contrary:

4 The wicked in his proud countenance does not seek God; God is in none of his thoughts." therefore

6 …He gives more grace. Therefore He says: "God resists the proud, But gives grace to the humble."" Psalms 10:4; James 4:6.

To seek God requires humility

8 "For My thoughts are not your thoughts, Nor are your ways My ways," says the Lord.

9 "For as the heavens are higher than the earth, So are My ways higher than your ways, And My thoughts than your thoughts." and

shows a recognition of the fact that "in Him we live and move and have our being..." Isaiah 55:8-9; Acts 17:28.

The Holy Spirit translates our communication with God

We are human and God's ways or thoughts we might not fully comprehend, meaning that we don't always want to pray for God's will or know what we should be praying for. We might not even be aware that we are praying for the wrong things. We are encouraged that the Holy Spirit helps us with our prayers as written:

26 Likewise the Spirit also helps in our weaknesses. For we do not know what we should pray for as we ought, but the Spirit Himself makes intercession [g]for us with groanings which cannot be uttered.

27 Now He who searches the hearts knows what the mind of the Spirit is, because He makes intercession for the saints according to the will of God. Romans 8:26-27.

Even when we might pray for the wrong things or pray for our will to be done and not His, because He loves us that much, He has the Holy Spirit help to translate our prayers so that they are still made conformable to His will. It might seem like God is not answering our prayers but He always does. It just might not be according to our will but is always according to His will. We might not recognize how He answers because we will be expecting a certain response from Him, but He always responds.

His response might not be what we prayed for or wanted but He always responds. Sometimes it might even feel like He is ignoring us and some may be angry at Him because He does not respond the expected way to grant our wishes. Our own parents did not always grant our requests and we might not have liked it but later on we realized and acknowledged that it was for our own good they did not. Things always work out for our good and for the best even though it might not be what we asked for or wanted as promised: "we know that all things work together for good to those who love God, to those who are the called according to His purpose." Romans 8:28.

The Holy Spirit helps us understand when God communicates with us

God reveals His will to us through the help of the Holy Spirit. Without the Holy Spirit we cannot understand God's Word and it is just like reading another book. It is a spiritual book and takes the Spirit to enable our understanding as written:

12 For as the body is one and has many members, but all the members of that one body, being many, are one body, so also is Christ.

13 For by one Spirit we were all baptized into one body—whether Jews or Greeks, whether slaves or free—and have all been made to drink [g]into one Spirit.

14 For in fact the body is not one member but many. 1 Corinthians 2:12-14.

The Holy Spirit helps us to understand what God reveals in His Word. His primary objective is for us to understand the truth about who God is, how much He loves us as He endeavors to reconcile humanity to Himself, and all the truth regarding this great conflict between good and evil we see in our lives and around us. Without the Holy Spirit's aid:

39..."Can the blind lead the blind? Will they not both fall into the ditch? ...

25 They grope in the dark without light, And He makes them stagger like a drunken man." Luke 6:39; Job 12:25.

The Holy Spirit helps us to understand Jesus Christ who is the truth as is written:

6 Jesus said to him, "I am the way, the truth, and the life. No one comes to the Father except through Me...

13 However, when He, the Spirit of truth, has come, He will guide you into all truth; for He will not speak on His own authority, but whatever He hears He will speak; and He will tell you things to come.

14 He will glorify Me, for He will take of what is Mine and declare it to you...John 14:6; and 16:13-14

Asking and receiving

God is our Father and we are His children. The love that we can have for our children is deep and most parents will do anything especially if it's for their children's good. If fallen sinful human beings like us can have such deep love for our offspring, how deep is God's love for us His children? His love is deeper and He wants the very best for you. Some of you are parents and you know there are certain things you will not give your children though you love them deeply. If you know it will be no good for them and has the potential to hurt them, why grant them the request. The deeper your love, the more you want the best for them. God is no different and His love is deeper. There are certain things we might want, but He knows that they will only serve to hurt us as written:

2 You lust and do not have. You murder and covet and cannot obtain. You fight and [b]war. [c]Yet you do not have because you do not ask.

3 You ask and do not receive, because you ask amiss, that you may spend it on your pleasures.;...

9 "So I say to you, ask, and it will be given to you; seek, and you will find; knock, and it will be opened to you.

10 For everyone who asks receives, and he who seeks finds, and to him who knocks it will be opened.

11 If a son asks for [e]bread from any father among you, will he give him a stone? Or if he asks for a fish, will he give him a serpent instead of a fish?

12 Or if he asks for an egg, will he offer him a scorpion?

13 If you then, being evil, know how to give good gifts to your children, how much more will your heavenly Father give the Holy Spirit to those who ask Him! James 4:2-3 and Luke 11:9-13.

As children ask their parents for things, we ask God to grant our requests but He does not always grant them, at least not in the way we expect. If you have a child who asks for a chainsaw as a toy, you will not give it to them because you know that it will hurt them. If you are truly a loving parent, as much as you want to grant all your child's wishes, you will not give to them what you know will hurt them. God is the same way. What is not good for us? Anything that will shift our focus from Him or serve to derail us on the way to salvation is not good for us. It might also be the right thing, but just at the wrong time. God however is eager to answer the prayer to grant us the Holy Spirit because the Holy Spirit plays an instrumental role in keeping us on track to salvation and eternal reconciliation to God.

Anything that we might desire with all our being, if it has the potential of drawing us away from God or destroying our relationship with Him is something He is not eager to answer. His will is our salvation. Any issues that we would like to bring to God's attention, we should be open minded and willing to accept that it might not be for our good which brings it in conflict against God's will and purpose for us which is our salvation. If it is falls within the broader purpose of your salvation He will grant it. Our will mostly desires for things that separate us from God but we are encouraged to make our requests known to Him according to His will as written:

10 Your will be done On earth as it is in heaven...

14 Now this is the confidence that we have in Him, that if we ask anything according to His will, He hears us. Matthew 6:10; 1 John 5:14.

Holy Spirit crucial for salvation

The Holy Spirit plays a pivotal role in drawing us to God and maintaining our daily relationship with Him. He works as our conscience in different situations, helping us to think about our choices and their consequences. To desire to draw closer to God, to desire to please God and do His will, all these things are possible only by the working of the Holy Spirit as written: "it is God who works in you both to will and to do for His good pleasure." Philippians 2:13. Seeing that salvation is found in responding to the working of the Holy Spirit in our lives, by rejecting Him, we reject the only means of reconciliation to God as written:

19 Do not quench the Spirit....

30 And do not grieve the Holy Spirit of God, by whom you were sealed for the day of redemption...

31 Therefore I say to you, every sin and blasphemy will be forgiven men, but the blasphemy against the Spirit will not be forgiven men.

32 Anyone who speaks a word against the Son of Man, it will be forgiven him; but whoever speaks against the Holy Spirit, it will not be forgiven him, either in this age or in the age to come. 1 Thessalonians 5:19; Ephesians 4:30; Matthew 12:31-32.

The Holy Spirit is a person and so can be grieved? How is that possible, you may ask? The Holy Spirit is God! He is one of the three: the Father, the Son and the Holy Spirit. They are three but one as God or the Godhead. We do not understand how it is and not much is revealed in the Word, but as all 3 God plays different functions in His efforts of reconciling humanity to Himself. In Genesis 1:26, God is spoken of as plural. "And God said, Let us make man in our image..." The Son is also known as the Word for we read that Christ or the Word created the world and The Godhead or God comprises the Father, the Son and the Holy Spirit as written, "He who has seen Me has seen the Father" and "in Him dwells all the fullness of the Godhead [f]bodily;" it means God or the Godhead is seen completely in Christ. John 14:9; Colossians 2:9. When you see Christ you have seen God!

The Holy Spirit is how God works to draw us back to Him. He is likened to a fire as seen in the following verses:

16 John answered, saying to all, "I indeed baptize you with water; but One mightier than I is coming, whose sandal strap I am not worthy to loose. He will baptize you with the Holy Spirit and fire...

3 Then there appeared to them [b]divided tongues, as of fire, and one sat upon each of them.

4 And they were all filled with the Holy Spirit and began to speak with other tongues, as the Spirit gave them utterance....Luke 3:16; Acts 2:3-4.

It can be likened to a spiritual fire which burns in believers empowering them to do God's will. It is this fire that helps us to be a light to those around us, revealing the character of God through our lives as written:

14 You are the light of the world. A city that is set on a hill cannot be hidden.

15 Nor do they light a lamp and put it under a basket, but on a lampstand, and it gives light to all who are in the house.

16 Let your light so shine before men, that they may see your good works and glorify your Father in heaven. Matthew 5:14-16.

Because of the Holy Spirit we are like lights in a world in the darkness of sin, revealing God's love through our lives. When the Holy Spirit burns in us we are hot and this is what Jesus refers to when He says:

15 I know your works, that you are neither cold nor hot. I could wish you were cold or hot.

16 So then, because you are lukewarm, and neither [k]cold nor hot, I will vomit you out of My mouth. Revelation 3:15-16.

Heat is present where there is a fire. If the fire is put out or quenched, there is no light or heat. The stronger the fire burns, the hotter it is and the brighter the flame. The stronger the presence of the Holy Spirit, the more our works glorify God revealing more of His character that He is Love.

How do we quench or grieve the Holy Spirit?

The Holy Spirit's objective is your salvation and doing God's will is His desire for you. When we deliberately choose to go against God's will, He keeps working in us through our conscience trying to get us back on track. The less we do God's will as revealed by the Holy Spirit weakens this spiritual fire as it gets dimmer shedding less light. The voice of your conscience weakens to a whisper until finally you don't hear it anymore. By constantly rejecting the working of the Holy Spirit it can get to the point where the fire is finally quenched and the light goes out.

This happens when we constantly reject His work our consciences, and live a life that is contradictory to God's will. He is grieved when it gets to the point that no matter how much He works in your heart, or what He does to get you back on track, He realizes that you do not respond and your heart is hardened. Essentially He gives up on you and it takes much to get the Holy Spirit to this point but even He has a limit. Let us not quench the Holy Spirit by hardening our hearts and becoming unresponsive to His work in our hearts. Rejecting Him is rejecting salvation because His work is what helps you to be saved.

21
WHO IS IN CONTROL?

The ability to have enough control to abstain completely from obviously harmful things like recreational drugs and to indulge in good things to moderation is self-control or temperance. Self-control even extends to how we manage our emotions, thoughts and how we generally maintain our conduct with other people. It is therefore important to have self-control seeing that it determines not only physical health but social, emotional and therefore spiritual health as well. Is it safe to say that when one lacks self-control, they are not in control? That is why it is called self-control; to control oneself. If one cannot control themselves when it comes to a habit or behavior, good or bad, they are not in control. If one cannot control themselves that means someone or something else has to be in control. If you are not in control and being controlled then you are in bondage!

What is bondage?

There are two entities in bondage: the master and the slave. The slave is held captive by the master. The slave serves the master and anything that has a dominating influence over us we become a slave to. Servitude implies work or the bearing of burdens. This work can be indulgence in a destructive habit like drug abuse. If one is a slave, they labor or bear burdens completely to a dominating influence's will and not at theirs therefore they are not in control but being controlled. If you indulge in a habit or behavior to your expense or injury but cannot stop and continue to do so, you have become a slave. You know it is bad or harming you and that you do not want to indulge in it but continue doing so to your hurt. A slave is held captive against his/her will and labors not for their own benefit, therefore:

1. Subject to something/someone's will – a master.

2. Not free to do what he/she
3. Work/bear burdens against will

Bondage for those Christ healed came in many forms such as dreadful diseases like Leprosy or demon possession. They were laboring as it were as they were under constant oppression from their circumstances. These were things which in their own power or ability they could not overcome. There are many today who are dealing with issues that no physician can help or any medication can cure. Bondage comes not only in the form of incurable disease, but also addictions and emotional burdens. Those that are bound are usually so against their will and remain in that state until they are set free only by Power greater than that which keeps them in bondage.

Types of Bondage

Addiction

Addiction is a type of bondage where one continues to use a substance or partake in a behavior despite adverse dependency consequences. Generally the word is associated with substance abuse but it can be broadly referred to anything that is habit forming which has the potential to be destructive to any aspect of life, not just physical well being alone.

These are just some of the most prevalent types of addictions:
- Alcohol
- Drug
- Sugar
- Chocolate
- Anorexia
- Eating
- Bulimia
- Binge eating
- Stress eating
- Exercise
- Work
- Shopping
- Gambling
- Sex
- Pornography

- Internet
- Cigarette
- Television
- Coffee
- Solitaire and other computer/Video Games
- Social networking

These are just some of the more common addictions. The need for doing these things can become compulsive and persistent even when the one addicted knows that the addiction might be destroying their health or other areas of their life. We realize that addiction is a type of bondage because it is characterized by:

1. Loss of control (Lack self control)
2. Compulsive preoccupation (working or doing it even when they don't want to)
3. Continuing habit despite negative consequences (powerless to deliver oneself from circumstances)

The even bigger problem is that addiction can occur with anything. Things that are normally harmless or even good in themselves can become addictive and eventually take over other areas of life they are not supposed to. Social networking has become one of those things. Anything that can hold us in bondage has the potential to destroy health, not only physically as in substance abuse, but also emotionally, mentally and spiritually. Addiction is intemperance or the lack of self control whether in good things like eating food or the indulgence in a harmful substance and it is bondage and how the devil holds us in captivity physically, because he knows that:

…19 your body is the temple of the Holy Spirit who is in you, whom you have from God, and you are not your own?

20 For you were bought at a price; therefore glorify God in your body [g]and in your spirit, which are God's…

31 Therefore, whether you eat or drink, or whatever you do, do all to the glory of God. 1 Corinthians 6:19, 20; 10:31.

The devil can also hold us in bondage through physical means like eating which are not necessarily harmful but become so through intemperance when we lose self control and cause us to sin against our bodies which God would have us to treat as a temple for the indwelling of His Spirit.

How can addiction affect our lives?
1. <u>Steals</u>
- Time from your relationships
- Time from your job
- Time from <u>GOD</u>

2. <u>Kills</u>
- Relationship with spouse and family
- Relationship with others
- Relationship with GOD
- And might even <u>kill you through bad health, disease or accidents</u>

3. <u>Destroys</u>
- Every aspect of your life

Any addiction, no matter how innocent or harmless it may seem has the potential to steal, kill or destroy some or all aspects of our daily lives especially your relationship with God and becomes a type of bondage!

Emotional and mental bondage

- Depression
- Bitterness
- Unforgiveness
- Guilt
- Shame
- Envy
- Anger
- Resentment
- Humiliation
- Fear
- Racist

The devil desires to hold us in captivity in any form whenever the opportunity presents itself. The opportunities present themselves when he sees that one has a tendency towards certain habits or behavior, or a certain character flaw or attitude. He can also capitalize on circumstances which lead to depression, for example, and strive to keep the person in this state and to worsen it.

Spiritual Bondage

The root of all bondage is sin. When we do not love God and put Him first in our lives or love others as we would want to be loved ourselves, we sin. Sin is when we do things that are contrary to the commandments (see Matthew 22:37-39). Daily we fail to do unto others as we would have them do unto us in many situations and yet that is what God requires of us as is written:

20 If someone says, "I love God," and hates his brother, he is a liar; for he who does not love his brother whom he has seen, [d]how can he love God whom he has not seen? 1 John 4:20.

The soul functions as God made it to when we love him with all our hearts and our neighbor as we love ourselves, but when we fail to do this, the soul ends up in an unhealthy state which is the spiritual disease of sin. Our bodies are the temples for the indwelling of His Spirit so we should keep them holy. Any form of addiction means that another entity other than God who created us takes His rightful place in our lives, because we love whatever it may be more than God.

Whatever the action against our bodies through the addiction, we will not be treating our bodies as His temple so we sin. Any emotions that hold us in bondage are also sin because through them we do not treat others as we would want to be treated. They are also not welcome in the temple as well, therefore not in our lives because they have a negative effect on our relationships with God and with others. Even when these emotions do not lead to any physical action, sin can take place in the heart/mind as is written:

21 You have heard that it was said to those [d]of old, 'You shall not murder, and whoever murders will be in danger of the judgment.'

22 But I say to you that whoever is angry with his brother [e]without a cause shall be in danger of the judgment. And whoever says to his brother, 'Raca!'[f] shall be in danger of the council. But whoever says, [g]'You fool!' shall be in danger of [h]hell fire. Matthew 5:21-22.

We are all judged by the same Law and the requirements are for us to love our neighbor as ourselves. When He sees us He looks at our actions and not our physical characteristics. The basis of God's Law is to do unto others as you want them to do unto you. It is not to love those of a certain race better than others because God does not esteem some higher than others but we are all equal in His eyes. He judges people not based on the color of their skin or which race they belong to but based on their actions, whether they are evil or good as is written:

10 I, the Lord, search the heart, I test the [e]mind, Even to give every man according to his ways, According to the fruit of his doings. Jeremiah 17:10.

We are not commanded to love only a certain type of neighbor but to love our neighbor, that is why Christ died for all of us so that whoever believes on Him should not perish but have eternal life. The verse does not say He died for certain or specific races or groups in the world but for the whole world. Racism has no place in the soul temple just as much as unforgiveness.

Another common example of emotional bondage to the devil is through unforgiveness. It is not easy to forgive and is in fact impossible for us to do so on our own. God has to help us to do so by His power to set us free. Forgiving others and being forgiven by God are two sides of the same coin. You cannot be forgiven by God if you cannot forgive others of the wrong they have done to you:

14 "For if you forgive men their trespasses, your heavenly Father will also forgive you.

15 But if you do not forgive men their trespasses, neither will your Father forgive your trespasses." Matthew 6:14, 15.

The power it takes for God to forgive all your sins is the same power it takes for God to help you forgive a wrong which seems unforgivable. It is the same power it takes to love those you do not desire to love. It is the same power it takes to erase the feeling of guilt, shame or being unforgiving even of yourself for something you did. Just as God can forgive all your sins against Him and even forget them, He can help you to forgive and forget, as is written:

25 I, even I, am He who blots out your transgressions for My own sake; And I will not remember your sins....

8 The Lord is merciful and gracious, Slow to anger, and abounding in mercy.

9 He will not always strive with us, Nor will He keep His anger forever.

10 He has not dealt with us according to our sins, Nor punished us according to our iniquities.

11 For as the heavens are high above the earth, So great is His mercy toward those who fear Him;

12 As far as the east is from the west. Isaiah 43:25; Psalms 103:8-12.

Christ came to give us life and to set us free

The devil came to steal, kill and to destroy every aspect of our lives or our very lives, while Christ came to set us free and to ensure that we have life abundantly as is written:

10 The thief does not come except to steal, and to kill, and to destroy. I have come that they may have life, and that they may have it more abundantly.

13 I have raised him up in righteousness, And I will [d]direct all his ways; He shall build My city And let My exiles go free, Not for price nor reward," Says the Lord of hosts.

61 "The Spirit of the Lord God is upon Me, Because the Lord has anointed Me To preach good tidings to the poor; He has sent Me to [a]heal the brokenhearted, To proclaim liberty to the captives, And the opening of the prison to those who are bound. John 10:10; Isaiah 45:13 and Isaiah 61;1.

When we are the devil's captives through these things, we become his slaves and become subject to his will:

18 For I know that in me (that is, in my flesh) nothing good dwells; for to will is present with me, but how to perform what is good I do not find.

19 For the good that I will to do, I do not do; but the evil I will not to do, that I practice. Romans 7:18, 19.

When you keep gambling even though you know it is destroying your finances, your marriage, your family and even your career, you have become a slave. If you cannot stop drinking or doing drugs, you have become a slave. When you cannot forgive someone for whatever wrong they did to you, you have become a slave. If you keep lying and cannot stop lying, you are in bondage and are a slave. These are all examples of how we might continue to do things that we are well aware are taking us on a path to self destruction but are absolutely powerless to break away from. The devil's will is exercised in our lives because:

16 Do you not know that to whom you present yourselves slaves to obey, you are that one's slaves whom you obey, whether of sin leading to death, or of obedience leading to righteousness?...

Most assuredly, I say to you, whoever commits sin is a slave of sin. Romans 6:16 and John 8:34.

Christ came that He can free those who are laboring against their will through addictions whether substance or habit, who are carrying emotional burdens like unforgiveness, shame, bitterness or guilt; who are doing these things and hate to do them but cannot stop in their own power and continue to do them because they are slaves as is written:

28 Come to Me, all you who labor and are heavy laden, and I will give you rest.

29 Take My yoke upon you and learn from Me, for I am [f]gentle and lowly in heart, and you will find rest for your souls.

30 For My yoke is easy and My burden is light." Matthew 11:28-30.

Even sickness which is also a type of bondage, Christ can free us from as seen in the miracles of healing He performed. There is nothing that He is unable to free us from if we believe. He is more than capable of restoring us to good health physically and spiritually if we believe. He came to set us free from our captivity to the devil that we might have life and have it abundantly. He desires that we have the best health not only physically but more importantly, spiritually. He came to deliver us from physical and spiritual bondage, if we believe.

Lack of self control as a form of Idolatry

Bondage is a type of idolatry because anything which we allow to take over our lives, controls us, takes up our time and energy not only from God but also our neighbor becomes an idol and takes God's rightful place in our lives. Bondage is idolatry because:

3 You shall have no other gods before Me....

16 And what agreement has the temple of God with idols? For you[f] are the temple of the living God." Exodus 20:3; 2 Corinthians 6:16

God hates idolatry which is why it is the first of the Ten Commandments, to have no other gods before Him. Whenever anything, no matter how innocent or harmless it might seem starts controlling our lives in one way or the other and starts negatively affecting our relationships with others and especially with God, it has become an idol, as is written:

3 Son of man, these men have set up their idols in their hearts, and put before them that which causes them to stumble into iniquity...

6 Therefore say to the house of Israel, 'Thus says the Lord God: "Repent, turn away from your idols, and turn your faces away from all your abominations…" Ezekiel 14:3, 6.

An idol does not have to be carved out of stone or wood. Anything that we esteem more than God in our hearts becomes an idol. If a person captivates one's life to the point of being an obsession, that person has become an idol. In this world are self-confessed idolaters who adore celebrities such as actors or musicians to the point of actually calling them idols. Whether it be a substance, sport, food, car, house, girlfriend, boyfriend, celebrity, money, career, job, hobby, attitude, emotional state; anything that steals you away from a healthy relationship with God and with your neighbor becomes an idol and you become an idolater in your heart.

It can be unforgiveness. If you hold onto baggage and refuse to forgive, then unforgiveness in itself has become an idol to you! It can be racism! It can be a philosophy or belief system contrary to God We see here then that bondage of any sort becomes sin because God hates idolatry and it is sin.

When we sin the devil is our master and takes God's rightful place in our lives. Through idolatry of any form we are indirectly worshiping the devil because he uses these different forms of bondage to become our master and to hold us his captives. All forms of bondage become sin no matter how harmless they seem because through them we allow the devil to control our lives.

Not natural for us to do God's will

We are naturally inclined to have the devil's will work in our lives as it is not natural for us to do God's will. What we call human nature is our flesh or carnal nature which is subject to the devil by default. We are married to sin by the vows of birth into this inherited sinful nature. It is not natural and in fact impossible for us to do God's will on our own. We are by human or carnal nature, selfish, self centered, proud and inclined to put ourselves before others in varying degrees.

To love God on our own is thoroughly impossible because we are born with this nature that is by default subservient to the devil. We know of only one master from birth and unless God intervenes to break the bondage and that is if we choose Him to be our new Master, we can die the devil's slaves serving him through sin. We are naturally the devil's slaves as is written:

5 Behold, I was brought forth in iniquity, And in sin my mother conceived me.

12 Therefore, just as through one man sin entered the world, and death through sin, and thus death spread to all men, because all sinned. Psalms 51:5 and Romans 5:12

Our human or carnal nature is naturally at odds with God and cannot of its own be subject to God, "Because the [c]carnal mind is enmity against God; for it is not subject to the law of God, nor indeed can be. 8 So then, those who are in the flesh cannot please God." Romans 8:7, 8.

What we call human nature or the carnal mind is actually an enemy of God seeing that it is contradictory to God's will and thus not natural for it to be subject to His law and cannot be. As long as we are in the flesh or in the carnal it is impossible for us to do God's will in our lives and thus cannot please Him. It is impossible because our master is not Christ but the devil. The devil holds us in captivity through our carnal nature and as long as he is master, he will not let us go as is written:

6 He who struck the people in wrath with a continual stroke, He who ruled the nations in anger…

17 Who made the world as a wilderness And destroyed its cities, Who [f]did not open the house of his prisoners?' Isaiah 14:6, 17.

As our slave master, he does not want to let us go but whips us continually to work for him the works of the flesh which is sin and to keep us in some sort of bondage whether it is emotional, mental or physical. He wants to keep us laboring for him through bondage and does not have any intentions of releasing any of his slaves with the only desirable outcome being our death in sin and therefore separation from God.

Thank God that He sent Jesus Christ to set us free because though we have a mighty and strong slave master from whom we cannot flee in our own power, Christ is mightier than the devil and can thus deliver us from any bondage and set us free, as is written:

17 But He, knowing their thoughts, said to them: "Every kingdom divided against itself is brought to desolation, and a house divided against a house falls.

18 If Satan also is divided against himself, how will his kingdom stand? Because you say I cast out demons by Beelzebub.

19 And if I cast out demons by Beelzebub, by whom do your sons cast them out? Therefore they will be your judges.

20 But if I cast out demons with the finger of God, surely the kingdom of God has come upon you.

21 When a strong man, fully armed, guards his own palace, his goods are in peace.

22 But when a stronger than he comes upon him and overcomes him, he takes from him all his armor in which he trusted, and divides his [g]spoils. Luke 11:17-22.

When we are the devil's slaves, our hearts are like the palace talked about in these verses and he is like the strong man running the palace. He is at peace because he is strong and continues to hold us in bondage until someone else comes along who is stronger than he to overthrow and spoil him. By default he runs the palaces in our hearts and only when we allow Christ to come into our hearts who is stronger can the devil be overthrown and we be delivered from all bondage.

How does Christ set us free?

Christ is the desirable master of the two but he can only set us free when we choose Him and allow Him into the palaces of our hearts so that he can overthrow the devil as is written:

20 Behold, I stand at the door and knock. If anyone hears My voice and opens the door, I will come in to him and dine with him, and he with Me...

28 Come to Me, all you who labor and are heavy laden, and I will give you rest.

29 Take My yoke upon you and learn from Me, for I am [f]gentle and lowly in heart, and you will find rest for your souls.

30 For My yoke is easy and My burden is light." Revelation 3:20 and Matthew 11:28-30.

Our carnal or human nature is naturally selfish as it is the devil's will working in us. He is selfish and so for us to break away from the bondage to him we have to deny ourselves. When we hold onto self and refuse to deny ourselves, we continue to allow the devil mastery in our lives as that selfishness started with him.

It is because of this selfishness, the desire to gratify self that we end up in bondage. When we gratify self through one form or another, we become easy prey for the devil. Bondage to recreational drugs illustrates this very well. The desire or lust in the flesh for a substance and the indulgence to gratify it leads to more dependence and thus addiction and bondage. It can be food, video games, prescription drugs, wealth, etc; anything that we cannot stop indulging in to the point of losing control becomes bondage. The devil easily traps us because of this lust in our flesh to gratify a habit, a want, anything that causes us not to rest until that gratification takes place, as is written:

15 Do not love the world or the things in the world. If anyone loves the world, the love of the Father is not in him.

16 For all that is in the world—the lust of the flesh, the lust of the eyes, and the pride of life—is not of the Father but is of the world.

17 And the world is passing away, and the lust of it; but he who does the will of God abides forever. 1 John 2:15-17.

How does the devil ensnare us and keep us in captivity?

13 Let no one say when he is tempted, "I am tempted by God"; for God cannot be tempted by evil, nor does He Himself tempt anyone.

14 But each one is tempted when he is drawn away by his own desires and enticed.

15 Then, when desire has conceived, it gives birth to sin; and sin, when it is full-grown, brings forth death. James 1:13-15.

15 And He said to them, "Take heed and beware of [c]covetousness, for one's life does not consist in the abundance of the things he possesses." Luke 12:15.

The devil entices us with the things of the world which causes many to covet for them. For some the drive to have a career comes first and becomes the sole purpose of life at the expense of their relationship with God and loved ones. They forget that the company can close tomorrow and just as today they have a job it might be gone tomorrow. Others put their all into buying a dream house which they don't know they might lose. Some may even accomplish their dreams only for their lives to be cut short suddenly when they didn't care to invest in the most important thing of all, a relationship with God and Eternal life.

The devil is more effective at using things which are harmless or good in themselves like acquiring a house or climbing up the corporate ladder. These examples only become harmful in our lives when they become the very reason for our existence and everything else revolves around them. Anything that becomes the center of life especially at the expense of relationship with your neighbor and most importantly that with God becomes an idol. The devil effectively uses things of the world to trap us if we are not careful as he strives for us to gratify the lust of the flesh and the eyes. Through coveting for them, self is gratified which is why the first step is self denial or not gratifying the carnal desires of our selfish nature.

    We are not in control in our lives therefore we lack self-control as the devil is naturally our master. He is our master by default because we are born into a sinful nature. The devil came to steal, kill and destroy and that is his objective in our lives. Though we might not realize this, we are his slaves as long as we sin or are in any sort of bondage. The other is our Great Physician Christ who is the more desirable Master and His goal is to give us life abundantly. We have to choose Him to be our Master and that is how He sets us free from bondage to the devil in any form. That is how we cease from our works in the flesh and bearing burdens for the devil whether physical addictions, emotional, mental or spiritual and how we rest.

22
REST

For physical health we learned that it is important to take some time to rest from the business of life. It allows the body to focus on things like repair and speeds up healing. When the soul is resting what exactly is it resting from?

There are 4 types of labor which we rest from:
- Works of the flesh
- Righteousness by works
- Cares of life
- Works of Righteousness

Most of us are working one or a combination of some or all these works. To those who are tired of working any of these works is the following invitation:

28 Come to Me, all you who labor and are heavy laden, and I will give you rest.

29 Take My yoke upon you and learn from Me, for I am [f]gentle and lowly in heart, and you will find rest for your souls.

30 For My yoke is easy and My burden is light." Matthew 11:28-30.

Works of the flesh

We have seen how the devil enslaved humanity through sin. Slavery as we learned is involuntary labor usually at something that does not benefit and eventually destroys the slave. Sin is called works of sin because when we sin, we are working for the devil as said in scripture:

19 Now the works of the flesh are evident, which are: [d]adultery, [e]fornication, uncleanness, lewdness,

20 idolatry, sorcery, hatred, contentions, jealousies, outbursts of wrath, selfish ambitions, dissensions, heresies,

21 envy, [f]murders, drunkenness, revelries, and the like; of which I tell you beforehand, just as I also told you in time past, that those who practice such things will not inherit the kingdom of God. Galatians 5:19-21.

When Christ sets us free, we cease from being slaves and stop the works of the flesh which is sin. It is important to note that the devil has no intention of freeing any slaves as is written, "opened not the house of his prisoners" Isaiah 14:17 (KJV). The devil and demons are foes that we are no match against. It takes one stronger than they to free us and to keep them at bay as is written, "No one can enter a strong man's house and plunder his goods, unless he first binds the strong man. And then he will plunder his house." Mark 3:27.

We find this rest in Jesus Christ and only in Him because He is the only one strong enough to bind these strong foes and as long as we remain connected to Him by faith, there is nothing they can do. Outside of Christ there is no rest but bondage through sin. The devil wants us to work for him until we die in our sins. Freedom is only found in a continuous abiding relationship with Him. It has to become a lifestyle, that is the only way. What happens often is that a person can be set free by Christ but if that connection is not maintained, the devil and his minions see an opportunity to come back to the house and reclaim what they lost as is written:

24 "When an unclean spirit goes out of a man, he goes through dry places, seeking rest; and finding none, he says, 'I will return to my house from which I came.'

25 And when he comes, he finds it swept and put in order.

26 Then he goes and takes with him seven other spirits more wicked than himself, and they enter and dwell there; and the last state of that man is worse than the first." Luke 11:24-26.

If we do not maintain our connection to Christ after being freed, we are in danger of enabling these demons to return and bring reinforcements with them. They want to make sure that it is even harder for you to break away from their grip. They make sure you work even harder than before which is why sometimes those who had a connection to Christ, if they don't maintain it can end up worse than they were before. This rest is only found in daily carrying your cross, dying to self, and in maintaining communion with Him through His Word and prayer. That is the only way to stay free by keeping Christ in your heart, and to keep these evil spirits at bay which are bent on reclaiming you as their own and working you to death in your sins.

Rest from the cares of life

27 Do not labor for the food which perishes, but for the food which endures to everlasting life, which the Son of Man will give you...John 6:27.

In the parable of the Sower, some of the seed fell among the thorns and sprung up but was choked by thorns and the meaning is given by Christ that one hears the Word and receives it but the cares of this life, and the deceitfulness of riches choke it that it does not bear fruit in the life. (Matthew 13:7, 22).

There are many who hear the Word of God and understand, but are unable to come to a place of practicing a life of trusting in God to provide for their needs because of fear. They fear that if they do not do something about their problem, they will not overcome it. It is actually in these circumstances that God can show Himself on their behalf, because He helps those who cannot help themselves. He will not do for you what He knows you can do for yourself.

If there appears to be no solution for the problem, that is the very opportunity for God to work so that your faith in Him will be increased when you see how He would have helped you to overcome what seemed impossible. They do not understand how a God who they cannot see can provide for their needs, and take matters into their own hands using what they can see or handle. The more pressing the needs, the less likely they are to trust and believe that God will provide.

It is a shallow faith which appears good when circumstances are good, but is exposed by trials that it is not in God but in one's own means and methods. There are many as an example who have families and when a job requires them to work on Sabbath, they are quick to rationalize that God would have them take care of their families, even though God would also have us to keep the Sabbath Holy which is the fourth commandment. Just because there is a pressing need, does not mean we should not keep one of God's commandments if it seems impossible to do both. The same God who would have you keep the Sabbath Holy, is the same God who knows your needs:

8 "Therefore do not be like them. For your Father knows the things you have need of before you ask Him.

31 "Therefore do not worry, saying, 'What shall we eat?' or 'What shall we drink?' or 'What shall we wear?'

32 For after all these things the Gentiles seek. For your heavenly Father knows that you need all these things.

33 But seek first the kingdom of God and His righteousness, and all these things shall be added to you. Matthew 6:8, 31-33.

By seeking to do His will regardless of our circumstances, He has promised to add all these things to us, which implies that since He already knows our need before we even ask, He will bring these things into our lives without much action on our part.

Deceitfulness of riches

Riches can have the same effect on faith as worrying about how needs will be met. Riches can be deceitful because they can give a sense of false security. One who lacks nothing might be less inclined to seek God because there is no need to or. In lack, one feels hopeless and resorts to whatever they can do which is visible or tangible instead of trusting God to provide; in plenty on the other hand, trust is put in the tangible and visible riches deceiving one not to seek God. In both, trust is not put where it needs to be in God but for entirely different reasons. Against the deceitfulness of riches we are warned:

26 For what profit is it to a man if he gains the whole world, and loses his own soul? Or what will a man give in exchange for his soul?

7 For we brought nothing into this world, [d]and it is certain we can carry nothing out.

8 And having food and clothing, with these we shall be content.

9 But those who desire to be rich fall into temptation and a snare, and into many foolish and harmful lusts which drown men in destruction and perdition.

10 For the love of money is a root of all kinds of evil, for which some have strayed from the faith in their greediness, and pierced themselves through with many sorrows.

4 Do not overwork to be rich; Because of your own understanding, cease!

5 [a]Will you set your eyes on that which is not? For riches certainly make themselves wings; They fly away like an eagle toward heaven.

19 "Do not lay up for yourselves treasures on earth, where moth and rust destroy and where thieves break in and steal;

20 but lay up for yourselves treasures in heaven, where neither moth nor rust destroys and where thieves do not break in and steal.

21 For where your treasure is, there your heart will be also. Matthew 16:26; 1 Timothy 6:7-10; Proverbs 23:4-5 and Matthew 6:19-21.

Rest from Righteousness by works

It is very easy to get into the trap of trying to impress God with our works. There are many who are tired because they are working hard to impress God but they are wearing themselves out in vain. You can't! I can't! No one can! When you think you have done something really impressive, you are reminded that, "…Verily every man at his best state is altogether vanity;… and all our righteousnesses are as filthy rags; and we all do fade as a leaf…" Psalms 39:5; Isaiah 64:6 (KJV). God is not impressed at all because your best is nothing to Him and you are wasting your time. He hopes that when we realize that it is futile to impress Him and work our way into Heaven, we will heed the invitation in Matthew 11:28-30 to find rest for our souls.

All we are invited to do is to rest in Him. We get tired because we are doing the work but when we rest in Him, we don't get tired because He does all the work:

13 for it is God who works in you both to will and to do for His good pleasure.;…

20 I have been crucified with Christ; it is no longer I who live, but Christ lives in me; and the life which I now live in the flesh I live

by faith in the Son of God, who loved me and gave Himself for me. Philippians 2:13; Galatians 2:20.

When we rest in Him, He lives in us and gives us the desires to do good and works through us to fulfill them according to His will. Only when He is living in us can He work through us to please Him. We can we get weary and worn out when He is the one doing all the work because:
28 Have you not known? Have you not heard? The everlasting God, the Lord, The Creator of the ends of the earth, Neither faints nor is weary. His understanding is unsearchable.
29 He gives power to the weak, And to those who have no might He increases strength.
31 But those who wait on the Lord Shall renew their strength; They shall mount up with wings like eagles, They shall run and not be weary, They shall walk and not faint. Isaiah 40:28-29, 31.

The works of righteousness are simply as a result of us being connected to Him. As long as that connection is maintained then we continue to rest in Him. As long as we rest in Him, we are resting in His works of righteousness on our behalf. There is nothing we do other than to make sure we maintain a connection to Him by daily dying to self so that He lives in and through us. He does the rest! Christ illustrated this best when He talked about the vine in John chapter 15.
1 "I am the true vine, and My Father is the vine dresser...
4 Abide in Me, and I in you. As the branch cannot bear fruit of itself, unless it abides in the vine, neither can you, unless you abide in Me.
5 "I am the vine, you are the branches. He who abides in Me, and I in him, bears much fruit; for without Me you can do nothing. John 15:1, 4-5.

The branch does not do any work to bear fruit. Its part is to remain connected to the vine. By being connected it bears fruit. If it is disconnected it stops bearing fruit and starts dying. The life and strength to bear is found in being connected to the vine. The only time we work is when we work the works of the flesh which is sin. We do not work to be righteous because He is doing all the work through us as His vessels to carry out His will. The fruit are the by-product of the branch being connected to the vine. It does not actively do any work to bear the fruit. When we are in the flesh, sin reigns and we labor through sin being disconnected from Christ.

Rest in His works of Righteousness

When we are in the Spirit, we are connected to Christ and He does the work on our behalf and we bear fruit. Because of the connection to Christ and as we maintain the connection, we continue to bear fruit. This is why Paul contrasts the results of being in the flesh and in the spirit when he says:

22 But the fruit of the Spirit is love, joy, peace, long suffering, kindness, goodness, faithfulness,

23 [g]gentleness, self-control. Against such there is no law…

9 (for the fruit of the [b]Spirit is in all goodness, righteousness, and truth)…Galatians 5:22-23 and Ephesians 5:9.

In Galatians 5:19-21, we learned that the works of the flesh are the works of sin. On one end we have works which lead to sin, and on the other, fruit which lead to Righteousness. In sin we are laboring spiritually for the devil, while fruit of the Spirit are a result of being connected to Christ. There is no effort involved to bear the fruit, but because of the branch's connection to the Vine, it produces fruit. The Vine is the one working to produce the fruit, and the branch's purpose is to carry or manifest the fruit.

The fruit is seen on the branches. If the branch disconnects from the Vine, it produces no fruit and in fact begins to die immediately. We are the branches and people are to see God's works of righteousness through our lives which is why it is written:

35 By this all will know that you are My disciples, if you have love for one another." John 13:35.

We can Let us therefore cease from our labors to be righteous and find rest in Him. Our only labor if you want to call it that is to believe in His works on our behalf as in the following account:

28 Then they said to Him, "What shall we do, that we may work the works of God?"

29 Jesus answered and said to them, "This is the work of God, that you believe in Him whom He sent."John 6:28-29.

There remains therefore a rest to the people of God.
10 For he that is entered into his rest, he also hath ceased from his own works, as God did from his.
11 Let us labor therefore to enter into that rest lest any man fall after the same example of unbelief. Hebrews 4:9-11.

The Sabbath

The Sabbath is an emblem, a symbol of God's works on our behalf. Our part is to just believe and to rest in His works for us. His works on our behalf "the works were finished from the foundation of the world." Hebrews 4:3.

The Lord created everything in six days and then rested on the seventh day:

1 Thus the heavens and the earth, and all the host of them, were finished.

2 And on the seventh day God ended His work which He had done, and He rested on the seventh day from all His work which He had done.

3 Then God blessed the seventh day and sanctified it, because in it He rested from all His work which God had created and made. Genesis 2:1-3.

The Ten Commandments were given on Mt. Sinai in grand fashion in which "the people witnessed the thunderings, the lightning flashes, the sound of the trumpet, and the mountain smoking; and when the people saw it, they trembled and stood afar off." Exodus 20:18. Of those Ten Commandments, the fourth is about the Sabbath:

8 "Remember the Sabbath day, to keep it holy.

9 Six days you shall labor and do all your work,

10 but the seventh day is the Sabbath of the Lord your God. In it you shall do no work: you, nor your son, nor your daughter, nor your male servant, nor your female servant, nor your cattle, nor your stranger who is within your gates.

11 For in six days the Lord made the heavens and the earth, the sea, and all that is in them, and rested the seventh day. Therefore the Lord blessed the Sabbath day and hallowed it. Exodus 20:8-11.

According to the Vine Expository Dictionary, Hallow means "to make holy" (from hagios, "holy"), signifies to set apart for God, to sanctify, to make a person or thing the opposite of koinos, "common;" it is translated "Hallowed," with reference to the name of God the Father in the Lord's Prayer. When something is Hallowed, it is set apart for God making it not like any other common day.

It was treated as such by the Patriarchs before the Ten Commandments were given on Mt. Sinai because in the Genesis account of creation, He Hallowed it right after finishing Creation. It did not start with the Jews but had been hallowed since Creation. This is also emphasized when Manna falls from Heaven to feed the Israelites in the wilderness as seen in the following verses.

4 Then the Lord said to Moses, "Behold, I will rain bread from heaven for you. And the people shall go out and gather [a]a certain quota every day, that I may test them, whether they will walk in My law or not.

5 And it shall be on the sixth day that they shall prepare what they bring in, and it shall be twice as much as they gather daily..."

16 This is the thing which the Lord has commanded: 'Let every man gather it according to each one's need, one omer for each person, according to the number of persons; let every man take for those who are in his tent.'"

17 Then the children of Israel did so and gathered, some more, some less.

18 So when they measured it by omers, he who gathered much had nothing left over, and he who gathered little had no lack. Every man had gathered according to each one's need.

19 And Moses said, "Let no one leave any of it till morning."

20 Notwithstanding they did not [b]heed Moses. But some of them left part of it until morning, and it bred worms and stank. And Moses was angry with them.

21 So they gathered it every morning, every man according to his need. And when the sun became hot, it melted.

22 And so it was, on the sixth day, that they gathered twice as much bread, two omers for each one. And all the rulers of the congregation came and told Moses.

23 Then he said to them, "This is what the Lord has said: 'Tomorrow is a Sabbath rest, a holy Sabbath to the Lord. Bake what you will bake today, and boil what you will boil; and lay up for yourselves all that remains, to be kept until morning.'"

24 So they laid it up till morning, as Moses commanded; and it did not stink, nor were there any worms in it.

25 Then Moses said, "Eat that today, for today is a Sabbath to the Lord; today you will not find it in the field.

26 Six days you shall gather it, but on the seventh day, the Sabbath, there will be none."

27 Now it happened that some of the people went out on the seventh day to gather, but they found none.

28 And the Lord said to Moses, "How long do you refuse to keep My commandments and My laws?

29 See! For the Lord has given you the Sabbath; therefore He gives you on the sixth day bread for two days. Let every man remain in his place; let no man go out of his place on the seventh day."

30 So the people rested on the seventh day. Exodus 16:4-5, 16-30.

The Israelites were in the wilderness as they made their way from Egypt to Canaan. It was a desert wilderness in which the approximately 4 million-strong nation would not have been able to survive the journey with no food or water. In the raining of Manna is an object lesson that God is ultimately our Sustainer. He consistently fed them and provided water in the desert as well, but also gave them what was sufficient so that they would not be tempted to hoard manna for the future in case it stopped falling.

He didn't allow them to keep extra Manna but to take what was sufficient for the day. Any extra which was unused would rot overnight rendering it inedible. It was for them to trust that God indeed knew their need and would supply it daily. He supplied them with Manna the forty years they wandered in the wilderness. If God provided food and water in a desert wilderness, surely He can provide for us today in a time of need. In addition to this lesson, He showed them the importance of the Sabbath.

All week long they had to take what was sufficient or the extra unused Manna would go bad. On the 6th day however, they were instructed to take a double portion; one for the 6th day and the other for the Sabbath, because no Manna would fall on the Sabbath. It was the only time that the Manna would not go bad, and the extra portion would be sufficient for the Sabbath with no left-overs. And those who would still go out to get Manna due to unbelief would find none. In this miracle of preserving the Manna, people would see the importance of the Sabbath.

The Ten Commandments were given to the Israelites after they left Egypt. These are people who on account of being in a foreign pagan country, and upon years of slavery, had somewhat forgotten the God of their forefathers. The spectacular way in which God gave the Law to them was to remind them of who God was. This is why when Moses delayed returning from Mt. Sinai; upon Aaron giving in to their demands, made a golden calf and they worshiped it in Exodus 32, because they were so quick to forget.

The spectacular way in which God descended on Mt. Sinai to deliver the Law by speaking it in the hearing of the whole nation, was to be a reminder to them that He was their One and Only True God who is a Living God, that there is no other, and that this Law was written by His own hand on the tablets of stone. It was not written by Moses or the Angels, but by God Himself:

12 Then the Lord said to Moses, "Come up to Me on the mountain and be there; and I will give you tablets of stone, and the law and commandments which I have written, that you may teach them..."

18 And when He had made an end of speaking with him on Mount Sinai, He gave Moses two tablets of the Testimony, tablets of stone, written with the finger of God. Exodus 24:12 and 31:18.

The Commandments of God are Holy just as He is Holy and speaking of the Law Jesus said:

17 "Do not think that I came to destroy the Law or the Prophets. I did not come to destroy but to fulfill.

18 For assuredly, I say to you, till heaven and earth pass away, one [b]jot or one [c]tittle will by no means pass from the law till all is fulfilled.

19 Whoever therefore breaks one of the least of these commandments, and teaches men so, shall be called least in the kingdom of heaven; but whoever does and teaches them, he shall be called great in the kingdom of heaven. Matthew 5:17-19.

In His own words, there has never and will never be a change of the Law till heaven and earth pass away. If there has ever or will ever be a change before His return, it will be a change not sanctioned or recognized in Heaven. This is the Law that is so unchangeable that, rather than change it to accommodate sinners, had Christ die in the sinner's place so the price could be paid of breaking it because "the wages of sin is death, but the gift of God is eternal life in Christ Jesus our Lord." Romans 3:23. Now that we have established how grand and unchangeable the Law is, what day is the Sabbath.

The Sabbath day

There is a lot of contention upon this topic, with most of Christendom keeping Sunday as Sabbath. What does scripture say the Sabbath day is? The following are some verses on the Sabbath when Jesus was here on earth.

Jesus taught on the Sabbath

21 And they went into Capernaum; and straightway on the sabbath day he entered into the synagogue, and taught. Mark 1:21.

2 And when the sabbath day was come, he began to teach in the synagogue: and many hearing him were astonished, saying, From whence hath this man these things? and what wisdom is this which is given unto him, that even such mighty works are wrought by his hands? Mark 6:2.

16 And he came to Nazareth, where he had been brought up: and, as his custom was, he went into the synagogue on the sabbath day, and stood up for to read. Luke 4:16.

31 And came down to Capernaum, a city of Galilee, and taught them on the sabbath days. Luke 4:31.

6 And it came to pass also on another sabbath, that he entered into the synagogue and taught: and there was a man whose right hand was withered. Luke 6:6.

10 And he was teaching in one of the synagogues on the sabbath. Luke 13:10.

During His whole ministry, He never once mentioned that the Sabbath day was changed. If it was something as important as a change with one of the Ten Commandments, He would have said something, but as we learned earlier, not one part of God's Holy Law will be changed.

The Apostles taught on Sabbath after Jesus' death and ascension

42 And when the Jews were gone out of the synagogue, the Gentiles besought that these words might be preached to them the next sabbath. Acts 13:42.

44 And the next sabbath day came almost the whole city together to hear the word of God.. Acts 13:44.

21 For Moses has had throughout many generations those who preach him in every city, being read in the synagogues every Sabbath. Acts 15:21.

2 And Paul, as his manner was, went in unto them, and three sabbath days reasoned with them out of the scriptures...Acts 17:2.

4 And he reasoned in the synagogue every sabbath, and persuaded the Jews and the Greeks. Acts 18:4.

The Apostles likewise followed in Christ's footsteps and taught on the Sabbath day. Just as it was customary for Christ to teach on the Sabbath day, it was also for the Apostles, and what they learned from Christ they practiced and taught new believers to do the same as we see here in Paul's letter to Titus:

9...holding fast the faithful word as he has been taught, that he may be able, by sound doctrine, both to exhort and convict those who contradict. Titus 1:9.

Jesus Himself before He ascended to Heaven encouraged His disciples to teach what He taught them:

19 Go [c]therefore and make disciples of all the nations, baptizing them in the name of the Father and of the Son and of the Holy Spirit,

20 teaching them to observe all things that I have commanded you...Matthew 28:19-20.

When asked about what the greatest commandments where, He said:

37...'"You shall love the Lord your God with all your heart, with all your soul, and with all your mind.'

38 This is the first and great commandment.

39 And the second is like it: 'You shall love your neighbor as yourself.'

40 On these two commandments hang all the Law and the Prophets." Matthew 22:37-40.

The first 4 commandments are about loving God and the last 6 loving our neighbor. (See Exodus 20:3-17)
These are the things He commanded and that those who are believers and follow Christ are to practice and teach others to do the same. If Christ taught that the Law is unchangeable, never mentioned of any change to the Sabbath while here and His Apostles taught new believers on the Sabbath, how did most of the Christian world end up keeping Sunday as the Sabbath?

Sabbath change: The Conversion of Constantine

Constantine was the first so-called Christian emperor of the Roman Empire. The story of his conversion has become very well known to students of ancient history. He was marching forth to fight the battle of Milvian Bridge when he had some kind of vision, and saw a flaming cross in the sky. Underneath the cross were the Latin words meaning "In this sign conquer." Constantine took this as an omen that he should be a Christian, and his army as well.

He declared all his pagan soldiers to be Christians, and became very zealous to build up the power and prestige of the church. Through his influence great blocks of pagans were taken into the Christian ranks. But, friends, they were still pagan at heart, and they brought in much of the paraphernalia of sun-worship to which they continued to be devoted. We mentioned in a previous broadcast about the adoption of Christmas and Easter into the church. At the same time, many other customs were Christianized and appropriated into the practice of the church as well.

Sun Worship

Mithraism or sun-worship was the official religion of the Roman Empire at the time. It had an official worship day on which special homage was given to the sun. That day was called "The Venerable Day of the Sun." It was the first day of the week, and from it we get our name Sunday. When Constantine pressed his pagan hordes into the church they were observing the day of the sun for their adoration of the sun god. It was their special holy day. In order to make it more convenient for them to make the change to the new religion, Constantine accepted their day of worship, Sunday, instead of the Christian Sabbath which had been observed by Jesus and His disciples. Remember that the way had been prepared for this already by the increasing anti-Jewish feelings against those who were accused of putting Jesus to death. Those feelings would naturally condition many Christians to swing away from something which was held religiously by the Jews. It is therefore easier to understand how the change was imposed on Christianity through a strong civil law issued by Constantine as the Emperor of Rome. [1] It says this:

"On the venerable Day of the sun let the magistrates and people residing in cities rest, and let all workshops be closed. In the country, however, persons engaged in agriculture may freely and lawfully continue their pursuits: because it often happens that another Day is not so suitable for grain sowing or for vine planting: lest by neglecting the proper moment for such operations the bounty of heaven should be lost." [2]

Chamber's Encyclopedia says this:

Unquestionably the first law, either ecclesiastical or civil, by which the Sabbatical observance of that Day is known to have been ordained, is the edict of Constantine, 321 A.D.

Following this initial legislation, both emperors and Popes in succeeding centuries added other laws to strengthen Sunday observance. What began as a pagan ordinance ended as a Christian regulation. Close on the heels of the Edict of Constantine followed the Catholic Church Council of Laodicea (circa 364 AD):

Christians shall not Judaize and be idle on Saturday (Sabbath), but shall work on that Day: but the Lord's Day, they shall especially honor; and as being Christians, shall, if possible, do no work on that day. If however, they are found Judaizing, they shall be shut out from Christ. [3] The following is an excerpt from sabbathtruth.com:

Historical Accounts

"Constantine made the initial pronouncement and legal decree about the change, while the Catholic Church reinforced that act in one church council after another. For this reason, many, many official statements from Catholic sources are made, claiming that the church made the change from Saturday to Sunday.

Here is a statement from Dr. Gilbert Murray, M.A., D.Litt., LLD, FBA, Professor of Greek at Oxford University and he wrote: "Now since Mithras was the sun, the Unconquered, and the sun was the Royal Star, the religion looked for a king whom it could serve as a representative of Mithras upon earth. The Roman Emperor seemed to be clearly indicated as the true king. In sharp contrast to Christianity, Mithraism recognized Caesar as the bearer of divine grace. It had so much acceptance that it was able to impose on the Christian world its own sun-day in place of the Sabbath; its sun's birthday, the 25th of December, as the birthday of Jesus." History of Christianity in the Light of Modern Knowledge.

Looking a bit further into historical statements, Dr. William Frederick says: "The Gentiles were an idolatrous people who worshiped the sun, and Sunday was their most sacred day. Now in order to reach the people in this new field, it seems but natural as well as necessary to make Sunday the rest day of the church. At this time it was necessary for the church to either adopt the Gentile's day or else have the Gentiles change their day. To change the Gentiles day would have been an offense and stumbling block to them. The church could naturally reach them better by keeping their day." There it is, friends, a clear explanation by Dr. Frederick as to how this change happened. Another statement very parallel to this one is found in the North British Review.

But let's move on to a statement from the Catholic Encyclopedia, Vol. 4, p. 153. "The church after changing the day of rest from the Jewish Sabbath or seventh-day of the week to the first, made the third commandment refer to Sunday as the day to be kept holy as the Lord's day."

Catholicism Takes Credit for the Change

From the Catholic Press newspaper in Sidney, Australia. "Sunday is a Catholic institution and its claims to observance can be defended only on Catholic principles. From the beginning to end of Scripture there is not a single passage that warrants the transfer of weekly public worship from the last day of the week to the first."

The Catholic Mirror of September 23, 1894, puts it this way: "The Catholic Church for over one thousand years before the existence of a Protestant by virtue of her divine mission, changed the day from Saturday to Sunday."

To point up the claims we're talking about, I want to read from two Catechisms. First, from the Convert's Catechism of Catholic Doctrine by Reverend Peter Giermann. "Question: Which is the Sabbath day? Answer: Saturday is the Sabbath day. Question: Why do we observe Sunday instead of Saturday? Answer: We observe Sunday instead of Saturday because the Catholic Church in the Council of Laodicea transferred the solemnity from Saturday to Sunday."

Second, from Reverend Steven Keenan's Doctrinal Catechism we read this: "Question: Have you any other way of proving that the Church has power to institute festivals of precept? Answer: Had she not such power, she could not have done that in which all modern religionists agree with her; she could not have substituted the observance of Sunday, the first day of the week, for the observance of Saturday, the seventh day; a change for which there is no Scriptural authority."

Then from Cardinal Gibbons' book, The Question Box, p.179, "If the Bible is the only guide for the Christian, then the Seventh-day Adventist is right in observing Saturday with the Jew. Is it not strange that those who make the Bible their only teacher should inconsistently follow in this matter the tradition of the Catholic Church?"

One more statement taken from the book, The Faith of Millions, p. 473. "But since Saturday, not Sunday, is specified in the Bible, isn't it curious that non-Catholics who profess to take their religion directly from the Bible and not from the Church, observe Sunday instead of Saturday? Yes, of course, it is inconsistency but this change was made about fifteen centuries before Protestantism was born, and by that time the custom was universally observed. They have continued the custom even though it rests upon the authority of the Catholic Church and not upon an explicit text from the Bible. That observance remains as a reminder of the Mother Church from which the non-Catholic sects broke away like a boy running away from home but still carrying in his pocket a picture of his mother or a lock of her hair." [4]

The Bible speaks of these changes

"We learned earlier that no where in Scripture is the change for Sunday to be hallowed instead of the Sabbath. In fact the Bible speaks of an entity which will try to change the Law, in the dream that Daniel had in Daniel 7 when the dream is being explained to Him:

23 "Thus he said: 'The fourth beast shall be A fourth kingdom on earth, Which shall be different from all other kingdoms, And shall devour the whole earth, Trample it and break it in pieces.

24 The ten horns are ten kings Who shall arise from this kingdom. And another shall rise after them; He shall be different from the first ones, And shall subdue three kings.

25 He shall speak pompous words against the Most High, Shall persecute[j] the saints of the Most High, And shall intend to change times and law. Then the saints shall be given into his hand For a time and times and half a time.

26 'But the court shall be seated, And they shall take away his dominion, To consume and destroy it forever.

27 Then the kingdom and dominion, And the greatness of the kingdoms under the whole heaven, Shall be given to the people, the saints of the Most High. His kingdom is an everlasting kingdom, And all dominions shall serve and obey Him.' Daniel 7:23-27.

To summarize as this is a topic for study in itself, there were 4 major kingdoms throughout history which fit the prophetic descriptions closest in Daniel 7: Babylon the lion like beast in verse 4, Medo-Persia the bear like beast in verse 5, Greece the leopard-like beast in verse 6 and Rome the ten-horned beast in verse 7. The Roman church started towards the demise of the Roman empire, with the compromise of Christianity with Paganism as we saw with the rule of Constantine. They grew stronger till they became a persecuting power of those who were protesting them, the Protestants, during the Dark Ages. The Book of Revelation also alludes to Papal Rome in the following text:

1 Then [a]I stood on the sand of the sea. And I saw a beast rising up out of the sea, having [b]seven heads and ten horns, and on his horns ten crowns, and on his heads a blasphemous name.

2 Now the beast which I saw was like a leopard, his feet were like the feet of a bear, and his mouth like the mouth of a lion. The dragon gave him his power, his throne, and great authority.

3 And I saw one of his heads as if it had been mortally wounded, and his deadly wound was healed. And all the world marveled and followed the beast.

4 So they worshiped the dragon who gave authority to the beast; and they worshiped the beast, saying, "Who is like the beast? Who is able to make war with him?"

5 And he was given a mouth speaking great things and blasphemies, and he was given authority to [c]continue for forty-two months.

6 Then he opened his mouth in blasphemy against God, to blaspheme His name, His tabernacle, and those who dwell in heaven.

7 It was granted to him to make war with the saints and to overcome them. And authority was given him over every [d]tribe, tongue, and nation.

8 All who dwell on the earth will worship him, whose names have not been written in the Book of Life of the Lamb slain from the foundation of the world. Revelation 13:1-8.

The four beasts of Daniel 7 are depicted as part of Antichrist, or the beast, because the papacy incorporated pagan beliefs and practices from all four empires. She clothed them in spiritual garb and spread them to the world as Christian teachings. Here is one of many supporting statements from history: "In a certain respect, she [the papacy] has copied her organization from that of the Roman Empire, has preserved and made fruitful the philosophical intuitions of Socrates, Plato, and Aristotle, borrowed from both Barbarians and the Byzantine Roman Empire, but always remains herself, thoroughly digesting all elements drawn from external sources."[5] This point definitely fits the papacy.

To identify the dragon, we go to Revelation chapter 12, where God's end-time church is pictured as a pure woman. In prophecy, a pure woman represents God's true people or church (Jeremiah 6:2 Isaiah 51:16). Revelation chapters 17 and 18 show the fallen churches which are symbolized by a fallen mother and her fallen daughters.) The pure woman is portrayed as pregnant and about to deliver. The dragon crouches nearby, hoping to "devour" the baby at birth. However, when the baby is born He evades the dragon, fulfills His mission, and then ascends to heaven. Obviously the baby is Jesus, whom Herod tried to destroy by killing all the babies in Bethlehem (Matthew 2:16). So the dragon represents pagan Rome, of which Herod was a king. The power behind Herod's plot was, of course, the devil (Revelation 12:7-9). Satan acts through various governments to accomplish his ugly work in this case, pagan Rome.

We will quote just two supportive references from history, though there are many:

(1) "The Roman Church ... pushed itself into the place of the Roman World-Empire, of which it is the actual continuation. ...The Pope ... is Caesar's successor." [6]

(2) "The mighty Catholic Church was little more than the Roman Empire baptized. Rome was transformed as well as converted. The very capital of the old Empire became the capital of the Christian Empire. The office of Pontifex Maximus was continued in that of Pope." [7] So this point also fits the papacy. She received her capital city and power from pagan Rome. [8]

More false teachings of the Catholic Church

Now that we understand how Sunday came to be accepted as the Sabbath when it is not, there are more teachings the Roman Catholic church teaches that are not Biblical. God has many people who are Roman Catholics just as He has many of other faiths who are not yet following Christ according to the Word of God, But He loves them and desires to save as many as choose to believe in Christ and confess Him as their Savior. That is why it is important to understand what God expects from us and to separate from any teachings that are not Biblical as we are warned:

8 'These people [c]draw near to Me with their mouth, And honor Me with their lips, But their heart is far from Me.

9 And in vain they worship Me, Teaching as doctrines the commandments of men...

1 Now the Spirit [a]expressly says that in latter times some will depart from the faith, giving heed to deceiving spirits and doctrines of demons. Matthew 15:8-9 and 1 Timothy 4:1.

The following are some of the teachings of the church as found in the Catechism of the Catholic Church (CCC), which are false because they are not in line with the Word of God:

The Catholic church is the one true church

CCC 2105 "The duty of offering God genuine worship concerns man both individually and socially. This is 'the traditional Catholic teaching on the moral duty of individuals and societies toward the true religion and the one Church of Christ.' By constantly evangelizing men, the Church works toward enabling them 'to infuse the Christian spirit into the mentality and mores, laws and structures of the communities in which [they] live.' The social duty of Christians is to respect and awaken in each man the love of the true and the good. It requires them to make known the worship of the one true religion which subsists in the Catholic and apostolic Church. Christians are called to be the light of the world. Thus, the Church shows forth the kingship of Christ over all creation and in particular over human societies."

Infallibility of the Catholic Church

CCC 2035, "The supreme degree of participation in the authority of Christ is ensured by the charism of infallibility. This infallibility extends as far as does the deposit of divine Revelation; it also extends to all those elements of doctrine, including morals, without which the saving truths of the faith cannot be preserved, explained, or observed."

Only the Roman Catholic Church has authority to Interpret Scripture

CCC 100, "The task of interpreting the Word of God authentically has been entrusted solely to the Magisterium of the Church, that is, to the Pope and to the bishops in communion with him."

The Bible teaches that reading the Scripture is the responsibility of every believer which is why it is written: "Study to shew thyself approved unto God, a workman that needeth not to be ashamed, rightly dividing the word of truth." 2 Timothy 2:15 (KJV). The following is an excerpt from E.G. White's book, The Great Controversy, on Scriptures being a safeguard in a believer's life:

"Satan well knew that the Holy Scriptures would enable men to discern his deceptions and withstand his power. It was by the Word that even the Savior of the world had resisted his attacks. At every assault, Christ presented the shield of eternal truth, saying, "It is written." To every suggestion of the adversary, he opposed the wisdom and power of the Word. In order for Satan to maintain his sway over men, and establish the authority of the papal usurper, he must keep them in ignorance of the Scriptures. The Bible would exalt God, and place finite men in their true position; therefore its sacred truths must be concealed and suppressed. This logic was adopted by the Roman Church. For hundreds of years the circulation of the Bible was prohibited. The people were forbidden to read it or to have it in their houses, and unprincipled priests and prelates interpreted its teachings to sustain their pretensions. Thus the pope came to be almost universally acknowledged as the vicegerent of God on earth, endowed with authority over Church and State." [9]

The Pope is the head of the church and has the authority of Christ

CCC 2034, "The Roman Pontiff and the bishops are 'authentic teachers, that is, teachers endowed with the authority of Christ, who preach the faith to the people entrusted to them, the faith to be believed and put into practice.' The ordinary and universal Magisterium of the Pope and the bishops in communion with him teach the faithful the truth to believe, the charity to practice, the beatitude to hope for."

The Roman Catholic Church is necessary for salvation

CCC 846, "How are we to understand this affirmation, often repeated by the Church Fathers? Re-formulated positively, it means that all salvation comes from Christ the Head through the Church which is his Body: Basing itself on Scripture and Tradition, the Council teaches that the Church, a pilgrim now on earth, is necessary for salvation: the one Christ is the mediator and the way of salvation; he is present to us in his body which is the Church. He himself explicitly asserted the necessity of faith and Baptism, and thereby affirmed at the same time the necessity of the Church which men enter through Baptism as through a door. Hence they could not be saved who, knowing that the Catholic Church was founded as necessary by God through Christ, would refuse either to enter it or to remain in it."

Sacred Tradition equal to scripture

CCC 82, "the Church, to whom the transmission and interpretation of Revelation is entrusted, does not derive her certainty about all revealed truths from the holy Scriptures alone. Both Scripture and Tradition must be accepted and honored with equal sentiments of devotion and reverence'."

Forgiveness of sins, salvation, is by faith and works

CCC 2036, "The specific precepts of the natural law, because their observance, demanded by the creator, is necessary for salvation."

CCC 2080, "The Decalogue contains a privileged expression of the natural law. It is made known to us by divine revelation and by human reason."

CCC 2068, "so that all men may attain salvation through faith, Baptism and the observance of the Commandments,"

Full benefit of Salvation is only through the Roman Catholic Church

"For it is only through Christ's Catholic Church, which is "the all-embracing means of salvation," that they can benefit fully from the means of salvation,," (Vatican 2, Decree on Ecumenism, 3).

Grace can be merited

CCC 2010, "Moved by the Holy Spirit and by charity, we can then merit for ourselves and for others the graces needed for our sanctification."

CCC 2027, "Moved by the Holy Spirit, we can merit for ourselves and for others all the graces needed to attain eternal life, as well as necessary temporal goods."

The merit of Mary and the Saints can be applied to Catholics and others

1477, "This treasury includes as well the prayers and good works of the Blessed Virgin Mary. They are truly immense, unfathomable, and even pristine in their value before God. In the treasury, too, are the prayers and good works of all the saints, all those who have followed in the footsteps of Christ the Lord and by his grace have made their lives holy and carried out the mission in the unity of the Mystical Body."

Penance is necessary for salvation

CCC 980, "This sacrament of Penance is necessary for salvation for those who have fallen after Baptism, just as Baptism is necessary for salvation for those who have not yet been reborn."

Purgatory

CCC 1031, "The Church gives the name Purgatory to this final purification of the elect, which is entirely different from the punishment of the damned. The Church formulated her doctrine of faith on Purgatory especially at the Councils of Florence and Trent. The tradition of the Church, by reference to certain texts of Scripture, speaks of a cleansing fire:

CCC 1475, "In the communion of saints, "a perennial link of charity exists between the faithful who have already reached their heavenly home, those who are expiating their sins in purgatory and those who are still pilgrims on earth. Between them there is, too, an abundant exchange of all good things." In this wonderful exchange, the holiness of one profits others, well beyond the harm that the sin of one could cause others. Thus recourse to the communion of saints lets the contrite sinner be more promptly and efficaciously purified of the punishments for sin.

Indulgences

CCC 1471, "The doctrine and practice of indulgences in the Church are closely linked to the effects of the sacrament of Penance. What is an indulgence? 'An indulgence is a remission before God of the temporal punishment due to sins whose guilt has already been forgiven, which the faithful Christian who is duly disposed gains under certain prescribed conditions through the action of the Church which, as the minister of redemption, dispenses and applies with authority the treasury of the satisfactions of Christ and the saints.'

'An indulgence is partial or plenary according as it removes either part or all of the temporal punishment due to sin.' The faithful can gain indulgences for themselves or apply them to the dead."

CCC 1478, "An indulgence is obtained through the Church who, by virtue of the power of binding and loosing granted her by Christ Jesus, intervenes in favor of individual Christians and opens for them the treasury of the merits of Christ and the saints to obtain from the Father of mercies the remission of the temporal punishments due for their sins. Thus the Church does not want simply to come to the aid of these Christians, but also to spur them to works of devotion, penance, and charity.

CCC 1498, "Through indulgences the faithful can obtain the remission of temporal punishment resulting from sin for themselves and also for the souls in Purgatory."

CCC 1472, "...On the other hand every sin, even venial, entails an unhealthy attachment to creatures, which must be purified either here on earth, or after death in the state called Purgatory. This purification frees one from what is called the "temporal punishment" of sin..."

Mary (there are many false doctrines concerning Mary found in Roman Catholicism, here are a few)

Mary is Mediatrix, CCC 969, "Therefore the Blessed Virgin is invoked in the Church under the titles of Advocate, Helper, Benefactress, and Mediatrix.'"

Mary brings us the gifts of eternal salvation, CCC 969, "Taken up to heaven she did not lay aside this saving office but by her manifold intercession continues to bring us the gifts of eternal salvation..."

Mary delivers souls from death, CCC 966, "...You [Mary] conceived the living God and, by your prayers, will deliver our souls from death."

Prayer to the saints

CCC 2677, "By asking Mary to pray for us, we acknowledge ourselves to be poor sinners and we address ourselves to the 'Mother of Mercy,' the All-Holy One. We give ourselves over to her now, in the Today of our lives. And our trust broadens further, already at the present moment, to surrender 'the hour of our death' wholly to her care."

The Communion elements become the actual body and blood of Christ

CCC 1374, "In the most blessed sacrament of the Eucharist "the body and blood, together with the soul and divinity, of our Lord Jesus Christ and, therefore, the whole Christ is truly, really, and substantially contained."

CCC 1376, "The Council of Trent summarizes the Catholic faith by declaring: "Because Christ our Redeemer said that it was truly his body that he was offering under the species of bread, it has always been the conviction of the Church of God, and this holy Council now declares again, that by the consecration of the bread and wine there takes place a change of the whole substance of the bread into the substance of the body of Christ our Lord and of the whole substance of the wine into the substance of his blood. This change the holy Catholic Church has fittingly and properly called transubstantiation."

References:

1. https://www.sabbathtruth.com/sabbath-history/how-the-sabbath-was-changed
2. Schaff's History of the Christian Church, vol. III, chap. 75.
3. https://amazingdiscoveries.org/S-deception-Sabbath_change_Constantine
4. https://www.sabbathtruth.com/sabbath-history/how-the-sabbath-was-changed
5. Andre Retif, The Catholic Spirit, trans. by Dom Aldhelm Dean, Vol. 88 of The Twentieth Century Encyclopedia of Catholicism (New York, Hawthorne Books, 1959), p. 85.
6. Adolf Harnack, What is Christianity? trans. by Thomas Bailey Saunders (New York: Putnam, 2nd ed., rev., 1901), p. 270
7. Alexander Clarence Flick, The Rise of the Mediaeval Church (reprint: New York, Burt Franklin, 1959), pp. 148, 149.
8. https://www.amazingfacts.org/media-library/study-guide/e/4997/t/the-mark-of-the-beast
9. Ellen. G. White. The Great Controversy (1888). pp. 51.

25
FOUNTAIN OF LIVING WATER

We need to eat to live, and Christ likened himself to Bread or food, that whosoever believes in Him and eats Him will not hunger again but be resurrected on the day of His second coming and will have everlasting life with Him. We learned that eating Him is dwelling in Him and Him in us, and this only happens when we surrender our will and His is done in our lives. So eating Him is His will being done in our lives, which is for us not only to be resurrected at His second coming, but also to live forever with Him. Just as essential as Bread is for life, water is just as crucial as we learn this encounter Jesus had with a Samaritan woman at a well:

6 Now Jacob's well was there. Jesus therefore, being wearied from His journey, sat thus by the well. It was about the sixth hour.

7 A woman of Samaria came to draw water. Jesus said to her, "Give Me a drink."

8 For His disciples had gone away into the city to buy food.

9 Then the woman of Samaria said to Him, "How is it that You, being a Jew, ask a drink from me, a Samaritan woman?" For Jews have no dealings with Samaritans.

10 Jesus answered and said to her, "If you knew the gift of God, and who it is who says to you, 'Give Me a drink,' you would have asked Him, and He would have given you living water."

11 The woman said to Him, "Sir, You have nothing to draw with, and the well is deep. Where then do You get that living water?

12 Are You greater than our father Jacob, who gave us the well, and drank from it himself, as well as his sons and his livestock?"

13 Jesus answered and said to her, "Whoever drinks of this water will thirst again, 14 but whoever drinks of the water that I shall give him will never thirst. But the water that I shall give him will become in him a fountain of water springing up into everlasting life."

15 The woman said to Him, "Sir, give me this water, that I may not thirst, nor come here to draw." John 4:6-15.

The labor of drawing water

In the account of Jesus at the well, we see how He used a literal thing to draw attention to the more important spiritual significance of it. He asks her for water and yet tells her that if she knew who He really was, she would have asked for Living Water and He would have given her. He knows that she understands that she will always need water, and will thus have to come continually to draw it at the well, but He seeks to divert her mind to water which is not only living which if she drinks will not thirst again, but will be a well in her springing to eternal life.

She had even mentioned that the well is deep and He had nothing to draw with, how could He possibly draw water enough that she will never thirst again? She understood that there's labor involved and as long as she needs water, which is as long as she is alive, she will have to come to draw water. So she sees His point that, the water which He seeks to give her is not only a gift as there is no labor involved, but also that when she drinks this water, she will not thirst again but the water in her even becomes a well springing everlasting.

She understands the two extremes: that on one end she continually labors to draw water as long as she lives, and on the other, she is given water as a gift thus it involves no labor and not only will she not thirst again, but this water in itself becomes a well in her. One extreme there is continual need and on the other her need is not only met but it is met indefinitely. He was diverting her attention to the rest we saw a few chapters back. "Come unto me, all ye that labor and are heavy laden, and I will give you rest." Matthew 11:28.

He seeks those who realize that no matter how hard they labor to sustain their lives, he is the one who gives life and thus He provides for it. He seeks those who realize that life is a rat race, and that "What profit has a man from all his labor In which he [b]toils under the sun?...14 I have seen all the works that are done under the sun; and indeed, all is vanity and grasping for the wind." Ecclesiastes 1:3, 14. He knows that we worry about providing for the present and especially the future which we will not even be guaranteed to see, (Matthew 6:25-34 and James 4:15.)

We worry about things that He has already taken care of and made provision for, and we labor hard for them yet He has already promised to provide all these things. He has promised take care of us as written: "I have been young, and now am old; Yet I have not seen the righteous forsaken, Nor his descendants begging bread." Psalms 37:25.

A Spring that never runs dry

In the scripture from Ecclesiastes above, the writer considers all works done under the sun as vain. Our hearts are where our treasures are. Your treasure is whatever you make your life goal to pursue. Our labors on this earth, no matter how significant they might be, are considered vain, unless God works through us to achieve His end in our lives and the lives we might be able to impact. Ultimately, they all have to be grounded in God's will and Kingdom for them to actually have everlasting value:

19 Do not lay up for yourselves treasures on earth, where moth and rust destroy and where thieves break in and steal;

20 but lay up for yourselves treasures in heaven, where neither moth nor rust destroys and where thieves do not break in and steal.

21 For where your treasure is, there your heart will be also. Matthew 7:24-27.

We are constantly drawing water because we thirst and drink but are never satisfied. We substitute the Living Water with water of things or achievements in this life which can never satisfy. The rich continue to strive to get richer even though they are more than sufficiently wealthy. The powerful strive for absolute power if they can have their way. Many dedicate their whole lives to accolades and the applause of man, and even then it is not enough. If they could, they would all want more and still not be satisfied. Christ, the Living Water, is the "Desire of All Nations" Haggai 2:7, and only He can satisfy this thirst of the soul completely and sufficiently. How does one go from continuously drawing water, to having a well of Water springing up in them?

Drawing the Living Water

Just as for the Bread of Life which if one eats, they will not only be filled but it will give them life everlasting; so is the Living water which if one drinks will not thirst again but will also have everlasting life. Water is life and thus Living Water gives us life springing unto everlasting life which is a gift from God. Just as for the eating of the Bread means dwelling in Him and Him in us, this dwelling can only happen when we allow His will to be done in our lives. So us choosing for His will to be done in our lives is the eating of the bread, and so it is also drinking the Water of life. Us choosing his will over ours which is the devil's will working in us as we have already seen, enables us to dwell in Him and thus the drinking of the Water of Life giving us life eternal.

39 This is the will of the Father who sent Me, that of all He has given Me I should lose nothing, but should raise it up at the last day.

40 And this is the will of Him who sent Me, that everyone who sees the Son and believes in Him may have everlasting life; and I will raise him up at the last day." John 6:39, 40.

Just as the woman at the well who labored continually by drawing the water time and time again, He offered the Living Water as a gift to her, ensuring her that if she drinks this Living water, she will not thirst again but will live everlasting as a result of it; the acceptance of this gift is believing on the gift that he sent:

15 that whoever believes in Him should [c]not perish but have eternal life.

16 For God so loved the world that He gave His only begotten Son, that whoever believes in Him should not perish but have everlasting life.

17 For God did not send His Son into the world to condemn the world, but that the world through Him might be saved. John 3:15-17.

By believing in Christ, the Great Physician himself, we accept this Living Water and the Bread of Life which He is also:

35 And Jesus said to them, "I am the bread of life. He who comes to Me shall never hunger, and he who believes in Me shall never thirst...

47 Most assuredly, I say to you, he who believes [j]in Me has everlasting life. John 6:35, 47.

Can this well of Living Water run dry?

Only Christ can satisfy our thirst! As long as we are in a relationship with Him, we are satisfied and the well never runs dry. However, it can run dry if we lose our connection to Him. Life is only found in Christ. As long as we abide in Him, and Him in us we have access to the Living Water and do not thirst. As soon as one stops abiding in Him and the connection to Christ is broken, figuratively, the water runs dry because Christ is the Water as long as He abides in us and us in Him. A good way to describe this is in the following scripture:

4 Abide in Me, and I in you. As the branch cannot bear fruit of itself, unless it abides in the vine, neither can you, unless you abide in Me.

5 "I am the vine, you are the branches. He who abides in Me, and I in him, bears much fruit; for without Me you can do nothing.

6 If anyone does not abide in Me, he is cast out as a branch and is withered;...John 15:4, 6.

A branch starts to wither when it is cut off from Vine. It begins to wither, dry up and die, and cannot produce fruit anymore because it is disconnected from the life source. Likewise, the water dries up because one stops abiding in the Spring, the Source of the Living Water, Christ. If His will is for us to be saved, believing in Him is how we accept The bread of Life and the Living Water, and the eating and drinking is us dwelling in Him and Him in us (John 6:56).

How do we keep the Spring of Living Water running in us?

Abiding in the Vine is how the branch stays connected as we saw in John 15. Abiding in Christ is how we drink the Living Water. As long as we drink, it never runs dry. We stop drinking and the Spring stops running.

24 Now he who keeps His commandments abides in Him, and He in him. And by this we know that He abides in us, by the Spirit whom He has given us. 1 John 3:24.

12 No one has seen God at any time. If we love one another, God abides in us, and His love has been perfected in us.

13 By this we know that we abide in Him, and He in us, because He has given us of His Spirit...

15 Whoever confesses that Jesus is the Son of God, God abides in him, and he in God.

16 And we have known and believed the love that God has for us. God is love, and he who abides in love abides in God, and God in him. 1 John 4:12, 13, 15, 16.

Whosoever keeps His commandments dwells in Him and He in him. His will is us dwelling in Him and Him in us, which is the keeping of the commandments. The keeping of the commandments is love as is written:

8 Owe no one anything except to love one another, for he who loves another has fulfilled the law.

9 For the commandments, "You shall not commit adultery," "You shall not murder," "You shall not steal," [b]"You shall not bear false witness," "You shall not covet," and if there is any other commandment, are all summed up in this saying, namely, "You shall love your neighbor as yourself."

10 Love does no harm to a neighbor; therefore love is the fulfillment of the law. Romans 13:8-10.

So, those who keep the commandments love their neighbor, and by doing so dwell in Him and He in them. Dwelling in Him is how we drink the Living water, and so by love or the fulfillment of the Law, we drink unto Eternal life. This is the Father's will for us and if we allow it to work in us, then He gives us the desire and empowers us to do what pleases Him; which is for us to love our neighbor as we love ourselves and love Him with all our hearts and this is how we drink the Living Water. So the only way to acquire the life giving properties of the Living water is to do God's will, love, which is the fulfillment of the Law. It is for the broken Law that Christ came:

4 who gave Himself for our sins, that He might deliver us from this present evil age, according to the will of our God and Father...

14 who gave Himself for us, that He might redeem us from every lawless deed and purify for Himself His own special people, zealous for good works. Galatians 1:4 and Titus 2:14.

Only by believing Him who gave himself for us to redeem us from iniquity, and to deliver us from this present evil world do we accept the sacrifice He made for us, and only by allowing His will to be done in our lives; to love our neighbor which is the fulfillment of the broken Law He came to die for, can we drink the Living water, hence can we live eternally.

Life is in the Water

It is important to understand that when we drink this Living Water we are alive indeed. Some might ask how we can be alive indeed if we are already alive as it is. When our Physician talks about life, He is talking about being alive in the spiritual sense. When you drink this Living Water, the Holy Spirit quickens you or gives you life and this life is what springs unto everlasting if you stay connected to the source of the Living Water, Christ because "It is the Spirit who gives life; the flesh profits nothing. The words that I speak to you are spirit, and they are life." John 6:63.

He is not talking about life in the physical but is always addressing the big picture which is life of the soul and that's more important. That is why Christ taught in parables because He would associate them to the deep spiritual things by relating the people to their everyday surroundings and situations. He knew that we are so literal or more inclined to understand things in the literal. In the above verse, He is saying that all that he talks about in John chapter 6 about the bread is not about their physical but is spiritual. These words are supposed to draw their attention to the more important quickening of the soul, as is written:

28 ...do not fear those who kill the body but cannot kill the soul. But rather fear Him who is able to destroy both soul and body in [h]hell. Matthew 10:28.

Anything that puts our bodies in danger or kills us in the flesh, only cuts our lives short on this earth. The thing to be more worried about is the death of the soul, which happens if one's soul is not healed of sin. Healing is by believing in Him, confession of sins, and surrender of one's will so that His will is done. His will works in us to will and do what pleases Him, which is to love Him with all our hearts and to love others as ourselves. This is how the Bread of Life is eaten and how the Living Water is drunk which then quickens our souls such that as long as we remain connected to the Source, Christ Himself, we will have everlasting life.

To show how when Christ is talking about life, he is talking in the spiritual sense. We have already seen what being dead in the physical sense is, that it's like being asleep. So when God is talking about us being dead, what exactly is He talking about? We saw earlier on in the book that He has diagnosed all humanity as having this terminal illness of sin. If it is terminal that means that we are all bound to die from it, unless if we are healed. So the ones who allow the Great Physician to heal them, do not die but live because the life threatening terminal illness has been taken away from them. Even though we are alive in the physical sense, we all have this spiritual leprosy of sin, and unless we are healed from it, we will surely die which is death of the soul.

Unless we are healed now when we are physically alive, if we die or sleep in our sins, we will surely die the death of the soul because of sin. So with this in mind let us see what is said in the Word about being dead and alive in God's eyes.

24 Most assuredly, I say to you, he who hears My word and believes in Him who sent Me has everlasting life, and shall not come into judgment, but has passed from death into life.

25 Most assuredly, I say to you, the hour is coming, and now is, when the dead will hear the voice of the Son of God; and those who hear will live...

23 For the wages of sin is death, but the [h]gift of God is eternal life in Christ Jesus our Lord. John 5:24, 25 and Romans 6:23.

We have all been diagnosed with the sin "For all have sinned, and come short of the glory of God;" Romans 3:23. So as a result of sin we have all committed, we are all dead spiritually and unless we are healed from sin "…shall surely die." Genesis 2:17.

Watery grave: Baptism

It's only fit that while we are on this subject of life and death, that we draw our attention to a very important role that water plays in the healing process. The only condition for a person to enter the Kingdom of God, that it is to be born again as we learn in the conversation Jesus has with Nicodemus. What is to be born again and what does this have to do with water? This next passage sheds some light on this:

3 ..."Most assuredly, I say to you, unless one is born [a]again, he cannot see the kingdom of God."

4 Nicodemus said to Him, "How can a man be born when he is old? Can he enter a second time into his mother's womb and be born?"

5 Jesus answered, "Most assuredly, I say to you, unless one is born of water and the Spirit, he cannot enter the kingdom of God.

6 That which is born of the flesh is flesh, and that which is born of the Spirit is spirit.

7 Do not marvel that I said to you, 'You must be born again.'

8 The wind blows where it wishes, and you hear the sound of it, but cannot tell where it comes from and where it goes. So is everyone who is born of the Spirit." John 3:1-8.

Christ is tells Nicodemus about the condition for Salvation or the basic and most essential step to the healing process. To enter the Kingdom of God, one has to be born again. No one will enter Heaven with their sinful nature. The people who enter the Kingdom are people who are born again and only they who are such can enter the Kingdom. Those who are born again have no sin, and they are the ones who will enter the kingdom as no sin will enter Heaven because

1 ...I saw a new heaven and a new earth, for the first heaven and the first earth had passed away;...

27 But there shall by no means enter it anything [q]that defiles, or causes an abomination or a lie, but only those who are written in the Lamb's Book of Life. Revelation 21:1, 27.

Except one be born again; except one have their sins washed away and to live a new life by God's power, they cannot see Heaven. Like Christ, we die, to the carnal or old nature by being crucified with Him as is written:

20 I have been crucified with Christ; it is no longer I who live, but Christ lives in me; and the life which I now live in the flesh I live by faith in the Son of God, who loved me and gave Himself for me. Galatians 2:20.

But here is the interesting part! The same power that raised Jesus Christ from the dead, is the same power that raises us from death to our old nature to a new life, as we see in the following verses:

2...How shall we who died to sin live any longer in it?

3 Or do you not know that as many of us as were baptized into Christ Jesus were baptized into His death?

4 Therefore we were buried with Him through baptism into death, that just as Christ was raised from the dead by the glory of the Father, even so we also should walk in newness of life.

5 For if we have been united together in the likeness of His death, certainly we also shall be in the likeness of His resurrection,

6 knowing this, that our old man was crucified with Him, that the body of sin might be [a]done away with, that we should no longer be slaves of sin.

7 For he who has died has been [b]freed from sin.

8 Now if we died with Christ, we believe that we shall also live with Him,

9 knowing that Christ, having been raised from the dead, dies no more. Death no longer has dominion over Him.

10 For the death that He died, He died to sin once for all; but the life that He lives, He lives to God.

11 Likewise you also, [c]reckon yourselves to be dead indeed to sin, but alive to God in Christ Jesus our Lord. Romans 6:2-11.

If the old nature is crucified with Him, we shall likewise rise like He did to a newness of life by His power. If we are in the likeness of His death by also being crucified to self, or the old life, we shall also be in the likeness of His resurrection. By death Christ overcame sin and will not die again but lives unto God, likewise if we are planted in the likeness of His death and die to self, we shall also rise with Him and are dead to sin but alive to God through Jesus Christ. What this is saying is that the old life is dead because the driving force behind it is dead which was self or the carnal nature, and a new life is born which has no fellowship with sin, therefore when we are truly born again and have died to self, our new nature which is spiritual is as good as dead to sin because it has no fellowship with it. The new nature because of the second marriage is now dead to sin but alive to God because God is the one working in him. This is likened in the whole of Romans chapter 7 to a marriage.

1 Or do you not know, brethren (for I speak to those who know the law), that the law [a]has dominion over a man as long as he lives?

2 For the woman who has a husband is bound by the law to her husband as long as he lives. But if the husband dies, she is released from the law of her husband.

3 So then if, while her husband lives, she marries another man, she will be called an adulteress; but if her husband dies, she is free from that law, so that she is no adulteress, though she has married another man. Romans 7:1-3.

A man and a woman are supposed to be married for life, and only death would be the reason for the marriage to end in God's eyes. Our old nature's struggles with sin is likened to a woman married to a husband who is not good. As bad as the husband is, the only way to discontinue this marriage would be upon his death. Dying to our old nature is what it takes to break this union and only death. Upon the death of the first husband, we, the woman, are then able to be married to Christ the new husband in a union that is legally recognized by God. Only death to break off the first union so that the second union can be consummated to the good and ideal husband Jesus Christ.

Just as marriage is legally not recognized to two husbands at the same time, one cannot be married to sin and to Christ at the same time. As long as the old husband is alive, then Christ can not enter into a union with the person legally in God's eyes.

4 Therefore, my brethren, you also have become dead to the law through the body of Christ, that you may be married to another—to Him who was raised from the dead, that we should bear fruit to God.

5 For when we were in the flesh, the sinful passions which were aroused by the law were at work in our members to bear fruit to death.

6 But now we have been delivered from the law, having died to what we were held by, so that we should serve in the newness of the Spirit and not in the oldness of the letter. Romans 7:4-6.

This is why to experience God's Transforming life-changing Power, one has to die to their old nature so that figuratively they are married to Christ in a union that God will recognize. One has to be dead to the old nature. In Revelation Christ says

15 "I know your works, that you are neither cold nor hot. I could wish you were cold or hot.

16 So then, because you are lukewarm, and neither [k]cold nor hot, I will vomit you out of My mouth. Revelation 3:15-16.

Being hot is being married to the new husband Christ, and being cold is being married to the old husband sin. To be lukewarm, is to try to marry both at the same time, which God does not want. The reason is because many believers do not actually die to their old nature, but learn to modify their behavior so that in appearance, they are in the marriage to Christ. They are actors which is what hypocrite means. Visibly, they appear to be playing the part of a born again Christian but the old nature is very much alive. They try to fool God that the old husband is dead, and that they are legally open to be married to Christ, but He can read the heart and knows if that is the case (1 Samuel 16:7). They act the part but do not actually live it. When we are in this state, we know and desire to do the right thing, but the power to do it we lack which is why we keep fall.

21 I find then a law, that evil is present with me, the one who wills to do good.

22 For I delight in the law of God according to the inward man.

23 But I see another law in my members, warring against the law of my mind, and bringing me into captivity to the law of sin which is in my members.

24 O wretched man that I am! Who will deliver me from this body of death?

25 I thank God—through Jesus Christ our Lord! Romans 7:21-25

This is why Christ discouraged us from being like the Pharisees who outwardly were very pious but inwardly were dead (Matthew 23:27). Remember, a person begins to live when Christ enters the heart "that Christ may dwell in your hearts through faith" Ephesians 3:17. My prayer for you and I: that we are truly dead to our old nature and that Christ is empowering us to live a new life; That we are not acting the part because we can fool people, but we cannot fool God who sees our hearts.

Death as self denial

Christ died once and will not die again, and so if we die to self, and the Spirit truly resurrects us to a new life by marrying us to the second husband Christ, we become alive to God and as long as we stay married to Christ and are empowered by His Spirit, we become dead indeed to sin and alive unto Him. So we are crucified to self, as is written, "Whosoever will come after me, let him deny himself, and take up his cross, and follow me." Mark 8:34. By taking up the cross we die to self. Dying to self means that we deny our selves, deny our will for our lives and thus surrender to His will so that His is done in our lives. Our will loves sin, and we love our way, but as we saw earlier, it is an illusion and it is actually the devil's will working in us. By allowing the devil's will to work in us, we allow him to divert us from having God's will being to be done in our lives,
39 This is the will of the Father who sent Me, that of all He has given Me I should lose nothing, but should raise it up at the last day.
40 And this is the will of Him who sent Me, that everyone who sees the Son and believes in Him may have everlasting life; and I will raise him up at the last day. John 6:39, 40.

Even if our will might be for something which seems harmless in itself, if it diverts our lives from God's will which is for us to be saved, no matter how innocent or harmless in itself, the devil succeeds because "The thief does not come except to steal, and to kill, and to destroy. I have come that they may have life, and that they may have it more abundantly." John 10:10. He steals us away from the big picture which is for us to be saved and to live Eternally with God; he diverts our attention, focus and energy on things which are vain and temporary.
He kills us while we are preoccupied with chasing these vanities as in the parable of the rich fool in Luke chapter 12, and he destroys the very things that we set our attention, focus and energy on. Many have made their life goal to be rich and might achieve great wealth only to lose it in recessions; built their lives around dream homes

only to lose them in foreclosures in a heart beat; built great careers only to be laid off at their prime or closure of the company they worked for. Others still have attained all these things only to lose their health at the prime of their success, as is written "Your riches are corrupted, and your garments are moth-eaten.

Your gold and silver is cankered; and the rust of them shall be a witness against you, and shall eat your flesh as it were fire. Ye have heaped treasure together for the last days." James 5:2, 3. God's will is for us to be saved and sometimes out of mercy allows things to happen in our lives to move us to seek him because He desires that none be lost but all to be saved. When we die to self, surrender our will so that His will is done, we will be able to follow him as is written, "These are the ones who were not defiled with women, for they are virgins. These are the ones who follow the Lamb wherever He goes. These were redeemed from among men, being first fruits to God and to the Lamb." Revelation 14:4.

They follow Him wherever he goes because His will works in them which is for them to be saved. Anything which can be a snare to them and prevent them from achieving this goal of Eternal Life with our Savior they let it go, no matter how innocent or good it may seem, if it diverts attention, focus and energy from this goal, they can lose Salvation because of it which is why they follow Him wherever He goes. The path might require us dropping things which we love so much but as innocent or harmless or good they may be, if they rob our attention, focus and energy from the big picture which is for us to be saved, they are a diversion and the devil's tools in stealing us away from God.

The more they seem to be innocent, harmless, or even good, the more dangerous the snare if those things own and direct our lives, but steal us away from Him or from Him working His will in our lives which is to save us. Anything which goes from being a part of our lives to owning us, holds us in captivity, and no matter what it is, if it captivates us to the point of us ignoring the opportunity to be healed by the Great Physician and to live Eternally, it is a diversion and a tool that the devil uses.

12 Therefore do not let sin reign in your mortal body, that you should obey it in its lusts.

13 And do not present your members as [d]instruments of unrighteousness to sin, but present yourselves to God as being alive

from the dead, and your members as instruments of righteousness to God.

14 For sin shall not have dominion over you, for you are not under law but under grace.

15 What then? Shall we sin because we are not under law but under grace? Certainly not!

16 Do you not know that to whom you present yourselves slaves to obey, you are that one's slaves whom you obey, whether of sin leading to death, or of obedience leading to righteousness?

17 But God be thanked that though you were slaves of sin, yet you obeyed from the heart that form of doctrine to which you were [e]delivered.

18 And having been set free from sin, you became slaves of righteousness. Romans 6:12-18.

Not under the law but under Grace

For us to get the opportunity to be healed is Grace, because we did not deserve it as all have sinned, and also there was no way we could repay the debt of sin except by death, as the wages of sin is death. Grace is this opportunity for us to be healed, no matter how sick we are with sin and is open to all who realize they are sick and accept the invitation to be healed by the Physician. "Therefore by the deeds of the law there shall no flesh be justified in his sight: for by the law is the knowledge of sin." Romans 3:20.

The Law reminds us of our obligation to our neighbor and to God, but in itself does not offer a solution of how to fulfill it's requirements therefore, "because the law brings about wrath; for where there is no law there is no transgression." Romans 4:15. It shows us our obligation to God and to man, and so when we fall short of it, it reminds us that we have messed up. If the Law is spiritual, there is no way we can fulfill its requirements in the flesh or in our carnal nature.

When we are born again, we are born of the Spirit, and thus by the Spirit we are able to fulfill the requirements of the Law. So when we die to self, we die to sin but are alive to God. If the husband who moved us to sin is dead, and we are married to a new husband, Christ, then sin has no dominion over us or control over us, and so we are no longer under the Law but under Grace. Being under the Law means it continually reminds us that we are messing up, which we are bound to when we are in the flesh because we are in bondage to it and labor or work the works of sin against our will (Romans 7:18-20).

As long as we are in the flesh we keep falling and sinning, and thus the Law keeps reminding us that we have fallen short of its requirements. So Paul is asking if we should sin because we are no longer under the law but under Grace. We are under the Law or under its reminders as long as we keep sinning. We keep sinning because we are in the flesh and still married to the first husband the flesh or carnal nature. Only when we are married to Christ and thus empowered by the Spirit to fulfill the requirements of the Law, can we not break it and this can only happen if God's Power is working in us "for it is God who works in you both to will and to do for His good pleasure." Philippians 2:13.

His good pleasure is that we fulfill the Law, for it is for a broken Law that He came and died, that whosoever believes on Him will not perish but have everlasting life. When we are married to Christ, we are not under the Law because we are fulfilling its requirements. As long as we are married to Christ, His will works in us and it is for us to fulfill the requirements of His Law. So being under the Law meaning it reminds us of our falling short in fulfilling its obligations.

So being under Grace, means we are empowered by Christ to fulfill the Law which we broke and He came to die for that if we believe on Him, we might live. So Grace fulfills the Law. There are many who misinterpret this that they can sin willfully because Grace gives them a license to do so since they are no longer under the Law but under Grace. But Grace fulfills the Law as we have seen here. It is the ability for us to fulfill the Law which we are thoroughly incapable of fulfilling on our own in our own strength but through Christ who strengthens us (Philippians 4:13). Grace is our marriage to Christ and thus our ability to fulfill His Law because He keeps the law for us.

Grace not a license to sin

The marriage to Christ takes place when we are born again of the Spirit and only when we are born again of the Spirit, can we fulfill the requirements of a Law which is spiritual, and worship God in spirit and in truth, for He is a spirit and those who worship Him must worship Him in spirit and in truth. So Grace is far from being a license to sin as is written;

11 For the grace of God that brings salvation has appeared to all men,

12 teaching us that, denying ungodliness and worldly lusts, we should live soberly, righteously, and godly in the present age,

13 looking for the blessed hope and glorious appearing of our great God and Savior Jesus Christ,

14 who gave Himself for us, that He might redeem us from every lawless deed and purify for Himself His own special people, zealous for good works. Titus 2:11-14.

Grace requires that we die to self, deny ungodliness and worldly lusts which are because of our marriage to the first husband self, that we live life as those who are expecting Him to return again who gave Himself for us so that He could redeem us from all iniquity, to even purify us and make us a people zealous of good works. These are all things which we can not do in the flesh no matter how much we can try and convince ourselves, and fool ourselves. This can only be achieved by being truly born again of the Spirit and thus married to Christ.

Water baptism as symbol of death to self

The grave which is signified by water at baptism is but an emblem of the death of the old man and a public testimony or confession to others that one has forsaken their old life, and desire to live a Godly life by His power:

32 Therefore whoever confesses Me before men, him I will also confess before My Father who is in heaven…

33 But whoever denies Me before men, him I will also deny before My Father who is in heaven. Matthew 10:32-33.

Being immersed in water is a type pointing to the death of self and his/her burial. The rising out of the water, the new spiritual nature is born who lives not for self but for God and His will is done and by His Spirit. The Power behind the resurrection is the same power that empowers to live a new life. That's why being immersed in water is a fitting type as it signifies that the old man with his sinful tendencies has been buried and the new man is born as one rises from the water, to a newness of life which is sinless by the power of the Spirit. Any form of baptism that does not illustrate the burial of the old man through immersion in water falls short of the significance God desired it to be given. If one is sprinkled with water for example, in the spiritual sense one is saying that the old man never died and continues to live.

Should infants be baptized?

The other thing is that baptism is only done when one acknowledges that they are a sinner that is sick with sin and in need of healing. That the first husband self or the flesh or the sinful nature has been directing their lives, by bondage to the devil for whom they labor through the works of sin. They desire not to be married to self no longer, and so to die and be buried in water. The first husband self remains buried as he is dead, but the Spirit then creates a new person breathing life into them, and resurrecting them from the watery grave just as Christ did on the third day.

When the Spirit quickens this person, they are at that point married to the second husband Jesus Christ and since the wife is subject to the husband, us being the wife, we are subject now to His will and it starts working in us to will and to do of His good pleasure. One who acknowledges that they are a sinner should have an understanding of what sin is and so infant baptism is not baptism. How can an infant who does not know anything be baptized? The one being baptized has to acknowledge their sin, and desire to start a new life by Christ's power as the healing takes place when they are separated from the first husband by death to self, and are married to the second who is Christ by the Spirit who then empowers them to live a new life according to God's will.

Any form of baptism short of immersion in water does not do justice to the type which God was illustrating, and thus misrepresents the process that He hopes we understand as taking place in the life of the individual being baptized. The type or being immersed in water itself is an emblem and if the person is immersed in water, it does not mean anything if in their heart they are unwilling to let go of the old life and to really live a new life by the Spirit of God. Yes they have made a public testimony that they forsake the old life and its ways, but in their heart have not invited the new husband Christ and have not allowed the Spirit to quicken them to a newness of life.

It is just like keeping the Sabbath. If one observes the type to the letter but does not understand or appreciate the real meaning of the Sabbath; which is rest from our efforts to sustain our lives as if we created ourselves, as the one who created us will sustain us if we trust him; rest from our works of sin and rest from the troubles and burdens that life can bring our way as without God's help they would certainly crush us, this is rest. The Sabbath is a reminder of all this and when we appreciate it, we by faith allow God to give us rest from all these things. God desires one thing, that we understand the spiritual significance of all these things as when we understand, the hope is that by faith these things come to life in our lives. Again, God would have us to understand the spiritual significance of all these things.

Thief on the cross

Though one may go into the watery grave, the real baptism takes place when quickened by the Holy Spirit to a new life, when they truly desire to live a new life by God's power and to forsake the old ways. Ideally, birth of the Spirit should take place when one goes in the watery grave but that is not always the case. In fact there may not be many who have had this happen. Most have the birth of the Spirit take place later when they truly in their heart desire to die to self, and surrender completely to Christ. He desires complete surrender though most of us surrender partially but we are enjoined to go all the way as is written,

34...Whoever desires to come after Me, let him deny himself, and take up his cross, and follow Me.

35 For whoever desires to save his life will lose it, but whoever loses his life for My sake and the gospel's will save it. Mark 8:34-35.

These things can happen if the Spirit starts working in that life, that's the only way old ways can truly be forsaken. Baptism in itself is still important because it is a public testimony that one has chosen to live a new life and are serious about pursuing God's way for their life and before He ascended up to heaven, He said:
19 Go [c]therefore and make disciples of all the nations, baptizing them in the name of the Father and of the Son and of the Holy Spirit,
20 teaching them to observe all things that I have commanded you; and lo, I am with you always, even to the end of the age." [d]Amen. Matthew 28:19, 20.

So if possible all who believe should be baptized. Now as I said, it is an emblem, a public testimony to the world that one has chosen to follow God and forsake their old ways for Him. In the case that one does not get an opportunity to be baptized but give their life to Christ on their deathbed or something, they are still saved. What matters most is if the person accepts Christ and are saved even if it is last minute. A good example is the thief on the cross. If one has an opportunity, then it is hoped that they can get baptized, and also that their baptism is real in the spirit, so that the Spirit truly quickens them from then on and gives them the power to live a new life.

Without desire on their part to live a new life or to forsake sin and the old ways, without them inviting the Spirit into their life because only by His power can one live a new life, the baptism is just a spectacle or ceremony. Real baptism is in the Spirit, when the Spirit comes into that person's life and starts transforming that life and enables God's will to work, the end result which is resurrection unto Eternal life at His second coming. But the immersion in water is a confession to man, a public testimony that one has decided to "follow the Lamb wherever He goes." Revelation 14:4.

24
WHILE IT IS TODAY

Now that we have established the role the laws of health play in returning to good health for the soul and maintaining it, in the miracles of healing Christ performed are important things to note which apply to us today as well.

They heard about Him

Everywhere Christ went, the crowds were overwhelming. Once people heard that He had the power to do what seemed impossible, word would spread and crowds would follow Him. As His fame grew, so did the crowds of those coming seeking to be delivered from their burdens. We read about Him that He literally walked this Earth, and the same Power He demonstrated in delivering the masses then is the same Power available today to deliver you from what seems impossible to overcome.

28 And immediately His fame spread throughout all the region around Galilee...

45 However, he went out and began to proclaim it freely, and to spread the matter, so that Jesus could no longer openly enter the city, but was outside in deserted places; and they came to Him from every direction. Mark 1:28 and 45.

24 Then His fame went throughout all Syria; and they brought to Him all sick people who were afflicted with various diseases and torments, and those who were demon-possessed, epileptics, and paralytics; and He healed them. Matthew 4:24.

Hope born in their hearts

Once people heard of Christ's Power, hope was born in their hearts. Once they heard about this Man who had helped many by taking away their seemingly impossible circumstances to overcome, their despair gave birth to hope that they also could be delivered. I don't know what your burden is but I know that what seems impossible for you is not impossible for God because all things are possible for Him.

37 For with God nothing will be impossible. Luke 1:37.

18 While He spoke these things to them, behold, a ruler came and worshiped Him, saying, "My daughter has just died, but come and lay Your hand on her and she will live." Matthew 9:18.

1 And again He entered Capernaum after some days, and it was heard that He was in the house.

2 [a]Immediately many gathered together, so that there was no longer room to receive them, not even near the door. And He preached the word to them.

3 Then they came to Him, bringing a paralytic who was carried by four men.

4 And when they could not come near Him because of the crowd, they uncovered the roof where He was. So when they had broken through, they let down the bed on which the paralytic was lying.

5 When Jesus saw their faith, He said to the paralytic, "Son, your sins are forgiven you." Mark 2:1-5.

Hope made them act immediately

Once hope was born in their hearts, it gave rise to faith. Hope by itself would not be enough. At the realization that here was One who could deliver them, they would stop at nothing to get to Him so that He could heal them. Some were carried to Him, others crawled or dragged along. One unable to move on His own was lowered through the ceiling to get around the crowds and get to Christ. Another even climbed a tree to catch a glimpse of He would set him free from greed and covetousness and to set his eyes on Heavenly treasures. All you have to do is reach out to Him and ask Him to deliver you from your burden, whatever it may be. Just as they did not think about how He was going to do it, they just focused on He who they believed was able to do it! Ask Him and He will do the rest.

20 And suddenly, a woman who had a flow of blood for twelve years came from behind and touched the hem of His garment.

21 For she said to herself, "If only I may touch His garment, I shall be made well." Matthew 9:20-21.

He came to free as many as He could

During Jesus' brief ministry here on earth, He saw as many people as He could, delivering them from their immediate circumstances and hoped they would understand His broader mission which was to give life to them if they believed in Him. His mission continues today. If you receive Him and believe, not only your body but also your soul, and He can also give you the right to become the children of God and be able to live forever.

35 Then Jesus went about all the cities and villages, teaching in their synagogues, preaching the gospel of the kingdom, and healing every sickness and every disease [i]among the people. Matthew 9:35.

12 But as many as received Him, to them He gave the [e]right to become children of God, to those who believe in His name:

13 who were born, not of blood, nor of the will of the flesh, nor of the will of man, but of God. John 1:12-13.

He was here for a limited time

Jesus was extremely busy and whenever word got out on where He was, people would immediately make their way to Him. There was no guarantee that He would be in a place for long, and He was constantly moving as He healed the masses. When He passed through a town, there was no guarantee of reaching Him even if among the crowd. His ministry was brief at only three and a half years. There might be some who doubted Him or His ability to help them and their hesitation to act when He was in their midst proved to be their loss.

37 When they found Him, they said to Him, "Everyone is looking for You."

38 But He said to them, "Let us go into the next towns, that I may preach there also, because for this purpose I have come forth."

39 And He was preaching in their synagogues throughout all Galilee, and casting out demons. Mark 1:37-39.

Whenever He was in a place, those who did not act thinking they would get another opportunity in the future missed out on Him delivering them from their circumstances. Other towns He did not return to because they were unbelieving even though He performed great works there. Ignoring the pleas of the Holy Spirit which is your conscience, can grieve Him which would be unfortunate because without the Holy Spirit's help, you cannot be saved. Just as Christ gave up on Jerusalem and the other towns mentioned in the scriptures below because of their unbelief, He cannot plead with you forever if you refuse to believe.

20 Then He began to rebuke the cities in which most of His mighty works had been done, because they did not repent:

21 "Woe to you, Chorazin! Woe to you, Bethsaida! For if the mighty works which were done in you had been done in Tyre and Sidon, they would have repented long ago in sackcloth and ashes.

22 But I say to you, it will be more tolerable for Tyre and Sidon in the day of judgment than for you.

23 And you, Capernaum, who[e] are exalted to heaven, will be brought down to Hades; for if the mighty works which were done in you had been done in Sodom, it would have remained until this day.

24 But I say to you that it shall be more tolerable for the land of Sodom in the day of judgment than for you." Matthew 11:20-24.

37 "O Jerusalem, Jerusalem, the one who kills the prophets and stones those who are sent to her! How often I wanted to gather your children together, as a hen gathers her chicks under her wings, but you were not willing!

38 See! Your house is left to you desolate;

39 for I say to you, you shall see Me no more till you say, 'Blessed is He who comes in the name of the Lord!' " Matthew 23:37-39.

He came to minister to as many as He could and especially knowing He would have a limited time, so he could not afford to spend too much time in one place since there were so many in other places who needed His help.

Such is the case for us as well. He is doing the work of healing and forgiveness of sins right now, but not indefinitely. Just as we learned that the Holy Spirit can be grieved, the Holy Spirit helps us to respond to Christ's love and to accept His sacrifice for our sins. He pleads with us but not forever, and if we grieve Him by rejecting His pleas then we would have rejected the only means of being healed from sin by Christ (Ephesians 4:30). Time is also limited in the sense that life can end abruptly. If it ends and you have not accepted Christ, the opportunity to be healed from sin is forever lost "...for him who is joined to all the living there is hope, for a living dog is better than a dead lion." Ecclesiastes 9:4. Tomorrow is not guaranteed and you do not know when you will die so it is wise to respond to the pleas of the Holy Spirit and to be healed while you have the opportunity. While you are still alive, do not procrastinate lest you also get to the point where the Holy Spirit is grieved and gives up on saving you. "Take heed, brethren, lest there be in any of you an evil heart of unbelief, in departing from the living God. But exhort one another daily, while it is called To day; lest any of you be hardened through the deceitfulness of sin…To day if ye will hear his voice, harden not your hearts…" Hebrews 3:12-13, 15.

Seek the Lord while it is today! Do not put it off till tomorrow because you are not promised tomorrow!

Book Ordering and Contact info

For speaking engagements, book orders and other enquiries, please email wtbtradio@gmail.com

For updates on future work, follow at gumroad.com/lamptomyfeet

Like us on facebook:
facebook.com/lamptofeet

Pdf version available for order at gumroad.com/lamptomyfeet

Paperback and Kindle versions at amazon.com/author/tapiwachiwawa

Book orders can be shipped anywhere in the US, but shipping & handling will be finalized at the time of the order. Orders of less than 10 book orders can be ordered directly from Amazon. For orders of more than 10 books, please contact us for discounts.

11-50 books $15.99 each
51-100 books $13.99 each
101-500 books $11.99 each
501 or more books $9.99 each

www.ingramcontent.com/pod-product-compliance
Lightning Source LLC
Chambersburg PA
CBHW070554100426
42744CB00006B/270